MARX'S
DAUGHTERS

MARX'S
DAUGHTERS

ELEANOR MARX
ROSA LUXEMBURG
ANGELICA BALABANOFF

RONALD FLORENCE

The Dial Press New York   1975

Library of Congress Cataloging in Publication Data

Florence, Ronald.
    Marx's daughters.

    Bibliography: p.
    Includes index.
    1. Aveling, Eleanor Marx, 1855–1898. 2. Luxemburg,
Rosa, 1870–1919. 3. Balabanoff, Angelica, 1878–1965.
4. Marx, Karl, 1818–1883. I. Title.
HX23.F55   335.4′0922 [B]   75–9576
ISBN 0-8037-5432-9

Manufactured in the United States of America

First printing

Cover and book design by Batten & Kreloff

PREFACE

This book began as an exploration of the lives of Karl Marx's daughters. As I began to probe those twisted and strange lives, I realized that their tragedies were due not so much to family heritage or ideological inheritance, but to the fact that they were women who had committed themselves to an ideology and a movement that remained ambivalent on the role that women should play in a man's world. I began to look at the lives of other women in the socialist movement, and settled on these three, Eleanor Marx, Rosa Luxemburg, and Angelica Balabanoff—only one of whom is a real daughter of Karl Marx—as illustrating different reactions to Marxism and to the socialist movement.

I have kept the original title of the book because in many ways, more than they would have acknowledged or realized, these women were so bound to an ideology and a movement that they were, and they remained, Marx's daughters.

The research for this book was supported by a grant from the National Endowment for the Humanities and by a faculty fellowship from Sarah Lawrence College. Certain sections were revised while I was a Fellow of the National Endowment for the Humanities and a Research Associate of the Twentieth Century Fund. Typing and clerical costs were supported by the State University of New York, College at Purchase, and the photographs are reproduced through the courtesy of the Photo Archive of the International Institute of Social History in Amsterdam. I am grateful for the support of these institutions.

I would also like to acknowledge the comments and criticisms of the friends and colleagues who have read the work at various stages. They may not agree with what I have written or how I have written it, but I appreciate their help and advice.

Chappaqua, New York
June 1974

CONTENTS

—You, young woman, who are going to cross this threshold, do you know what awaits you?

—I know.

—Cold, hunger, hostility, contempt, irony, shame, prison, disease, and death.

—I know, I am ready to endure all this.

—Even if all this were to come not only from your enemies, but also from your relatives and friends?

—Yes, even then.

—Are you even ready to commit a crime?

—I am ready for that too.

—Have you considered that you might be subject to a delusion, that you might find that you have sacrificed your young life in vain?

—I have considered this too.

—Enter, then.

—Imbecile! said someone.

—Saint! the echo answered.

—Turgenev, *Prose Poems*

THE FUNERAL

Karl Marx died on March 14, 1883, leaving two daughters, a half-shelf of published books and articles, several trunks of notes and manuscripts, and an estate valued at two hundred fifty pounds. Although he had lived in London for more than thirty-three years, he was still almost unknown to the English public. His magnum opus, *Das Kapital,* had yet to be published in English, and the only report of his death in the English press was a belated obituary by the Paris correspondent of the *Times*. Eleven people came to his funeral at Highgate Cemetery, six of them German émigrés, who, like Marx, had come to England in the wake of the repression that followed the unsuccessful revolutions of 1848.

Friedrich Engels, Marx's lifelong colleague and collaborator, delivered the eulogy at the funeral, reading in English for the benefit of the few there who could not understand German.

> On March 14, at a quarter to three in the afternoon, the greatest living thinker ceased to think. . . .
>
> Just as Darwin discovered the law of the development of organic nature, so Marx discovered the law of the development of human history: the simple fact, hitherto obscured by an overgrowth of ideology, that man must first of all eat, drink, have a roof over his head and clothe himself before he can pursue politics, science, art, religion, etc. . . .
>
> But that is by no means all. Marx discovered also the special law of motion governing contemporary capitalist methods of production and the bourgeois society which was created out of it. With the discovery of surplus value a light was suddenly created, while all earlier investigations, both those of bourgeois economists and socialist critics, were gropings in the dark.
>
> Two such discoveries would be enough for one lifetime. Happy the man to whom it is granted to make even one such discovery. But in every single field which Marx investigated—and he investigated very many fields, none of them superficially—in every field, even in that of mathematics, he made independent discoveries.

Such was the man of science. But this was not even half the man. . . .

For Marx was above all a revolutionary. His real mission in life was to contribute in one way or another to the overthrow of capitalist society and the state institutions which it brought into being, and to contribute to the liberation of the modern proletariat, which *he* was the first to make conscious of its own position and its own needs, conscious of the conditions of its emancipation. Battle was his element. . . .

Engels chronicled the newspapers for which Marx had written, the organizations in Paris, Brussels, and London which he had commanded, and the achievements of the International Working Men's Association which Marx had led.

And so it happened that he was the most hated and calumniated man of his time. Governments, whether absolutist or republican, deported him, and the bourgeois, whether conservative or ultra-democratic, vied with one another in heaping abuse on him. All this he brushed aside as though it were a cobweb, ignoring it, answering only when extreme necessity compelled him. And he died beloved, revered, and mourned by millions of revolutionary fellow-workers—from the mines of Siberia to California, in all parts of Europe and America—and I make bold to say that though he may have had many opponents he had hardly one personal enemy.

His name will endure through the ages, and so will his work!

Even allowing for the hyperbole that belongs in an eulogy, Engels had only slightly exaggerated his friend's achievements. Marx did not discover the law of human history. Nor the law of surplus value. As a revolutionary, he preferred to do battle from behind an editor's desk; he had spent far more of his energies on internecine fighting within the revolutionary movements than in any great assault on bourgeois society. He was certainly not the first to make the proletariat conscious of its needs and goals, and his mathematical discoveries were, to say the least, questionable. The organizations which he had led were singularly ineffective, and the International Working Men's Association had achieved its notoriety from inflated propaganda, not revolutionary deeds.

What Marx did do was write clearly and convincingly, indeed, brilliantly, about the industrial society that was emerging in Europe in the nineteenth century. In a series of manuscripts of the 1840s, most of which were not published, Marx had uncovered a tantalizing and seemingly inexorable progression—from the alienation of an individual worker in industrial society, to the alienation of a class, the proletariat, and then, through the mechanism of class struggle, to the inevitable revolution that would liberate all men from the suffering and alienation that had transformed and disfigured humanity. With exquisite logic, Marx demonstrated a necessary relationship between capitalism and the working class upon which its production was so

3

dependent. That same working class, he showed, would be the agency of the dissolution of capitalism and thus of human liberation, not on its own behalf, but on behalf of all humanity.

He had accurately predicted the outbreak of revolution in 1848, even to the point of declaring that "universal emancipation would be signaled by the crowing of the Gallic cock." And when the revolutions all over the European continent did not follow the chiliastic predictions of the *Communist Manifesto,* Marx analyzed what did happen in studies that are among the clearest and most convincing histories of revolutions ever written. In *Class Struggles in France* and in *The Eighteenth Brumaire of Louis Bonaparte,* Marx unfolded the history of the revolution of 1848 not in the crude terms of economic determinism, but in a subtle interweaving of those psychological, social, political, and economic threads that spelled certain doom for the revolution. Although both studies are laced with the scalpel-sharp invective that was to be Marx's literary trademark, his theses are argued with a flexibility and balance that stand in sharp contrast to the cold, inexorable laws of human history so often attributed to Marxism.

In his later works of economic analysis and history, Marx tried to unravel and explain the complex development of capitalist society. In the *Critique of Political Economy,* and particularly in the one volume of *Capital* that was published in his lifetime, Marx used a plethora of concrete historical evidence to support his demonstration that the development of capitalism inevitably leads to an ever-widening gap between the capitalist class and the laboring class upon which capitalism depends.

He had achieved a brief notoriety at the time of the revolutions of 1848, and again at the time of the Commune in 1871, when his outspoken praise of the Communards led most European governments to mistakenly credit the International with the impetus and organization of the Paris revolution. But even at the time of his death, Marx's works were scarcely known to the public. *Capital* had been reviewed only by Engels when first published. The book was later translated into Russian and French, but it remained known only to a small circle of readers patient enough to wade through abstruse arguments, erudite language, and Marx's interposed ad hominem attacks on those who had crossed intellectual or political swords with him.

There was no significant political party in 1883 that considered itself modeled after the ideas of Marx, and no newspaper hewed to what could by any stretch of interpretation be called a "Marxist" line.

Yet by the 1880s the industrialization of Europe and America had passed the takeoff point. France had begun to catch up with, and Germany and the United States were beginning to surpass the industrial production of England. As Marx had predicted—along with, it should be acknowledged, many others—the growth of industrialization and urbanization produced a coherent and conscious working class, a class which in many situations no longer identified itself with the official goals and means of society. "The advance of industry, whose involuntary promoter is the bourgeoisie, replaces the isolation of the laborers, due to competition, by their revolutionary combination, due to association." Marx had written the prophecy in 1847; it was only beginning to become true in the 1880s. The corollary of Marx's prophecy remained to be tested: "What the bourgeoisie, therefore, produces, above all, is its own gravediggers. Its fall and the victory of the proletariat are equally inevitable."

The 1880s also saw the growth of organized labor movements, led in most cases by intellectuals who were versed in the wealth of literature that the social critics of the nineteenth century had produced. Many working-class leaders in France, Russia, Germany, and England read *Capital* in the 1880s. As its adherents discerned, the book was uniquely appropriate to the historical moment. Marx offered a distinction between the objective historical conditions necessary to achieve socialism and the subjective will of the proletariat needed to bring it about—a dichotomy that accorded very well indeed with the growing industrialization of European society and the revolutionary rancor engendered in a working class that increasingly felt the economic pressures and the political isolation or powerlessness that were to be their lot under the governments of Europe in the late nineteenth century.

The growth of Marxism as a movement offers a striking parallel to the growth of Christianity. In the beginning, with the Word, there were tiny groups, meeting in the wilderness; the catacombs of the Marxists were clandestine party meetings and rallies, to which the police relentlessly pursued them. This adversity produced a coherence of purpose, and the pronouncements of the Master were enough to control incipient dissent and rebellion within the movement. Then, with the death of Marx, the prophets and preachers of Marxism appeared everywhere—and, as in the case of Christianity, the movement soon acquired its saints, heretics, and martyrs. It was not long before the movement had achieved an institutionalization and codification that Marx would no longer have recognized.

Marx's later writings were marked by a qualified tone of "perhaps" that mitigated the harsh determinism and chiliasm of his earlier predictions. Especially in *Capital,* his tone was more critical and negative than predictive. *"Capital,"* he wrote in a letter to Ferdinand Lassalle, "is a presentation of the system, and through the presentation a critique of that system." But as his disciples tightened the loose associations of the labor movements into organized parties, his writings and theories became sacred texts, used to maintain the orthodoxy in what had become a fervent millenial faith. "There is but one path to the liberation of the working classes, and Karl Marx is its prophet," became more and more the figurative cry of a large segment of

5

the European labor movements. In the transformation of theory to religion, the distinctions between the preachings of the prophet and the wishes of the faithful often became blurred. Marx's true achievements were lost in hagiography, as generations of intellectuals on the Left took his historical and economic precepts and theories as panaceas or guidelines for a style of life. Most of the disciples called themselves Marxists, an appellation which Marx himself had eschewed with disdain.

Although Marx's ideas owed a great debt to the Hegelian philosophical tradition that he had studied and transformed, and to the French revolutionary tradition he had witnessed and analyzed, the mature ideas of Marxism were a product of the Victorian era. It was in the England of Queen Victoria that Marx witnessed the true ravages that industrialization could bring upon society. It was in the British Museum, that monument of Victorian pride, that he studied the Blue Books of factory inspectors that were to be his documentation of these horrors. Marxism started as a science—that is, Marx thought he had uncovered the science of history. With Marx's death the doctrine became a religion. Between those poles it spanned the nodes of Victorian thought.

Yet even as it was a product of the Victorian era, Marxism was a challenge to the most basic of Victorian values. For against the ideal of an ordered society, where men and women, workers and bosses, aristocrats and commoners, Englishmen and foreigners played their assigned roles, Marxism offered a vision of equality, between individuals and between men and women. That vision, even without a manifesto for action, was a challenge and a threat to the smug assumptions of an age of confidence.

The dream of equality was age-old, though usually presented as an utopian paradigm rather than a concrete goal. What made Marxism different was that it appeared to provide a mechanism to achieve that goal. The understanding of the inexorable flow of history gave the Marxists what they thought was a means to usher in the new era. Yet what the adherents saw as obvious insights into the laws of nature, bourgeois society treated as dangerous rhetoric.

The challenge to Victorian society was also a challenge to the Marxists. For even as the latter preached change, they perforce lived within the society they sought to remake. The men and women who questioned the class structures of Victorian society were frequently offspring of the privileged classes they sought to dismember; like Marx himself, many were bourgeois intellectuals, enjoying the advantages of middle-class life even as they worked for its downfall.

To the socialists, at least in theory, women were exactly equal to men, entitled to every right and privilege that men enjoyed. And in a world in which women were lesser creatures, confined to the home and subject to the judgment of men, a world in which women were thought to have no capac-

6

ity for rational thought, a world in which the fate of women was to suffer and be still, the rhetoric of Marxism was a powerful and revolutionary gauntlet thrown down to Victorian values.

In the sphere of politics and parliaments the socialists could plead and argue and campaign for the equality of women, knowing at the same time that little would change, at least in their own lifetimes. Many, enjoying the security and consistency of opposition, probably never hoped for change. But what would they do within their own movement where there were no obstacles to change? Almost unique among the great ideological movements of the nineteenth century, socialism numbered women among its leadership. Were they to be treated as "men"? Or should they be accorded special status and patronization? Could men who had been conditioned to believe that women were incapable of logical reasoning begin to listen to the arguments of women? Would men be persuaded by women? Or take orders from them? And could a movement as patriarchal in its origins and talmudic in its orthodoxy as Marxism ever adapt itself to the real, rather than the rhetorical, equality of women?

To answer these questions, even to touch upon the lives of the important women in the socialist movement, would require volumes. From Marx's contemporaries to Chiang Ching and Angela Davis, there have been dozens of women important in the spread and articulation of Marxism. Such a survey would surely include Klara Zetkin in Germany, Dolores Ibarruri ("La Pasionaria") in Spain, Alexandra Kollontai in Russia and perhaps Emma Goldman in the United States and Louise Michels in France. My purpose here is not to survey, but to illustrate; the three women I have chosen— Eleanor Marx, Rosa Luxemburg, Angelica Balabanoff—reflect a range of reactions to Marxism, as a life-style, as a doctrine, and as a movement. Their ideas and their lives illuminate that crucial era after the death of Marx, when Marxism emerged from relative obscurity to become one of the dominant ideologies of the world, and when women began to emerge from enforced silence to play a role in that ideology and in the world.

E L E A N O R
M A R X

Only one of Karl Marx's children was at the funeral in Highgate Cemetery, his youngest daughter Eleanor, known to family and friends alike as Tussy.* Next to her stood a rather repulsive Englishman named Edward Aveling, a stranger to at least some of the other mourners, but a man with a reputation in England. Before the graveside ceremony was over, rumors had already started about Tussy Marx and Edward Aveling. Within a year the rumors would be "scandals," and the scandals would multiply into what many called a socialist tragedy.

Tussy believed in Marxism as more than an economic and historical theory. For her it was an ethic, a value system applicable without exception to every aspect of the human experience. Marx had been content to live as a Victorian gentleman. Even as he wrote his painstaking and daring analysis of capitalism, he would speculate on the stock market, buy his wife embossed stationery, and relish the few bottles of excellent Bordeaux that he occasionally received as gifts from Engels. But for Tussy, Marxism was the mandate for a life-style, a preview of the future promised by the theory. In its suggestions of what the world might be, Marxism told Tussy how to live; she struggled to follow what she considered the dictates of that model.

When she translated her literal interpretation of Marxism into the life-style that it seemed to decree, Tussy offended the deepest mores of those who called themselves Marxists. To live *now* in a manner that someday, but only someday, might be possible, was to raise in its starkest form the problem of the disjunction between rhetoric and reality in socialism. Her life and her death raised questions that most socialists did not care to answer. Even less did they want to know what pain and what effort it would cost to build a stronghold for the mind and the will outside the makeshifts of human society.

* I have referred to the heroines of this book throughout by their first names or nicknames, not through any measure of condescension or disrespect, but to avoid the confusion that would ensue if Tussy were referred to as "Marx" or "Aveling." Although the same problem does not arise with Rosa Luxemburg or Angelica Balabanoff, I have kept to first names in the interest of consistency.

I

Tussy was born in 1855 in a tiny two-room flat on Dean Street, in the heart of the refugee tenements of Soho. Already six people were living in those two little rooms—their existence revolving around Karl Marx, the patriarch, whom they called "Mohr" (Moor) on account of his dark skin. Jenny, Marx's wife, was so devoted to him and so self-effacing that she began her autobiography: "June 19, 1843 was my wedding day." Her aristocratic upbringing in Germany, the years of cultivated life in Trier, where Karl Marx was the rather ungainly son of an upstart bourgeois family, were little more than occasional, remorseful memories. There were two daughters, Jenny and Laura, and a son, Edgar—all born during the terrible years of exile in Paris and Brussels from 1844 to 1847. There was also Helene Demuth, the Marxs' housekeeper, governess, maid, and cook. Marx described her in three words: *Demuth, Wehmuth, Hochmuth* (humility, sorrow, pride). When no one else could control Marx's alarming explosions of temper, wrote Wilhelm Liebknecht, who knew the family well, "Lenchen" "would go into the lion's den." If he growled, "she would give him such a piece of her mind that the lion became as meek as a lamb."

The very month of Tussy's birth, January 1855, eight-year-old Edgar developed signs of tuberculosis. The disease spread rapidly, and soon the child's every breath was a death rattle to the family listening in horror. In April the boy died in his father's arms, leaving Marx so distraught that friends feared he would leap into the grave when the coffin was lowered. His incredible love was transferred to Tussy, who arrived just in time to fill the gap. Speaking of his oldest and youngest daughters, Marx said, "Jenny is most like me, but Tussy is me."

The family took turns at spoiling the little girl. At the orders of a physician she was indulged with a diet of milk until she was five years old. The four older females of the house fondled her constantly. For nearly a year, Tussy suffered from whooping cough, and took advantage of the situation to insist upon open house being kept for every street child of the neighborhood. "The whole family became my bond slaves," wrote Tussy, "—& I have heard that as usual in slavery, there was general demobilization." But Tussy was spoiled by her father most of all. Though he joked that she was a sexual error—because he was so anguished at no longer having a son—he would carry her about on his shoulders, arranging flowers in her hair and telling her endless stories.

They were a warm family, if only because the close living in such small quarters left little choice. Privacy was unknown. The "study" where Marx worked was also the children's playroom. A police spy has left a charming description of the atmosphere:

In the whole apartment there is not one clean and solid piece of furniture. Everything is broken, tattered and torn, with a half inch of dust over everything and the greatest disorder everywhere. In the middle of the salon there is a large old-fashioned table covered with an oilcloth, and on it there lie manuscripts, books and newspapers, as well as the childrens' toys, and rags and tatters of his wife's sewing basket, several cups with broken rims, knives, forks, lamps, an inkpot, tumblers, Dutch clay pipes, tobacco ash—in a word, everything topsy-turvy, and all on the same table. A seller of second-hand goods would be ashamed to give away such a remarkable collection of odds and ends.

When you enter Marx's room smoke and tobacco fumes make your eyes water so much that for a moment you seem to be groping about in a cavern, but gradually, as you grow accustomed to the fog, you can make out certain objects which distinguish themselves from the surrounding haze. Everything is dirty and covered with dust, so that to sit down becomes a thoroughly dangerous business. Here is a chair with only three legs, on another chair the children are playing at cooking—this chair happens to have four legs. This is the one which is offered to the visitor, but the childrens' cooking has not been wiped away; and if you sit down, you risk a pair of trousers. But none of these things embarrass Marx or his wife. You are received in the most friendly way and cordially offered pipes and tobacco and whatever else there may happen to be; and eventually a spirited and agreeable conversation arises to make amends for all the domestic deficiencies, and this makes the discomfort tolerable. Finally you grow accustomed to the company, and find it interesting and original. This is a true picture of the family life of the Communist chief Marx.

On Sundays the entire family would troop to Hampstead Heath, often with friends like Liebknecht or an honored guest from abroad. At a brisk walk the journey would take one and a half hours, with an enormous hamper of food in tow. When finances allowed, the picnic provisions would be supplemented with shrimps or periwinkles bought at Jack Straw's Castle, a tavern overlooking the Heath. Then the children would spend a whole day with Marx's games (horseback riding was a favorite, with Karl playing the horse) and with the feast. The trip home assumed the pace of a forced march, as Marx would sing loudly old German patriotic songs, declaim passages from *Faust,* or tell stories.

Marx was a compulsive storyteller, rattling on not by the minute or hour, but, on long walks, "by the mile." When Tussy was old enough to speak she knew the Grimm tales well enough to object if a single syllable about the Noisy Goblin, King Drosselbart, or Snow White were omitted. But the stories she remembered best were a masterful series of narratives that "went on for months and months" about the curious life of Hans Röckle. As Tussy recalled:

Hans Röckle himself was a Hoffmann-like magician, who kept a toyshop, and who was always "hard-up." His shop was full of the most wonderful things—of wooden men and women, giants and dwarfs, kings and queens, workmen and masters, animals and birds as numerous as Noah got into the Ark, tables and chairs, carriages, boxes of all sorts and sizes. And although he was a magician, Hans could never meet his obligations either to the devil or to the butcher, and was therefore—much against the grain—constantly obliged to sell his toys to the devil. These then went through wonderful adventures—always ending in a return to Hans Röckle's shop.

What wondrous tales, these. No image could be more perfect for industrial society, the society that Marx had analyzed so carefully, than the toy maker. He was the truly human man, the man who created, who could identify with the products of his labor. Indeed, the shop of Hans Röckle was a microcosm of *Das Kapital,* a world filled with a panopoly of wondrous *things,* each made by a loving and laboring creator. The shop even had "workmen and masters," the medieval craftsmen whose world would be destroyed by the onslaught of machine industry.

Even more, the tales of Hans Röckle served as a marvelous autobiography of their creator. Marx saw himself, like Hans the toy maker, as a Promethean figure, a god who defied the gods by making men in his own image. In his doctoral dissertation, Marx had picked up the Promethean myth— "Just as Prometheus, having stolen fire from heaven, begins to build houses and settles on earth, so philosophy, having extended itself to the world, turns against the apparent world"—to describe his mission in writing philosophy. In 1843, after his newspaper, the *Rheinische Zeitung,* was banned, a drawing was published showing Marx chained to a printing press while the crowned eagle of Prussia fed on his liver. Prometheus turns up in *Capital* to represent the proletariat chained to capital. And Marx, who is said to have reread Aeschylus every year, was obsessed by the fear that his own liver would be consumed, like his father's, by cancer.

Yet Prometheus has his other side. The gift he has brought to man— fire—is far more destructive than any devouring bird. So too, Marx's gift— historical materialism—proves ultimately more powerful than the ravages of capitalist society. Hans Röckle, like his creator, has a price to pay for his defiance. When financial debts are not paid, the toys are sold to the devil, or the butcher. But they always go back to the creator. As Marx would put it, the expropriators will in the end be expropriated.

These stories were Tussy's education. Because she was sickly as a child, she was not sent to school. Instead she was tutored by her father at home, and his encyclopedic knowledge seemed to answer every question she could pose. When she was five or six, her father took her to a Roman Catholic church to listen to the music. Afterward she felt what she called "certain religious qualms,'' which she confided to Mohr. He then told her the story of the gospel in an historical materialist version: a tale of the poor carpenter whom the rich men killed. "He quietly made everything clear and straight," wrote Tussy, "so that from that hour to this no doubt could ever cross my mind again."

The stories were followed by novels. On her sixth birthday, Tussy was given *Peter Simple* by her father, followed by "a whole course of Marryat and Cooper." Marx read each novel as Tussy did, and they would discuss them in grave and serious tones. When Tussy, fired by Marryat's sea tales, decided to dress up as a boy and run away to sign up on a man-of-war, Marx assured her that it might very well be done, only nothing must be said about it until all plans were matured. Any fantasy was tolerated, even encouraged, if it would but remain their secret. Tussy learned early that literature could serve as an escape, that its fantastic plots—even the emotions and actions of literary heroes and heroines—could be a model, an alternative to the vagaries of life.

Tussy and her father were later caught up in the Scott mania that swept England in the 1860s. To her horror, she learned that she was descended, through her mother, from the detested Campbell clan. The pain was eased only by the enthusiastic plots of Marx for rousing the Highlands once again and reviving the "forty-five." Marx also read aloud from the books he loved most, so often that by the age of three Tussy had learned whole passages. Homer, the *Nibelungenlied, Gudrun, Don Quixote, The Arabian Nights*—any literature was ripe for Marx's reading and commentary.

The Bible of the household, though, was Shakespeare. Marx had inherited "Shakespearomania," as the family called it, from his father-in-law, Baron Ludwig von Westphalen, who could recite entire plays in both English and German. At three or four, Tussy knew whole passages by heart; by the age of six she could recite complete scenes. "My favorite scenes," she wrote, "were the soliloquy of Richard IIIrd ('I can smile and smile and be a villain,' which I *know* I loved because I had to have a knife in my hand to say it!) and the scene between Hamlet and his mother!" Tussy's mother sometimes played the Queen, and the line, "Mother, you have my father much offended," was a special attraction as Tussy would look at her father "very pointedly" when she spoke it.

These little family stagings were as important to Tussy's education as the tales of Hans Röckle. From the stories her father told, and from his ready answers to every question, Tussy had surely acquired a sense of materialist thought. Her childhood took in the very years when Marx was researching the factory labor reports in the British Museum and putting together the first volume of *Das Kapital,* a period when he was perhaps at the peak of his intellectual activities. The playlets in the living room were to add another dimension to this education, giving to Tussy Marx's own sense of the drama of history.

14

This was the missing element that was to convert his scientific theories of the 1840s into the passionate and righteous arguments of *Das Kapital*. In the early writings, even in the *Communist Manifesto,* Marx had tried to be coldly scientific, to reveal in absolute terms the mechanical levers that moved history. Although as early as 1843 he had written about the alienation that transformed a laborer from a man into an animal, Marx had not experienced firsthand the poverty and pain of the working classes. Although powerful and convincing, his writings remained the abstract arguments of an intellectual, as removed from the suffering of a laborer as Marx's own life. Then, during the first years he spent in London from 1849, when he arrived penniless, friendless, and disillusioned at the failure of the revolution he had predicted for Europe, Marx knew for the first time the anguish of not having enough money to eat from one day to the next. His family would live on a diet of bread and potatoes for weeks at a time, would be evicted from residence after residence for falling behind with the rent. They would live, six of them, in two tiny rooms, a flat no larger than the workers' cottages of industrial Manchester, and in those rooms Marx would learn what it meant to live a life without privacy, without the human dignity of returning home with a decent wage after a decent day of work. In the very rooms where he wrote the *Eighteenth Brumaire,* he would learn the insecurity of poverty and the excruciating pain of poverty's bedfellows, starvation and disease. The trips to pawnshops, the repossessions and evictions, the denial of credit, the impossibility of buying medicine that is needed, the fear of calling a doctor who cannot be paid, the awareness that children cannot go out in the winter because their coats and shoes have been pawned—all this Marx saw and felt for the first time in those years in London. "Never, I think, was money written about under such a shortage of it," said Marx.

The experience admitted a tone of drama to his writing. Where once the bourgeoisie and proletariat, the factory owner and worker, had been neutral gears in a great machine of history, they were now to be villain and hero in a titanic epic. The bourgeoisie of *Das Kapital* is pure villain, transfigured by "those passions which are at once the most violent, the basest and the most abominable of which the human breast is capable: the furies of human interest." It remains a class, rather than a collection of individuals, because Marx continued to adhere to his theoretical formulations and because he did not share the poetic cult of sensibility that so affected the intellectual life of the middle of the nineteenth century. Yet beneath the sheer hypnotizing logic of the book's abstract chapters there is always the concrete example, the single stinging phrase that brings the complex and elegant laws of economics down to the horrors of human life. Every formula becomes a penny from the worker's pocket, or sweat from his pores. The whole volume takes on a dramatic development, with the suspense heightened by the interposed chapters of abstraction, until the drama itself reaches the climax of the chapter on "The Working Day," with its horrifying contrast between the day of the worker and the wealth of the greedy exploiter. It is this portrayal of the human condition as a life and death struggle that has made Marx survive into an "ism" when so many other doctrines of the nineteenth century faded quickly into the dustbin of history.

Marx spoke of writing a play on the "Gracchi" for the children, and many times the Marx family would walk to Sadler's Wells to watch some Shakespeare play from the standing pit, since they could never afford seats. But most of all, it was the little family dramas, where every line could be worked and reworked until it showed the keenest of passion, that were Tussy's theater. Not surprisingly, for Tussy the theories of political economy that were written between the lines of her education came out in the form of a simple and dramatic struggle, with all of history its stage, the classes as its characters, and a predictable ending.

The worst years of Marx's London poverty had ended by the time Tussy was born. She had never known the deaths of two children as infants, nor the agonized death of little Edgar. She had not known the humiliation of the birth of a bastard son to Helene Demuth, and the scandalous rumors that accompanied the surrender of the child to a working-class foster family. Tussy never really knew those two crowded rooms, for when she was two years old a timely inheritance enabled the whole family to move to a modest house on Haverstock Hill, on the southern slope of Hampstead Heath. "A princely abode in comparison with the holes we had lived in before," wrote Tussy's mother. It was soon furnished with a collection of "second-hand rubbish."

Yet poverty was not so easily overcome. By the 1860s, Marx's two older daughters were becoming proper young ladies, scurrying off to private schools, and lessons in French, Italian, piano, and drawing. They were chosen bridesmaids for a society wedding, and the man who was composing diatribes against the excesses of the bourgeoisie found himself confronted with his daughters' demands for bonnets and cloaks that would be presentable.

Engels, who had returned to the detested work in his father's cotton trade in Manchester to support himself and Marx, was the main source of funds in those years. "I live at any rate too dear for my conditions," wrote Marx in an appeal,

> but it is the only means with which the children . . . can enter into connections and relations which can secure them a future. I believe, you yourself will be of the opinion that even from the mere commercial point of view a pure proletarian arrangement would be unsuitable here, although it would be all right if my wife and I were alone or the daughters were young.

16

Years later Marx would put his requests to Engels in more direct terms: "My circumstances are harassing . . . yet certain appearances must be maintained for the children's sake."

Appearances were maintained so well that Tussy remembered childhood as a warm Victorian home, one which provided almost every comfort and differed from her playmates' homes only in the aura of politics that pervaded every room. Marx read several English and continental newspapers daily and every mention of the American Civil War, or Bismarck's wars, or the parliamentary debates of Gladstone and Disraeli, or the pitiful adventures of Napoleon III, was noted, chronicled, tiraded, harangued. Unable to address kings and parliaments, Marx instead lectured to his family, and in tones that made the sarcasm of his articles in the New York *Tribune* seem like sincerity.

In politics, too, Tussy was her father's favorite. Her older sisters, Jenny and Laura, had reached that age of embarrassment when schooling was about to draw to a close and middle-class Victorian daughters faced the limited choice of a respectable profession, such as that of governess or tutoress; or marriage to a proper and eligible young man; or waning at home as a spinster. But Tussy was still young, still free to devote her energies to a grave if infantile interest in the politics that consumed her father.

She would write letters to her uncle in Holland to ask what he thought of the Polish uprising or the "Federals" in the American Civil War. When she convinced herself that "Abraham Lincoln badly needed my advice as to the war," Tussy wrote him long letters that her father promised to mail, but did not. And when the Fenians led an insurrection in Ireland in 1867, Tussy declared herself firmly on the side of "the convicted nation." For the occasion she even rewrote the English royal anthem:

> God save our flag of green
> Soon may it bright be seen
> God save the green.
> Send it victorious
> Peaceful and glorious
> God save our flag of green
> God save the green.

Tussy's feelings for Ireland were advanced by her friendship with Lizzie Burns, an Irish factory girl who lived on and off with Engels in Manchester. Engels maintained two residences in Manchester, an official town house in the center of the city, and a cottage in the proletarian outskirts, where he lived with Mary Burns until her death in 1863, and afterward with her sister Lizzie. Tussy was allowed to visit Engels ("Uncle Fred") often, and there she met the Burns sisters, the Irish agitators they sheltered, and their stories of maltreated and beleaguered Ireland. After a visit to Engels in 1868, Tussy returned home to declare: "Formerly I clung to a man, now I cling to a nation." So constantly was the phrase on her lips that she earned the nickname "The Poor Neglected Nation." Her letters were signed F.S., for Fenian Sister.

Tussy was in Manchester when Engels, having come to terms with his partner for the withdrawal of his capital and compensation for his goodwill in the firm, "reached the end of his forced labor." "I shall never forget the triumph with which he exclaimed: 'For the last time!' as he put on his boots in the morning to go to the office for the last time," wrote Tussy afterward. She knew of the financial help that Engels had given her father, for she had often helped him answer letters, and had seen the halves of five pound notes that Engels would enclose. But seeing Engels skip across the field on his way home that afternoon was perhaps the first time Tussy realized the sacrifices that had been made to give her and her sisters the "proper" upbringing that had been maintained "for the sake of appearances." The conditions of Engels' sale left him with enough money to settle an annual allowance of £350 on Marx, putting a permanent end to the days of aching financial worry.

Tussy's initiation to the realities of government was, for her, a precise illustration of every lesson her father had given in the wickedness and pettiness of European regimes. It came with the outbreak of war between France and Prussia in 1870, a conflict that captivated Marx's attention: "Both nations remind me of the anecdote of the two Russian noblemen accompanied by two Jews, their serfs. Nobleman A strikes the Jew of Nobleman B, and B answers: 'Schlägst du meinen Jud, schlag ich deinen Jud.' So both nations seem reconciled to their despots by being allowed, each of them, to strike at the despot of the other nation." Engels too observed the war carefully. A series of articles he wrote for the *Pall Mall Gazette* earned him the nickname of "General" among his friends and family.

The war caught Tussy's sister Laura and her husband, Paul Lafargue, in Paris. When Napoleon III's spectacular defeats boded the end of the Second Empire, the two set off for Bordeaux, where Paul's family lived, and where he hoped to rally republican support for a new France. In the midst of this excitement, Tussy and her oldest sister Jenny got permission to visit the Lafargues, perhaps to help take care of the baby while Paul carried on his political activities. They arrived in time to witness Napoleon's final defeat and the flight of the Lafargues to Spain with the French secret police in hot pursuit.

As the plot thickened, Jenny and Tussy followed the Lafargues to a Spanish border village where Paul was in hiding. On their return to France they were arrested on the French frontier, escorted by twenty-four gendarmes to the prefect's house, kept waiting under heavy guard, then removed to the house where they had been staying in Luchon.

The prefect had already interrogated the landlady and servants. When he returned to take on the two girls, then aged fifteen and twenty-five, he brought a full entourage: a *procureur général,* a *juge de paix,* a *juge d'instruction,* the *procureur de la republique,* and *gendarmes, mouchards,* and *agents* galore. He also brought along "a forbidding-looking creature—a most unwomanly woman" whose task it was to search the two suspected spies. When Tussy refused to allow the woman to undress her, the woman returned to the room with the *procureur de la république.*

"If you will not allow this woman to search you, I shall do so," he said.

"You have no right to come near a British subject," answered Tussy. "I have an English passport."

The *procureur* was unimpressed by the English passport, and the girls finally yielded to the search by the woman, who went through every item of their clothing, and ran her "spidery fingers" through their hair.

They were then taken to separate rooms and interrogated until two-thirty in the morning. Both sisters held out, even when confronted with the ridiculous "evidence" of an alleged plot. One of the magistrates had found a commercial letter of Lafargue's, in which reference was made to the export of sheep and oxen. The prefect proudly deciphered the letter as evidence of a conspiracy: "Oxen, sheep, intrigues, sheep-Communists, oxen-Internationals."

At last, a Mutt and Jeff trick broke Tussy down. The prefect read out a fabricated statement of charges to which Jenny had allegedly confessed. Tussy, fearing to contradict her sister, said, "Yes, it is so."

The entire episode came to nothing beyond the harassment of the girls. They spent another night in a *gendarmerie,* then were set free. But for Tussy, the adventure was a perfect introduction to the world of government that her father had written and spoken of so often. The buffoonery of the police—who "deduced" that a lamp for warming babies' milk was some diabolical machine used to discharge petroleum into the streets of Paris by the putative *petroleuses*—was a perfect example of the utter helplessness of the governments that Marx had always attacked with scorn. Most of all, the episode was proof of the power of Marx's writings and of the International. As Tussy explained the affair, ". . . all that because Lafargue is Mohr's son-in-law, for Lafargue had done nothing at all."

II

It was less than a year later that Tussy was introduced to an aspect of the real world that her "education" had not covered. She happened to be lying on the sofa at home one day, when a "sudden sexual initiation . . . [was]

effected by a prominent foreign follower of her father's.'' Rape or seduction? Old lecher or dashing young man? A thirdhand account by Havelock Ellis, the only record of the episode, gives no clues. It may not have happened at all, but shortly afterward, when she was seventeen years old, Tussy showed her first interest in a man other than her father.

It was after the fall of the Commune, when many of the Communards went into exile in London to avoid transportation to New Caledonia. Marx had been one of the few individuals outside France to salute the Commune, and his home in London became a haven for many of the refugees. His two unmarried daughters both spoke French fluently and they became natural hostesses. Before long they were being pursued by ardent French admirers.

Prosper Olivier Hippolyte Lissagaray was thirty-four, a Basque who dressed in dashing clothes and, it was rumored, carried a revolver under his coat. His ''reputation'' matched his dress, and gossip told racy tales of his exploits as a duelist and as a lover. He had been a journalist under the Empire, and had made efforts to rally a democratic opposition in Toulouse and later in Paris. Although never an official member of the Commune, he had served the cause in the National Guard, and during the heroic week of May, his newspaper, *Tribune du Peuple,* had advocated a fight to the finish with a marked accent of 1793. His methods of courtship were, as Tussy put it, ''highly compromising,'' but the dashing Frenchman caught her fancy, and she soon announced to her father that she was engaged.

Marx was furious. His middle daughter, Laura, had already married a Frenchman, Paul Lafargue, and his oldest, Jenny, was engaged to Charles Longuet, another Communard exile. Even in the latter case, Tussy's mother regretted that her daughter's choice had not fallen, for a change, on an Englishman or a German. Longuet was active in politics, as a follower of Proudhon, and his mother-in-law-to-be, who knew well the anxieties of being a political wife, entertained fears for her daughter. What made Tussy's engagement to Lissagaray even more distressing was her youth, and the fact that Lissagaray, a rebel in politics as well as in his reputation, gave no indication of becoming a follower of Marx. Although he frequented the house—until Marx banned him—he was of a very independent mind: His first short volume on the commune, *Huit journées de mai derrière les barricades,* as well as the famed history of the Commune which grew out of it, show no debt to Marx.

''Today I have written to Tussy,'' Marx said in a letter to Engels, ''and am sure that Herr Lissagaray will be obliged for the moment to put a good face on a bad business.'' Tussy protested. Marx was unmoved.

> I want nothing from him [Marx wrote in another letter to Engels] except that he would give proofs instead of phrases, that he would be better than his reputation, and that one could have a certain right to rely on him. You

will see from the answer [from Tussy] how the man continues to act. The damned thing is that I have to proceed with much consideration and foresight for the child's sake.

Lissagaray, with his ostentatious attire and his contempt for convention, seemed to awaken a desire for independence in Tussy. Using a letter of reference she had got from Engels in 1873, Tussy found herself a position at a boarding school for ladies run by a Miss Hall in Brighton. Marx probably consented to the move because he thought it would keep his daughter away from Lissagaray.

The move did not end the problem. Lissagaray visited Tussy in Brighton, and the conflict between love and filial duty left Tussy a nervous wreck, unable to work and finally confined to bed. Mrs. Anderson, the local physician kept changing diagnosis and prescriptions, but was unable to accomplish anything for the patient. Only one medicine seemed to help.

> I want to know, dear Mohr, when I may see L again. It is so *very* hard *never* to see him. I have been doing my best to be patient, but it is so difficult, and I don't feel as if I could be much longer.—I do not expect you to say that he can come here—I should not even wish it, but could I not, now and then go for a little walk with him? You let me go out with Outine, with Frankel,* why not with him?—No one moreover will be astonished to see us together, as everybody knows we are engaged. . . .
>
> When I was so very ill at Brighton (during a week I fainted 2 or 3 times a day) L cam[e to] see me, each time left me stronger and happier, and more able to bear the rather heavy load laid on my shoulders. It is *so* long since I saw him, and I am beginning to feel so very miserable notwithstanding all my efforts to be merry and cheerful. I cannot much longer.— Believe me, dear Mohr, if I could see him now and then it could do me more good than all Mrs. Anderson's prescriptions put together—I know that by experience.

A contest of wills between father and daughter over the daughter's choice of a beau was not unusual in Victorian England. Young women, dictated to in every decision of their lives, with their education, their friends, their activities, even their wardrobes prescribed by convention or by the wills of their fathers, often sought a relief from this oppression in flamboyant young lovers, sometimes foreigners, more often men who were just a little risqué in their politics or their reputations. A great blowup would ensue, with consternation on the part of father and mother and strong admonition about reputations and traditions, about the effect of scandal on present and future generations, and about ''decent people,'' ''God-given'' class distinctions, and

---

* Nicolai Isaakovitch Outine was a Russian emigré whom Marx once referred to as ''one of my dearest friends''; Leo Frankel was a Hungarian socialist who had been elected to the Commune.

the "control of base passions." Though some families suffered permanent ruptures over these infatuations or affairs, more often the wounds could be healed and a mutual pact of silence would bury the damage forever, as the daughter returned from her wayward path to choose or have chosen for her a proper and appropriate young man of the right family and with the proper standing. These affairs were no monopoly of the upper classes; indeed, every middle-class Victorian family with any pretensions to propriety faced the threat of what such a liaison could do to the family's good name. Social considerations, coupled with the father's concern for the means of his daughter's suitors, were usually enough to put a sudden and effective damper on nascent romances between bold adventurers and well-bred young ladies.

What made the contest of wills between Marx and Tussy extraordinary was that Marx was not, if we are to believe his writings, a typical Victorian gentleman and father. On such questions as marriage and the choice of mates, and on the very question of the liberation of women, he had discoursed often, and always to roughly the same effect. "The changing of an historical epoque is always determined as a function of the progress of women toward liberty," wrote Marx in *The Holy Family* in 1845, "because it is here, in the relationship of women with men, of the weak with the strong, that the victory of humanity over barbarity appears in the most obvious fashion. The degree of women's liberation is the natural measure of the degree of general emancipation." Or, later in the same passage: "No one, in fact, is more punished than the woman maintained in slavery."

With the onset of communism, Marx assured his readers in the *Communist Manifesto,* family relationships would also change, not into the vulgar communism of wives practiced already by the bourgeoisie with their wife trading and prostitution, but "because marriage will become a union of free beings, who will find in one another a reciprocal enrichment."

For Marx, this theoretical position was a direct and logical consequence of the altered relationships which would result in a different historical era. But just as piecemeal changes in the status of workers would not definitively change their relationship to the means of production, so piecemeal changes in human relationships were not possible in a bourgeois era. Thus in his own life Marx was thoroughly bourgeois, participating in the only kind of relationships he thought possible in a bourgeois era. And while Tussy may have thought her alliance with Lissagaray revolutionary, to Marx it was simply unwise.

His reaction was steeped with the middle-class horror against which he had so often tiraded. In letters to Engels he wrote of her "affliction," and of "this women's disease where the hysterical element plays into it." Women who assert themselves in spite of the advice of men were, for Marx, "hysterical." He had used the same language to describe his wife, who in the early 1850s was thoroughly distraught about the woes the family endured, the pains of being a political wife, and intermittent pangs of remorse for the comfortable aristocratic life she had left behind. Marx's analysis of what troubled his wife was simplistic, and, in its nineteenth-century diction, typical: "hysterical explosions," "eccentric emotions," and a "dangerous nervous state."

Marx's prescription for Tussy's ailment was equally simple and conventional: he would take her with him to Karlsbad, which had been prescribed for Marx's own liver ailments. Twice, in 1874 and again in 1876, Marx traveled to the Bohemian spa with his daughter. Each time the hundreds of cups of magic water from the *Brunnen,* the long promenades through the exquisite gardens, the fabled aura of civilization as people discussed Richard Wagner's love life and other *au courant* topics, and the precise regimen from morning until evening did wonders for Tussy's symptoms. Her appetite improved, the general nervousness abated, her complexion turned rosy once again. She dressed tastefully, even strikingly, in Karlsbad, wearing her hair down so that it blew to and fro in the breezes. Once again, she was Marx's little girl, and it seemed to Gertrude Kugelmann, the wife of one of Marx's friends, that she was allowed to follow her caprices like a pampered child. "Young women need to primp themselves," said Marx, as he admired and paraded his darling daughter.

Yet while Karlsbad cured some symptoms, it left the disease untreated. Tussy still asserted her independence. She smoked cigarettes incessantly, even in restaurants—still shocking behavior for women. And at one point she boldly showed Frau Kugelmann a letter she had received from Lissagaray. It began: "Ma chère petite femme."

Back in London, Marx yielded a little. Tussy was allowed to see Lissagaray again, although he was still forbidden to call on her at home. When he founded a review, *Rouge et noir,* she solicited articles from her father's friends. The journal failed, and Lissagaray turned his energies to writing his famous *Histoire de la Commune de 1871,* perhaps the best-known history of the Commune and a work which did much to legitimize it in the eyes of France and the rest of the world. Tussy insisted upon translating the book into English, and Marx, who recognized the merits of the work despite his opinions of the author personally, gave her advice on many points. He later revised and corrected her translation himself.

Tussy languished in London. She undertook occasional research for her father at the British Museum. She summoned up a dilatory interest in school board elections. She read the papers, including the job offerings. "A young lady desires an engagement as governess. She can give good references, and teaches *German,* French, *music* and drawing learnt abroad. TERMS 6 SHILL-

INGS a week!!!'' Tussy copied the advertisement from the *Times;* it could as well have been her own.

In 1875 Tussy noted the establishment of a London Medical School for Women. "It is of course chiefly an advantage for 'bourgeoises','' she wrote to a friend, "but it is always something and it is time that women too may be able to work, and have other occupations than dress.''

It was time. The ordained lot of Victorian woman was not very uplifting. Rich, middle-class, or poor, she was considered a "relative creature,'' whose brain was too small to permit her to reason or to pursue any connected line of thought. Her duty was to obey the males of the household, which left precious little freedom to pursue any career. And even should the males of her household be a particularly enlightened group, there were more than sufficient laws and social mores to discourage any career for a woman.

The duty of most Victorian women was to be married, and to serve their husbands as if they were lords and literal masters. If misfortune decreed that they were to remain single, they were to live quietly with their families, or take up a correct position as a governess or perhaps that of teacher in a proper boarding school. Women who chose to defy these choices usually ended up in either of two professions—prostitution or the stage, both patronized and condemned fulsomely by men. To families with any social aspirations, the latter choice by a daughter was not very different from the former.

Tussy elected the stage. In 1880 she gave her first recitation, at an evening entertainment held at a North London Hall for the benefit of the widow of a Communard. She read "The Pied Piper of Hamelin,'' the childrens' poem by Robert Browning. Eduard Bernstein, who saw the performance, wrote that she was "full of life,'' and that she "spoke with a wealth of modulation and earned a great deal of applause.''

As long as the performances were for socialist benefits, Marx did not mind. But he soon recognized the intensity of Tussy's involvement. "She is burning with eagerness to make for herself, as she believes she will in this way, an independent career as an artist,'' he wrote to Engels. "She is not frank; what I say is founded on observation, not on her own confession.''

In time Tussy made her confession. She had joined the New Shakespeare Society, and, through its founder, Frederick James Furnival, cultivated friendships with the members of the Dogberry, a private Shakespeare reading club. Soon club members were visiting the Marx house, discussing their idolization of Henry Irving's acting and planning their own careers. Tussy decided to ask her father to pay for dramatic lessons with a Mrs. Vexin. "I feel sorry to cost Papa so much,'' she wrote to her sister Jenny, then living in Paris, "but after all very small sums were expended on my education, compared at least to what is *now* demanded of girls—& I think if I do succeed it will have been a good investment. I shall try too, to get as much work as I can so that I may have a little money by the time I need it." The new work was as a "préer," writing précis of books and articles. "You see, dear," the letter continued, "I've a goodly number of irons in the fire, but I feel I've wasted quite enough of my life, & that it is high time I did something."

Marx opposed the independence of a dramatic career as he had opposed the independence of Tussy's relationship with Lissagaray. He refused to subsidize the acting lessons, and once again the collision between filial duty and her own mind's dictates took its toll on Tussy's health. Marx returned from a visit to Paris to find her "pale and emaciated." "For some weeks," he wrote to his daughter Jenny, "she has eaten nothing (literally). Her nervous system is in a pitiable state, whence continual insomnia, tremblings of hands, neuralgic convulsions of the face, etc."

They were all ill that year of 1881. Tussy's mother was dying of cancer of the liver; Marx was suffering from pleurisy and bronchitis; and Tussy, despite a regimen of taking iron, rest, and Turkish baths, still felt "seedy." For months the Marx house was like a hospital, as Helene Demuth ran from bed to bed to ply them with medications.

On December 2, Tussy's mother died. "My mother and I loved each other passionately," wrote Tussy, "but she did not know me as father did. One of the bitterest of many sorrows in my life is that my mother died, thinking, despite all our love, that I had been hard and cruel, and never guessing that to save her and father sorrow I had sacrificed the best, freshest years of my life."

Engels came when he heard the news and said, "Mohr is dead too." The words "nearly made me wild at him," wrote Tussy, but as she later realized, ". . . it was true." With the death of his wife Marx was a broken man, lonely, aging quickly, realizing that he would never finish *Das Kapital,* that the long-faded influence of the International would never be revived, that he would remain to the end an outsider in European politics, condemned to criticize from afar while a newer generation of socialist leaders put together the parties and programs of an emerging working-class movement. He clutched at the only family he still had, the only woman of the many who had once clustered around his patriarchal authority. Lenchen was still there to care for Marx, but only Tussy could listen and understand all that he had to say.

The demands on Tussy's devotion were stronger than ever before, and even Marx was aware of her reluctance. "Tussy is very laconic, and seems indeed to endure the sojourn with me only out of a sense of duty as a self-sacrificing martyr," he wrote to his daughter Laura. Yet Marx did nothing to make Tussy's decision easier, and there was no one to whom she could turn in her perplexity. She finally wrote to her oldest sister, Jenny, to present the quandary. Should she immediately become an actress and be independent? Or should she indefinitely follow the life of duty that seemed predestined, knowing that the chances of ever having a successful career on the stage were ticking away with each passing day?

> What neither Papa nor the doctors nor anyone will understand is that it is chiefly *mental worry* that affects me.—Papa talks about my having "rest" & "getting strong" before I try anything & won't see that "rest" is the last thing I need—& that I should be more likely to "get strong" if I have some definite plan & work than to go on waiting & waiting.

Jenny had just moved to Paris so that her husband could pursue his literary activities with Clemenceau's newspaper. In letters, she and Tussy compared their lives and dreams. Jenny had once acted in *Macbeth* on a London stage. At the urging of her parents, she had dropped her aspirations for the theater, and worked instead five days a week, for three years, as governess to the family of a Dr. Monroe, until in 1871, the Monroes made "the terrible discovery that I am the daughter of the petroleum chief who defended the iniquitous Communard movement." Shortly after her dismissal she met Longuet and was married.

> . . . I feel as if I were growing quite an idiot [wrote Jenny] since I have been entirely cloistered in this apartment nest. The cruelest of it all is that though I drudge like a nigger Longuet never does anything but scream at me and fumbles every minute he is in the house. I feel more sick of life than I can say—& if it were not for the poor children, I should soon know how to change my uncongenial existence. But enough—remember it is strictly *between us only that* I speak so frankly.

She went on to describe the woes of married life. The "two geese of servants" had quit, and Longuet kept postponing their replacement by saying the family would soon go to the seashore for a holiday, which, of course, never happened. The children were sick, one after another; the littlest had recurrent diarrhea ("The smell is frightful and not one of us could have stood it had not the child a room of his own. . . ."). Jenny was called upon to be "head cook and bottle washer" not only for her husband and children, but also for her mother-in-law, who daily accused her of laziness and of trying to squander Longuet's money.

By comparison, wrote Jenny, Tussy could look forward to a life of independence. ". . . I admit frankly that I rejoiced in your freedom and in your prospect of living the only free life a woman can live—the artistic one."

The arguments and advice were all stacked on the side of the theater, but

Tussy was still torn by the pull of her father. The quandary left her in a state approaching a nervous breakdown. She slept only six hours in a week, and took every manner of drugs. To no avail. She was constantly on the verge of hysteria. When Marx's own health seemed to improve, she concluded that he no longer needed her as a nursing companion. "If I only had a little money," she wrote to Jenny, "I should distinctly say this; go in for hard work with Mrs. Vexin—& then *see* (you may be sure I will make no rash plunge) what I can do. . . . You know, dear, I'm not a bit vain—& that if I err it is not from over-confidence but from distrust in myself—but in this I think I could get on. I have seen too often—& with such different people— that I can *move* an audience—& that is the chief thing."

Convinced finally that Tussy's nervous symptoms had reached a danger- ous state, Marx relented. He wrote to Engels: "I would not for anything in the world wish that the child should imagine herself to be sacrificed on the family altar in the form of the 'nurse' of an old man." The agreement seems to have been that Tussy could take the lessons and commit herself to the dra- matic career, but that she had to stop seeing Lissagaray. She agreed. Jenny saluted both decisions: "I congratulate you with all my heart and rejoice to think that one of us at least will not pass her life in watching over a pot-au- feu. I have no doubt you will succeed." And: "French husbands are not worth much at the best of times & at the worst—well, the less said of it—the better."

Within a week Tussy was on the stage, reading "The Pied Piper" and "The Bridge of Sighs," by Thomas Hood, a tragic story of a homeless girl who drowns herself in despair. Tussy earned all of two pounds for her ef- forts, but, as she wrote Jenny, "It is better to have tried and failed, than never to have tried at all." Soon she was in a constant whirl of meetings of the Shakespeare society, auditions, minor performances, and recitations. At the annual entertainment of the Browning Society, she did her "Pied Piper" and "Count Gismond," a chivalric epic. "The place was crowded," she wrote to Jenny, "& as all sorts of 'literary' & other swells were there I felt ridiculously nervous—but [got] on capitally." Elated with the forbidden sweets of independence, Tussy gushed on about a "crush" at Lady Wilde's, a benefit where Henry Irving himself would recite, a private reading for the president of the Royal Academy. She was scarcely a star, really no more than a star-struck initiate, but the glimpse of independence filled Tussy with rosy dreams of establishing herself among this galaxy of literary stars, of being truly herself, and of living a life free from the domination and tutelage of what her father once called "the dead weight of generations."

For more than a year, Marx ran away from death. The winter after his wife died was so cold that a continuous coal fire could not fight off his chills. Recurrent attacks of pleurisy could not be stemmed, and between at- tacks he coughed so horribly that his old afflictions, the boils and the ever troublesome liver, were scarcely noticed. The knowledge that Tussy—for all her love and sense of duty—was a less than enthusiastic companion, only added to the bleakness. His doctors finally ordered him to follow the sun to Algiers, where the warmth could be expected to cure. Marx went, but the journey was a slow one, through Paris—where he visited his two daughters—and through the calamities of missed trains and walks around strange stations in the cold rain. Algiers alternated between a burning heat that gave him a rash, and an unusually cold rain. He tried Monte Carlo. Again, the rain followed him like an evil omen. He spent the summer with his oldest daughter in Argenteuil, outside Paris, and there he could tell stories to his grandchildren, or play the horse for them, as he had done for his children. But the ill health pursued him, and visits to Enghien-les-Bains and Vevey brought the same cruel rain. "It is all my fault," he said. "I bring the bad weather with me."

His daughter Laura, then living in Paris with her husband, accompanied him to Vevey, after he had written to her of his fear of riding alone in a railway car: ". . . you see it is more or less your duty to accompany the old man of the mountain."

Nothing worked. For the next winter the doctors tried Ventnor, on the Isle of Wight. There Marx lived in a boardinghouse, alone, unable to write or read for any extended period. His powers of observation were acute enough to note the foibles of his fellow boarders, but he had no audience to listen to his tirades and harangues.

In January 1883, Jenny Marx Longuet, never quite recovering from complications following the birth of a fifth child, died. The news of her illness had been concealed from Marx. A telegram was sent to Tussy to announce the death and it was Tussy's duty to tell Marx. She hurried down to Ventnor, torturing her brain to prepare a careful speech. When she walked into the room, Marx sensed the news on her face. "Our Jennychen is dead," he said.

Marx moved immediately to London, where at least he could have the company of Helene Demuth and Tussy. His various afflictions, too numerous to list, were exacerbated by bronchitis and laryngitis, then an abscess in one lung. He died, alone, in his armchair, on March 14, 1883.

> Of my father I was so sure! [wrote Tussy]. For long miserable years there was a shadow between us . . . yet our love was always the same, and despite everything our faith and trust in each other . . . father, though he did not *know* till just before the end, felt he must trust me—our natures were so exactly alike.

The shadow between them was the chasm between two generations. Marx, for all his prescience and prophecy, remained a Victorian to the core.

He had been conventional in his mores and priggish in his attitudes to women. Once, when with a group of comrades he had begun singing *"Jung, Jung Zimmergesell,"* a mildly off-color German drinking song, he went out of his way to make sure that the women of the house were out of earshot. And when his wife had been intolerant of Engels' somewhat unorthodox relationships with the Burns sisters, he had never once spoken up in defence of Engels' mistresses or the moral legitimacy of Engels' relationships with these women. Thus, while he might praise the Communards for their new morality, and condemn them for having too many scruples to seize the funds of the Bank of France, he remained himself a prisoner of the very morality he condemned. In his world there had been no room for the New Woman that Tussy had become.

III

Edward Aveling was born on November 29, 1849, a few months after the Marx family settled in London. His father, the Reverend Thomas William Baxter Aveling, was a Congregational minister, one of those incurable Victorian optimists who reveled in the Great Exhibition of the Crystal Palace. "An eighth wonder of the world," he called it, especially its display of the British and Foreign Bible Society with copies of the Scriptures in more than one hundred fifty different languages and dialects. "The heart will thrill," he wrote, "as it reflects that by these the Church shall conquer the world for Christ." Aveling's mother was known only for her drinking—an attribute which has been singled out by those who have sought to explain Edward Aveling.

He was a sickly child, and careless nursing caused an injury to his spine which left him slightly stooped. Most of his early years he spent at home, reading Shakespeare, Defoe, and Fielding in his father's excellent library; on Sundays he was allowed only *Pilgrim's Progress*. Although fourth of six brothers, Edward was headstrong and assertive, even as a child. When asked whether he would take peas or potatoes at dinner, he promptly replied, "Both please." And although he was strictly forbidden to attend the theater, he would regularly sneak out to pantomimes at Drury Lane.

For his education he was sent to Harrow; from there to Taunton, where he studied medicine under a tutor for a year and a half; then finally to University College, London. He picked up awards and scholarships like so many coins in the street, until he took a D.Sc. in 1876, was elected a Fellow of the Linnaean Society and a Fellow of University College. His first appointments in a long string of teaching positions were at the North London Collegiate School for Girls (a pioneering institution), Lecturer in Comparative Anatomy at London Hospital, and Tutor in Science at King's College, London.

But Aveling's fame in London did not derive from his academic career. His education had taken place during those years when Darwin's theories of evolution were in open competition with both religious and established scientific authority. Darwin's notoriety made science popular by the 1880s, and the London public began attending lectures and experiments with the fervor that had once been reserved for the Sunday Mass. Many a budding academic could earn far more from coaching these new science students than from regular university appointments—especially those, like Aveling, who had early joined the Darwin supporters, and put Darwinian ideas into their lectures and tutoring sessions. With his loud check suits, his bright ties, and his easy familiarity with the latest in theater, arts, and books, Aveling became one of the most popular coaches among the young women who for the first time were taking science lessons.

"Aveling was one of those men," wrote H. M. Hyndman, "who have an attraction for women quite inexplicable to the male sex. Like Wilkes, ugly and even repulsive to some extent as he looked, he needed but half an hour's start of the handsomest man in London." Some who knew him said that there was a "fascinating touch of the diabolic about him," that he was handsome in a showy way, that women could not resist running their fingers through his hair. Others compared him to Quasimodo, called him "a repulsive creature," or, as a saying had it, "Nobody can be so bad as Aveling looks." Bernard Shaw, who knew him well, painted a rather circumstantial portrait:

> Now Aveling was not a handsome man. He was undersized, had the eyes of a basilisk, and it was said of him that he would have been interesting in a zoological museum as a reptile but impossible as a man. Short of actual deformation he had every aesthetic disadvantage except a voice like a euphonium of extraordinary resonance and beauty of tone.

As a teacher of science Aveling had a record of excellence. In other areas his performance had been somewhat less compelling. In 1872 he had married Isabel Campbell Frank, the plump and decorative daughter of a poulterer. They soon separated because her devout faith and Aveling's Darwinism could not accommodate themselves to the same household. She ran off with a priest and began spreading insulting rumors about her husband—most of which were quite true. "As a borrower of money and a swindler and seducer of women," wrote Shaw,

> his record was unimpeachable. On the same day he would borrow sixpence from the poorest man within his reach on the pretense of having forgotten his purse, and three hundred pounds from the richest to free himself from

30

debts that he never paid. He had the art of coaching for science examinations, and girl students would scrape money together to pay him in advance his fee for twelve lessons. The more fortunate ones got nothing worse for their money than letters of apology for breaking the lesson engagements. The others were seduced and had their microscopes appropriated.

It was through his coaching that Aveling met Annie Besant and the daughters of Charles Bradlaugh. Bradlaugh was then the leader of the Secularist Society, the leading movement of free thought in England. Annie Besant was already notorious in England for her much publicized separation from her husband on grounds of irreconcilable religious differences; the court had taken her children away from her because of her atheism. With Bradlaugh, as "C.B. and A.B.," she so popularized the free thinking movement, with its combination of utilitarian morality and an uncompromising belief in the possibility of the improvement of human conditions in the world, that membership grew to nearly six thousand by 1880. A.B., in her pursuit of education, began studying with Edward Aveling. In her *Autobiography* she wrote that he was an ideal teacher; he undoubtedly taught her more than the laboratory science she signed up for.

Aveling began to publish articles in the *National Reformer,* the journal of the Secularist Society—first anonymously, with the signature "E.D.," then, after a manifesto entitled "Credo Ergo Laborabo" ("I believe, therefore I shall work"), as an open advocate of free thought. For his first lecture to the movement he gave a talk on Shelley. Mrs. Besant, the chairman of the evening, declared to the audience afterward that "our mistress Liberty has won a new knight." As she later wrote, she was enraptured by the mere music of his speech, the "artistic charm" of his language, which was "exquisitely chosen" and "polished to the highest extent." Soon afterward the two of them went on a holiday together in the mountains of North Wales, and there began to exchange poetic compliments rather more romantic than allegorical. Before long, Aveling was writing passionate passages in the secularist journals describing the loveliness of Annie's face, form, and mind, and announcing that "she shall be the sole mistress of my life."

Bradlaugh welcomed Aveling to the movement as a man of intellect and standing, who would bring science to the campaign of the freethinkers. His articles added a breath of humor to the *National Reformer,* and a wealth of erudition to the movement. The stage at meetings soon enjoyed the presence of "the great Trinity in Unity," the triumvirate of C.B., A.B., and E.A. Aveling also gave a series of lectures for the movement, and after a lecture modestly entitled "The Sermon on the Mount," he took advantage of the secular rite that followed, designed to replace baptism, to name a child of one of the followers "Aveling Hope."

But Aveling was not a man to devote himself heart and soul to any movement, even a movement headed by a woman as dynamic and appealing as

Mrs. Besant. Although he worked in Bradlaugh's first campaign for parliament—a campaign which was to result in Bradlaugh's election, though as a freethinker he was allowed neither to take the oath of office, nor to affirm his loyalty, and thus could not take his seat—it was not long before Aveling was heating other irons in the London fires. Capitalizing on both his scientific credentials and the fame he had generated in his talks and writings for the Secularists, he got himself elected to the school board for Westminster. He also became a popular atheist lecturer, and even journeyed to Darwin's home to secure the support of the master for the doctrine of atheism.

"I am with you in thought," said Darwin, "but I should prefer the word Agnostic to the word Atheist."

"After all," said Aveling, "Agnostic was but Atheist writ respectable, and Atheist was only Agnostic writ aggressive."

Still, Darwin would not give his endorsement. He kept silent in order not to offend his churchgoing wife, a delicacy that Aveling would never understand. Aveling had to console himself with Darwin's admission that Christianity "is not supported by the evidence."

Aveling also took advantage of his already renowned voice. At the slightest provocation, he would give evenings of "Recitations from Poetry and Prose," ranging from Shakespeare to Bret Harte. For less serious occasions, he gave "Readings, Grave and Gay," featuring Edgar Allen Poe's "Bells," a piece he was to repeat often. At each reading he would be surrounded by a bevy of young girls, all thrilled at his erudition and his graceful ability to combine science with art. "Our aim is to gladden the life of man, and to remove all that saddens it," he would tell his appreciative audiences. "We love all forms of art. Free as children we can laugh, and sing, and dance to our heart's content."

He gave talks on Shakespeare, emphasizing the need for the unity which he, presumably, represented, between the scientific mind and literature. As a theatergoer he fell in with the circle who worshipped the muse of Henry Irving. That group not only flattered Aveling's sense of himself; they were also a little racier than "C.B. and A.B."

Aveling and Tussy Marx met in the reading room of the British Museum. In fact, although Tussy did not remember, they were meeting for a second time. The first had been around 1873, when Tussy was too interested in Lissagaray to notice any other man. Aveling had given a lecture on "Insects and Flowers" at the Orphan Working School in Hampstead. Afterward three members of the audience went up to meet the lecturer: "One of the three [Aveling recalled] was a not very tall, but very powerfully built, man, with a tremendous leonine head, and the strongest and yet gentlest eyes I think I ever saw. The second was a lady of singular refinement and high breeding.

The third was a young girl." These were Karl Marx, his wife, and Tussy. Marx congratulated the lecturer, but as long as Aveling remained associated with Bradlaugh, he had no further contact with the Marx family. Marx and Bradlaugh were intellectual rivals. Marx called Bradlaugh "a courtesan of Plon-Plon" and "the huge self-idolater." Bradlaugh returned the compliments, though minus the cleverness, by calling socialism a set of "half-baked, plausible sounding, economically unsound" ideas.

The reading room of the British Museum was a regular meeting place of the demimonde of London intellectuals. Aveling wrote a humorous account of meetings there, and recommended a separation of the sexes, so "there would be less talking and fewer marriages." Tussy, who earned occasional money by doing "devil's work" (research for other people) and who also checked Blue Books and other sources for her father, was a regular. Beatrice Potter, later the wife of Sidney Webb, met her there in the spring of 1883, about the time that Tussy met Aveling.

> Went in afternoon to British Museum and met Miss Marx in refreshment-room . . . [B.P. wrote in her diary].
>
> It was useless to argue with her—she refused to recognize the beauty of the Christian religion. She read the gospels as the gospel of damnation. Thought that Christ, if he had existed, was a weak-headed individual, with a good deal of sweetness of character, but quite lacking in heroism. "Did he not in the last moment pray that the cup might pass from Him?" . . .
>
> In person she is comely, dressed in a slovenly way, with curly black hair flying about in all directions. Fine eyes full of life and sympathy, otherwise ugly features and expression, and complexion showing the signs of an unhealthy excited life, kept up with stimulants and tempered with narcotics.

There is no record detailing the meeting of Aveling and Tussy, but in April 1883 the monthly *Progress,* a magazine of "advanced thought," carried a notice about the death of Karl Marx, which mentioned that Aveling and Tussy were at the funeral together. In fact, for several months they had been working together on the magazine: Aveling as a substitute for the editor, G. W. Foote, who was serving out a year in jail for blasphemy, and Tussy as his editorial assistant. The journal's articles mixed socialism with atheism, and seemed devoted in large part to attacks on Bradlaugh and the Secular Society. In the occasional poetry, Aveling published a chronicle of his new romance.

> The trill of a lark; the sound of a sea;
> Green grass growing on a salt-sown lea;
> The voice of a maid; a man's heart-strife;
> Strange hopes growing in a storm-tossed life.

Then later:

> They met, changed eyes. Changed hearts?
> Who knows? Turned, met again, again, were
> married. . . . That fatal day! Love comes and
> goes.

Aveling even seemed aware of Lissagaray, although her relationship with him had been broken off before he met Tussy:

> I tore at her robe till the breast outburst,
> And knew with a secret laughter
> His counterfeit lips had touched her first,
> Then mine in the real thereafter.

The romance raised nettles in every circle of the London intellectuals. Annie Besant, realizing that Aveling's intellectual shift from the secularists to the socialists had sexual overtones, answered with wrath: "My name is being used by a Miss Eleanor Marx . . . to give authority to a gross and scandalous libel on Dr. Edward Aveling. . . . Warning should be given of strangers who try to creep into our movement with the object of treacherously sowing discord therein." Annie Besant's letter to *Progress* did not tell the whole story, but Tussy was willing to explain her own view in a letter to a friend:

> I do not think it necessary that *I* should answer such a person as Mrs. Besant, from whom I consider abuse the best compliment. . . . The reason of this—"lady's" animosity is not far to seek. The one clear thinker and scientific student whose popularity *in the* Secularist Party almost equals Mr. Bradlaugh's—Dr. Edward Aveling, has joined the ranks of the Socialists, & Mrs. Besant does me the honour to make me responsible for this. I am very proud of Dr. Aveling's friendship for myself, but I hope I need not tell you that his conversion to Socialism is due to a study of my father's book & not to me.

Annie Besant struck her blow at Tussy in a review: "These sentences are, I fear, unintelligible, but Dr. Aveling is not in town and the copy is written by such a sloppy amanuensis that I have had to make the best of it throughout." Annie later took solace in evening duets with Bernard Shaw.

The socialists were equally distressed by Tussy's new friendship. Engels, who had inherited Marx's literary estate, and who would serve as surrogate father to Marx's daughters, invited Aveling along to the regular Sunday parties he held at his home on Regent's Park Road. The other socialists in attendance seemed to agree on their initial reaction to Aveling: "repulsive."

Try as they later might, most of them could never overcome their first impressions. The word stuck to Aveling's name with the tenacity of a Homeric epithet. But Tussy was fully aware of Aveling's reputation, and game to answer every accusation. She could even cite the absolute authority: "Poets, Mohr maintained, were green kittle-cattle, not to be judged by the ordinary, or even the extra-ordinary standards of conduct." Marx was talking about Heine, a poet he would have been unlikely to compare with Edward Aveling. But a well interpreted phrase from Scripture could prove anything.

Wilhelm Liebknecht had known the Marx family well enough to understand. "The worse the reputation, the brighter the merit," he wrote, "and it is not saying too much that just the badness of Dr. Aveling's reputation helped to gain him Eleanor's sympathy." It was true. For Tussy, who had struggled so long and so hard to be independent, who had rebelled against the proper and correct life of a Victorian lady, who had questioned the dreary destiny that seemed to face every woman of the nineteenth century—a quiet that stood out amidst what everyone called the "century of progress"—Aveling was a challenge. He had been at the cutting edge of movements that defied the Victorian norm—Darwinism, secularism, socialism—and like her father, he had thrived on the shock value of his ideas. Moreover, he was exciting, in his dress, his incredible, easy familiarity with the worlds of science and art, his infamously seductive voice, even his reputation, as checkered as those bright suits he wore. That he was still married, though long separated from his wife, only added to the excitement; it meant that after challenging the Church, the established order, and the Biblical story of creation, he was willing to affront the most sacred of Victorian institutions—marriage. Aveling may have seemed an amoral man to many, but to Tussy he was the precursor of the socialist society to come, already living his life in blithe disrespect for "bourgeois morality."

Yet there was a problem. Tussy wanted more than a casual affair with Edward Aveling. ". . . If you had ever seen my Father and Mother [she wrote], known what *he* was to me, you would understand better both my yearning for love, given and received, and my intense need of sympathy." The nineteenth century, while riddled with the love affairs that have made up its literature and scandals, was not so tolerant of the idea of a man and woman living together openly. A love affair was tolerated because it was ostensibly a secret, even if every concerned party and the public were privy to the secret. To live together openly, instead of being secretive, was not to play by the rules. It was to introduce a new and revolutionary order. "It is a curious fact," wrote Engels, in an article he contributed to *Progress,* "that with every great revolutionary movement the question of 'free love' comes to the foreground."

It was not really free love that Tussy wanted. Her generation believed that love strikes (or grows) but once, and she shared that belief. Ceremony or not, her relationship with Aveling was more than the chance encounter of sexual anarchy. Only to an age which could not talk of sex at all, and which characterized any movement or idea of the Left as "anarchy," was her desire to live openly with Aveling seen as free love.

Yet free love was the logical conclusion of many of the ideological movements of the nineteenth century—from socialism to free thinking to anarchism or the many utopian sects—although it was usually the critics of the movements, rather than the advocates, who pointed out the connection. The adherents to most causes were very reluctant indeed to admit that free love was one of their goals. In the *Communist Manifesto,* Marx and Engels mocked the outrage of the bourgeoisie at the idea of free love and pointed to the hypocrisy of the position:

> "But you communists would introduce community of women," screams the whole bourgeoisie in chorus.
>
> The bourgeois sees in his wife a mere instrument of production. He hears that the instruments of production are to be exploited in common and, naturally, can come to no other conclusion than that the lot of being common to all will likewise fall to the women.
>
> He has not even a suspicion that the real point aimed at is to do away with the status of women as mere instruments of production.
>
> For the rest, nothing is more ridiculous than the virtuous indignation of our bourgeois at the community of women which, they pretend, is to be openly and officially established by the communists. The communists have no need to introduce community of women; it has existed almost from time immemorial.
>
> Our bourgeois, not content with having the wives and daughters of their proletarians at their disposal, not to speak of common prostitutes, take the greatest pleasure in seducing each other's wives.
>
> Bourgeois marriage is in reality a system of wives in common and thus, at the most, what the communists might possibly be reproached with is that they desire to introduce, in substitution for a hypocritically concealed, an openly legalized community of women.

This was as close as Marx would come to admitting that communism would culminate in an abolition of marriage and the substitution of free love. In his own life, as we have noted, Marx firmly upheld the sanctity of the bourgeois family.

Engels was more open-minded on the question, in his writings (especially *The Origins of the Family, Private Property, and the State*) and in his relationships with Mary and Lizzie Burns. But he married Lizzie Burns on her deathbed, as if to legitimize the marriage in the eyes of an eternal society, and it could be said that his maintenance of double residences in Manchester—a proper one for business and a worker's cottage for love—was

nothing more than the usual double standard that men had always applied to
their affairs with mistresses.

In 1884 a play by Henrik Ibsen opened on the London stage. The play
was *Nora,* later to be known in English as *A Doll's House.* The version presented then was much altered (the title had been changed to *Breaking the
Butterfly,* which may give some idea of the changes). Only in the notes to
the play did Ibsen's intention still come through unambiguously:

> A woman cannot be herself in the society of the present day, which is an
> exclusively masculine society, with laws framed by men and with a judicial
> system that judges feminine conduct from a masculine point of view.

For the New Women of Victorian England, Ibsen's play had the impact of a
manifesto, calling upon them to end the era of "suffer and be silent." Outside the theater after the first performance a group of young women talked
excitedly about the play as the harbinger of a new era. Tussy Marx was one
of them.

For Tussy, parts of the play were like a memoir. In Act III, when Nora
has finally decided that she can no longer bear her life with Helmer, she
explains her youth to him:

> . . . While I was still at home I used to hear Father airing his opinions
> and they became my opinions; or if I didn't happen to agree, I kept it to
> myself—he would have been displeased otherwise. He used to call me his
> doll-baby, and played with me as I played with my dolls.

Later in the same scene Nora explains that she must educate herself. Helmer
answers her with condescension.

HELMER: You talk like an ignorant child, Nora—!

NORA: Yes. That's just why I must educate myself.

HELMER: To leave your home—to leave your husband, and your children!
What do you suppose people would say to that?

NORA: It makes no difference. This is something I *must* do.

HELMER: It's inconceivable! Don't you realize you'd be betraying your
most sacred duty?

NORA: What do you consider that to be?

HELMER: Your duty towards your husband and your children—I surely
don't have to tell you that!

NORA: I've another duty just as sacred.

HELMER: Nonsense! What duty do you mean?

NORA: My duty towards myself.

HELMER: Remember—before all else you are a wife and mother.

NORA: I don't believe that anymore. I believe that before all else I am a
human being, just as you are—or at least that I should try and become

one. I know that most people would agree with you, Torwald—and that's what they say in books. But I can no longer be satisfied with what most people say—or what they write in books. I must think things out for myself—get clear about them.

It was sometime that spring that Tussy thought things out about her relationship with Aveling. Her conclusion was much in Nora's spirit.

IV

"You must have known, I fancy, for some time that I am very fond of Edward Aveling," Tussy wrote to her sister Laura in June 1884, "—& he says he is fond of me. So we are going to 'set up' together. You know what his position is—& I need not say that this resolution has been no easy one for me to arrive at." Tussy announced her decision freely, proclaiming in letters that she and Aveling had been married "without the benefit of authorities."

> Edward Aveling & I are living together as man & wife. He is married. Our union cannot therefore be a legal one. It is true & real none the less. We are doing no human being the smallest wrong. Dr. Aveling is *morally* as free as if the bond that tied him years ago, & that had been severed for years before I even met him, had never existed. We have both felt that we were justified in setting aside all the false & really immoral bourgeois conventionalities, & I am happy to say we have received—the only thing we really care about—the approbation of our friends and fellow socialists.

As a New Woman, Tussy could not resist asserting the principle involved. She personally informed the headmistress of a school in which she had been teaching, inviting the certain dismissal that her finances could ill afford. It was an unnecessary gesture, but important to Tussy because it made a virtue of the necessity of the free union. On occasion Tussy could even squeeze a tone of moral self-righteousness into her letters to friends:

> . . . I can understand that people brought up differently, with all the old ideas & prejudices will think me very wrong, & if you do I shall not mind it, but simply "put myself in your place"—You know I have the power very strongly developed of seeing things from the "other side."

The free union effectively finessed the problem of Aveling's wife. But no relationship could escape Aveling's reputation and his past. No sooner had the "newlyweds" set up in a flat on Fitzroy Street than they had their first caller—Charles Bradlaugh, who had come to claim the love letters that Aveling had received over the years from Annie Besant.

Most of Tussy's friends were willing to accept the principle of the free union. "Aveling and Tussy," wrote Engels, "without the aid of officials, etc. are married, and now bathe in bliss in the mountains of Derbyshire. *Nota bene:* about this there must be no public report. The fact is that Aveling already has a legal wife which he cannot get free from *de jure* although he has for years been so *de facto*. This is fairly well known and even among the literary philistines fairly well accepted." But some friends, even if they supported the principle, could see that the relationship was not all it was supposed to be. "Dr. Aveling and Miss Marx have just come to see me," wrote Olive Schreiner to Havelock Ellis. "She is to be called Mrs. Aveling. I was glad to see her face. I love her. But she looks so miserable." For Tussy too, the realization slowly dawned that the relationship was not entirely what it once seemed: ". . . I am *very* lonely," she wrote to her friend Dollie Redford, "& I never felt lonelier than I do just now."

Olive Schreiner, now famous for her prophetic probing into the role of women in Victorian society, was a close friend of Tussy Marx. Both saw themselves as New Women, and in their questions and introspection they spoke with a frankness uncommon for their era. They had no compunction about discussing the effects of menstruation—the taboo of Victorian taboos—on their mental alertness, and later Olive would report these conversations to her friend Havelock Ellis. "The time of greatest and most wonderful mental activity," she reported, "is just after, and perhaps the last two days of the time too. With myself, while I am unwell every month my feelings are particularly sensitive and strong. . . . My acquisitive power, my power of learning is not at all weak at the time, but my feelings are so strong." Tussy's experiences, she reported, were even more remarkable, and could be the basis for a medical article by Ellis.

Despite the intimacy of her friendship for Tussy, and the fact that in a review Aveling had praised her first novel, *The Story of an African Farm,* for its "bold outspeaking" about the relations between men and women, Olive could not overcome her revulsion for Aveling.

> I am beginning to have such a horror of Dr. A., otherself [she wrote]. To say I dislike him doesn't express it at all; I have a fear and a horror of him when I am near. Every time I see him this shrinking grows stronger. . . . I love her, but *he* makes me so unhappy. He is so selfish, but that doesn't account for the feeling of dread. Mrs. Walters [a woman suffragist, and another of the New Women] has just the same feeling. I had it when I first saw him. I fought it down for Eleanor's sake, but here it is, stronger than ever.

Other friends, from the New Women and from the socialist circles, echoed Olive's feelings about Aveling. His behavior was consistent enough to assure that no new friends could be found.

Havelock Ellis got to know both Tussy and Aveling on a visit to the country. He was a careful observer, despite the clinical romanticism of his prose. Tussy he found "always a delightful personality, intelligent, eager, full of enjoyment." "It is perhaps a bodily trait of her powerful personality that I have never known a woman who on a long summer's day ramble diffused so potent an axillary fragrance." Aveling too he found an agreeable enough companion, although after a walk through the countryside he recalled that it was perhaps typical of Aveling that "with immense gusto" he would disregard notices warning against trespassers. Later Ellis discovered that Aveling, after living at the inn for weeks and ordering drinks without stint, had quietly decamped without paying the bill. "We were learning to know him," wrote Ellis.

Whatever others might think of Aveling or of their relationship, Tussy and Edward had much to hold them together. Both were passionately in love with the theater, though still outsiders, and they had come upon the stage at a time when innovations in playwriting, staging, and financing were making a revolution in the theater. Although the explanation for Aveling's intellectual conversion might remain a moot question, both were socialists, and would soon be important figures in the growing socialist movement in England. But more important than these intellectual and vocational bonds was the simple identity that both had as gadflies to the Victorian establishment. They sought to establish their "revolutionary" relationship as much for its shock value as for its companionship. The criticism of friends or enemies was a reassurance to them.

The great pursuit of Aveling's life was to be the stage. His asset was his magnificently resonant voice, the kind of voice that could turn enemies into followers. On the honeymoon that Edward and Tussy took in the Cotswolds, he read a section of Ibsen's *Ghosts,* then still in manuscript, for a group of friends. Even Olive Schreiner was impressed. "It is one of the most wonderful and great things that has long, long been written," she wrote to Ellis. ". . . I cried out loud. I couldn't help it."

But a voice alone was not an entry ticket to the inner sanctum of the London theater world, especially when other newcomers, some of extraordinary talent, were waiting in the wings. In January 1885, the Avelings played in "a third-rate comedy" with George Bernard Shaw. A month later, Shaw and Aveling joined the staff of the just founded *Dramatic Review,* though Aveling's contributions, in consideration of his reputation, were published under the pseudonym Alec Nelson. The only other place where he could get his dramatic criticism printed was *Neue Zeit,* the theoretical journal of German Social Democracy. There he could throw down the gauntlet to Victorian society: "Real problems, life questions (I speak always of England) are just as much tabooed on the stage as on the academic platform. . . . Our modern dramatists . . . are not in a position to understand the sham civilization at the end of the 19th century. . . . They do not appear to see the fact that we live in a transition age." Unfortunately, none of the influential people in the London theater world read the convoluted dialectic prose of *Die Neue Zeit*.

Eleanor did what she could to assist Edward in his efforts to set himself up as a dramatist, begging Olive Schreiner to induce her influential friends to read a one-act play that he had written, or dragging the play to Beerbohm Tree, whom she had once met. No one was interested. *A Test* was finally produced under Aveling's own direction, with the Avelings as stars. The *Dramatic Review* said the play was crudely constructed, with an unhappy ending that was merely "painful without really being dramatic." "Dr. Aveling," the review continued, "was manifestly out of his depth; but, on the other hand, Mrs. Aveling, as his wife, displayed a quite surprising amount of force and feeling." It was not an auspicious entrance onto the London stage.

The favorable comments on Tussy's performance were not enough to sweep her into the floodlights. Nonplussed, she determined to do something to "make people understand our Ibsen." She turned to the few individuals who, she believed, could really comprehend Ibsen. Even then she had to twist some wrists to get a cast together. George Bernard Shaw was urged to read the part of Krogstad, the blackmailer, in *Nora*. "It is not in the least necessary that you should be sane to do that," she wrote:

> Au contraire. The madder the better. . . . I wish some really *great* actors
> would try Ibsen. The more I study the greater I think him. How odd it is
> that people complain that his plays "have no end" but just leave you
> where you were, that he gives no *solution* to the problem he has set you!
> As if in life things "ended" off either comfortably or uncomfortably. We
> play through our little dramas, & comedies, & tragedies, & farces & then
> begin it all over again. If we *could* find solutions to the problems of our
> lives things would be easier in this weary world.

The reading took place in 1886, with Tussy as Nora, Aveling as Helmer, Bernard Shaw as Krogstad, and May Morris (the daughter of William Morris) as Mrs. Linde. The audience, wrote Tussy, was "just a few people worth reading 'Nora' to." One can almost hear them—Tussy resolute, perhaps too didactic, as she taught Helmer the lesson she had been afraid to teach her father; Aveling self-righteous, unable to shake off a cynical grin; Shaw leering at May Morris and munching caramels as he posed his impossible demands. The reading, probably the first presentation of unadulterated Ibsen in London, made no impact. The London theater world was not ready for either Ibsen or the Avelings.

Through their dramatic activities Tussy had met the novelist George

Moore, and through him she obtained the highly profitable assignment of translating Flaubert's *Madame Bovary*. Although the book had never appeared in English, it was well-known in England because "to the eternal honor of Flaubert," as Tussy wrote in the preface to her translation, the Imperial prosecutor had singled out the book for proscription, and a well-publicized trial had ensued.

Eleanor was fascinated by the character of Emma. Her situation seemed to sum up the dilemma of any woman caught in the quagmire of responsibilities and mores, dreams and illusions, that nineteenth-century society presented. Flaubert held up a mirror to society, in the Shakespearian idiom, and this, more than the adulterous plot of the novel, was what horrified French and, later, English society. It was only natural, wrote Tussy, that "some, recognizing their own image, should be shocked."

What made Emma unique was the problem of self-deception. "Her life is idle, useless," wrote Tussy:

> And this strong woman feels there *must* be some place for her in the world; there *must* be something to do—and she dreams. Life is so unreal to her that she married Bovary thinking she loves him. . . . In all literature there is perhaps nothing more pathetic than her hopeless effort to "make herself in love." And even after she has been false, how she yearns to go back to him, to something real, to a healthier, better love than she has known.

Like Ibsen's plays, the story and the very character of Emma had an autobiographical ring for Tussy. The trapped feeling, the eternal condescension of the men around her, the quiet joy in defying the sacred—all these Tussy had shared with Emma Bovary. The difference was that Tussy had an ideal in her life, her free and pure union with Aveling; and goals, socialism and drama. Emma's life was empty. In searching for an ideal Emma had become corrupt and base. "But for her surroundings," wrote Tussy, "she would be a monster and an impossibility." Given the surroundings—the stifling provincialism of Normandy that so mirrored the provincialism of values in the century of progress—Emma was inevitable. She was a woman whom Tussy could understand.

Tussy completed her translation in May 1886. Though far from being faultless, it remained for many years the only English version.

V

The middle-class audiences that were so shocked by Emma Bovary and the New Theater of the 1880s were the same people who discovered to their horror that socialism—the "red menace," as they called it—was rapidly making converts in their very midst. The socialist movement in England was in its nursery years when the Avelings were first "married," and both had ready qualifications as nursemaids—Tussy because of her name and her close relationship with Engels, and Aveling because of his oratorical skills, his well-known dispute with Bradlaugh, and his relationship with Tussy.

The only organization in London that called itself socialist was the Democratic Federation, a well-meaning group of intellectuals who could agree on goals, but could never agree on how to reach those goals. The acknowledged leader of the group was Henry Hyndman, the editor of *Justice,* and a man well-known for his overweening ambition, his business sense, and what some called his "impatience to play the dictator." Hyndman had read *Das Kapital* in French, and his own *England for All* borrowed heavily from Marx. When the acknowledgments in Hyndman's book cited only "a distinguished foreigner," without mentioning Marx's name, Marx and Engels gave Hyndman the cold shoulder, basing their objections not so much on the plagiarism as on the belief that borrowings from *Capital* had no place in a program at variance with its theories. Hyndman reciprocated, calling Engels the "Teutonic Grand Lama of Regent's Park Road."

The other leaders, the men whom Engels preferred, were Aveling, Belfort Bax, and William Morris. Bax was a militant internationalist, a prolific journalist, and a rather fervent enemy of Hyndman. Morris, after many years of studying Icelandic sagas and other medieval literature, was making his way from an admiration for the Middle Ages to an attempt to recreate the world of the medieval craftsman; socialism was a stop along that route. While Engels liked all three, he recognized their potential shortcomings as leaders of a militant socialist movement. ". . . The only honest men among the intellectuals," he called them, "—but men as impractical (two poets and one philosopher) as you could possibly find." We could also add George Bernard Shaw, who read *Das Kapital* in French at the British Museum and who joined the Avelings in their commute from the Ibsen Society to the Democratic Federation.

Tussy was the only woman in the group. She was accepted because of her name, her relationship with Engels and Aveling, and because, as Hyndman put it, she resembled Marx "as much as a young woman could." Tussy was well aware of the resemblance: "I, unfortunately, only inherited my father's nose (I used to tell him I could sue him for damages as his nose had distinctly entailed a loss upon me.)"

One of the great aspirations of the New Women was to be recognized for their innate talents or abilities. Tussy had a good education in socialist theory and the myriad of subjects that she had been introduced to by the master; she was an excellent speaker; and the enthusiasm and persistence that had enabled her to do research for her father could be a valuable asset in organizing the activities of the movement. But Tussy was Tussy *Marx* to the movement, and later she was Mrs. Edward Aveling.

43

Sexist discrimination was not the sole cause of Tussy's self-effacement in the socialist movement. She might have contributed some important ideas—perhaps a combination of a *real* sense of poverty and alienation with a theoretical explanation—that could have infused British socialism with new life. But there was little room in Tussy's life for her own conceptions. She was dominated by the ideas of others: her father, Edward Aveling, the literature she so loved. Karl Marx had made literature a living vision in those childhood stories, so much so that the tales of Hans Röckle were more familiar to Tussy than the real life of their author. And for Tussy, the world of Ibsen or Flaubert or even Edward Aveling was more vivid than the world she saw with her own eyes.

Despite their varied backgrounds and the obvious differences in their approaches to socialism, the group agreed on the goals of the movement. All would subscribe to a program of ends drafted by Tussy and Edward:

> Let us state in the briefest possible way what socialism means to some of us. (1) That there are inequality and misery in the world; (2) that this social inequality, this misery of the many and this happiness of the few, are the necessary outcome of our social conditions; (3) that the essence of these social conditions is that the mass of the people, the working class, produce and distribute all commodities, while the minority of the people, the middle and upper classes, possess these commodities; (4) that this initial tyranny of the possessing class over the producing class is based on the present wage system and now maintains all other forms of oppression, such as that of monarchy, or clerical rule, or police despotism; (5) that this tyranny of the few over the many is only possible because the few have obtained possession of the land, the raw material, the machinery, the banks, the railways—in a word, of all the means of production and distribution of commodities . . . (6) lastly, that the approaching change in "civilised" society will be a revolution. . . . The two classes at present existing will be replaced by a single class consisting of the whole of the healthy and sane members of the community, possessing all the means of production and distrubtion in common. . . .

Almost any one of the group could have written the passage, and all would subscribe to it as "socialism." They had all read Marx, and what they wrote included the basic conceptions of Marxism even if it did lack key references like "surplus value" or "dialectic." The codification of the religion was still many years off, and the dogma had yet to be defined by theoretical squabbling, heresies, and the fine textual nit-picking that came to characterize European socialism.

The problem for these socialist leaders was to bridge the gap between their new-found faith and the political movements of the masses. Most of them knew nothing about the real lives of the workers who played such an important role in their theories. To Bax they were the "antitheses to a bourgeois thesis." To Aveling, especially after he had read *Das Kapital* and turned out his *Student's Marx* for the coaching market, the workers were the source of complex algebraic equations on surplus value. To Hyndman, they were the raw stuff of revolution; though unconscious of history and of their role as agents, they would be the blind force that under his leadership would topple governments. To Morris, still filled with visions of singing sculptors carving the gargoyles of medieval cathedrals, the workers were good fellows and trusted artisans. To Shaw they were one part heroic dynamiters and three parts duffers and dupes. But none of these men who were counting so heavily on the workers had ever visited a slum house. As long as they had never seen how the workers lived, let alone actually talked with them, there was no reason why they should question any of their own theories.

Tussy was the first to visit the slums of London's East End. What she saw was something that no amount of theoretical discussion or reading could have prepared her for.

> A father, most "respectable man," with "excellent character," willing to do any work, and who is overjoyed at the prospect of earning 2/6 *a week* cleaning the streets for the vestry; eight children who for days have tasted nothing but bread, & who have not even that now; the mother lying on some straw, naked, covered with a few rags, her clothes pawned days ago to buy bread. The children are little skeletons. They are all in a tiny cellar. It is pitiable, but all around them people are in the same state. . . .

On a closer look, things were even worse. "I can't tell you the horrors I have seen," she wrote to her sister:

> One room especially haunts me. Room!—a cellar, dark, underground. In it a woman on some sacking & a little straw, her breast half-eaten away with cancer. She is naked but for an old red kerchief over her breast & a bit of soiled rags over her legs. By her side a baby of three & other children— four of them, the oldest just nine years old. The husband tries to "pick up" a few pence at the docks—that last refuge of the desperate—& the children are looking for bread. . . .

This was the truth of the working classes that even Marx had never seen. His writings had pointed up the horrors of alienation that workers suffer, the feeling of powerlessness and of being only an animal that haunts the wage laborer. But Marx's descriptions of working class life were derived exclusively from the Blue Books, the compilations of factory inspectors. He had never seen the horrors at first hand.

Following in his footsteps, the intellectuals who introduced socialism to

Britain also took an aloof stand. They were indeed concerned with the workers of England and of the whole world, but they did not allow their ethereal concern to be confused by the sentimentalism of a woman. The socialist movement had to win its battles on a grand scale, not with the compassionate bandaging of a Florence Nightingale.

The leadership of the Democratic Federation was a delicate coalition of prima donnas. Theoretical splits and personal rivalries were kept at a minimum only because almost everyone could unite against the martinet Hyndman and his insistence on parliamentary tactics. He seemed to oppose any activity that would put real life into the movement. He opposed a commemoration of the anniversary of Marx's death because it represented the "canonization of individuals" and thus was "contrary to the principle of Socialism." The intellectuals of the leadership he opposed because they were not working men, although his own foppish dress became something of a joke in the movement.

For Engels the last straw came when he discovered that Hyndman was attempting a translation of *Das Kapital*. Engels, as literary executor of the Marx estate, had already authorized his friend Sam Moore to make the official English version. To speed up things, Aveling was invited to assist, although his contributions were limited to the nontheoretical chapters. Tussy had the "devil's work" of looking up all the quotations from the Blue Books so errors of retranslation could be avoided.

Hyndman retreated on the translation dispute, and to pacify the Avelings, the name of the Democratic Federation was changed to the Social Democratic Federation, usually shortened to SDF. Tussy was even allowed to chair some meetings. But the abrasions could not be soothed with symbolic balms. The final split was catalyzed by that old albatross around Aveling's neck, Charles Bradlaugh. Bradlaugh publicly accused Aveling of peculating funds from the Practical Science Laboratory, a teaching venture of the Secularist Society. Hyndman leaped at the chance to eliminate his chief adversary, demanding that Aveling resign from the SDF if he could not clear his character. Morris and, of course, Tussy backed Aveling, setting the stage for a showdown.

Bernard Shaw watched the affair develop. Aveling, he wrote, was "a man to be thrown out of the window or shaken hands with cordially, as the case might be, but not such a fool as to let himself be elbowed out." Shaw was right, and Aveling did not even need recourse to his famous voice. He issued a simple public statement, a masterpiece of vagueness and sincerity:

> I am at the present time indebted in many sums to many persons. But I wish to say that to the best of my knowledge and belief all monies received by me as funds in trust for others have been fully accounted for. My monetary difficulties have to do with my poverty and my want of business habits alone.

It was probably funds provided by Morris, more than Aveling's statement, that cleared the air and saved the SDF.

Within weeks further charges were brought against Aveling—from a tailor who was never paid for a velvet waistcoat and jacket, and from Mme. Olga Novikoff, the "MP for Russia," who accused him of pocketing a collection that had been entrusted to him on behalf of some Slav cause.

By the end of 1884, the SDF did break up, supposedly over the issue of internationalism, but really over an irreconcilable split in personality. The Avelings and William Morris formed their own organization, the Socialist League, and thanks to Morris' funds, by February 1885 they had a journal, *Commonweal*.

Bernard Shaw ought to have been a natural for the new group, but by 1885 he was well on his way toward Fabianism. Already he was refusing to take part in various peace meetings that had been called to protest the war in the Sudan. On one occasion he was billed as "Comrade Shaw" for a rally. He failed to show, sending along a written excuse: "I am G. Bernard Shaw, of the Fabian Society, member of an individualist state, and therefore nobody's comrade."

With an executive committee of poets, that the Socialist League functioned at all was a constant miracle. Records were often chaotic, membership rolls were lost or weeks behind, finances were in constant disarray and rescued repeatedly at the last moment by Morris. But these poets were articulate and well-spoken, and *Commonweal* was a monthly forum in which they could combine visionary social thinking with artistic criticism, even if their theoretical purity came under question. Hyndman once asked, "Does Comrade Morris accept Marx's Theory of Value?" Morris replied:

> To speak frankly, I do not know what Marx's theory of value is, and I'm damned if I want to know. Truth to say, my friends, I have tried to understand Marx's theory, but political economy is not in my line, and much of it appears to me to be dreary rubbish. But I am, I hope, a Socialist none the less. It is enough political economy for me to know that the idle rich class is rich and the working class is poor, and that the rich are rich because they rob the poor. . . .

Tussy and Edward might not be so casual about Marx's theory of value, but they could work with a man like Morris.

One of the great sensations in the press in the early days of the League was the wave of sexual crimes that had overtaken London. W. T. Snead, the editor of the *Pall Mall Gazette,* had described some shocking cases in delicate purple prose, and he began a campaign to have the age of consent raised from thirteen to sixteen. A campaign force of "the Women of England," nearly two hundred strong, made a major issue of the question, until Parliament finally acted. The Socialist League endorsed the campaign, but in a *Commonweal* article Tussy explained her reservations. The age of consent, she pointed out, had little to do with sexual crimes, for as long as there were two classes, "the one literally in a position to buy, and actually buying, the bodies of the other," the crimes would continue. Her tone was not theoretical, but strident: "We, the women, must, above all the rest, bestir ourselves. . . . We need a deluge—aye! though it were one of blood—to wipe out our sin and wickedness of this society of ours. It is with those who would revolutionise society that our work as women lies."

This was the New Woman speaking.

The same year, a translation of August Bebel's *Women in the Past, Present and Future* was published in England. In Germany, it was already the most widely read appeal for the equality of women. Bebel saw the problem as a question of "sex-rule," arguing that the apparent "lesser capacities" of women were a consequence of historical conditions: "Geniuses do not drop down from the skies; they must have opportunity to form and mature. This opportunity woman has lacked until now. . . ." The solution, he believed, would only follow from the abolition of class rule: "We have absolutely no measure today by which to gauge the fullness of mental powers and faculties that will develop among men and women so soon as they shall be able to unfold amid natural conditions."

Tussy reviewed the book favorably in *Commonweal,* offering "marriages" such as her own as one mode of emancipation for women: "Both the oppressed classes, women and the immediate producers, must understand that their emancipation will come from themselves. Women will find allies in the better sort of men, as the labourers are finding allies among philosophers, artists, poets. But the one has nothing to hope from man as a whole, and the other has nothing to hope from the middle class as a whole."

Later, with Aveling, she further analyzed the whole issue in a pamphlet entitled *The Women Question*. The ideas of advanced women, according to the Avelings, including women's suffrage and higher education, were "based either on property, or on sentimental or professional questions." Weddings were nothing more than "business transactions," and "marriages thus arranged . . . seem to us . . . worse than prostitution." The argument sounded like the language of the *Communist Manifesto*. But the pamphlet took on a curiously autobiographical tone. A line from *Nora* summed it up: ". . . Home life ceases to be free and beautiful directly its foundations are borrowing and debts." Even a free marriage, they argued, could not truly work in a capitalist society. Not until "love, respect, intellectual likeness and command of the necessaries of life" could be assured by a socialist revolution would there ever be the harmonious blending of two lives that a true marriage should be. Without this revolution, any marriage would entail the bondage of master and slave, free and indentured, and neither would develop the full and independent life that a free union should mean.

It was a good description of their own situation. Wherever they went, whatever group or society they joined, the Avelings were dogged by Edward's rather casual attitude toward money—particularly other peoples' money. He had the abandon with funds that belongs to the very rich or the very poor. What he had, he spent. And what he did not have, he also spent. On a speaking tour he would go to a pub with a group of local workingmen. They would order lemonade; he would order a special vintage sherry. When the drinks were served, he would pause in his declamation, point to a poor stonemason, and say: "And you'll pay."

His credit should have been terrible. But every time he cleared himself of a scandal it would be restored for a few days, and in a spree of borrowing he could raise enough to support his most outlandish squandering for a while. Few, if any, of these loans seem to have been repaid, except when Aveling used Bernard Shaw's ploy. Shaw would borrow a half-crown for a cab, then send a postal order to repay the sum the next morning. When asked to explain, he said: "Oh! It is my habit to show punctilious accuracy in small money matters, so that when the time comes I may pull off my big coup with success. To achieve that it is absolutely essential to acquire a reputation for rigid and undeviating accuracy in small debts. The commonplace man does not understand that." Aveling, no commonplace man, understood the idea well. By moving from organization to organization—the intellectual history of the Avelings could be written in terms of Edward's financial scandals—and providing occasional careful explanations, he could usually get by even without repaying the half-crowns.

VI

In 1886, Wilhelm Liebknecht of the German Social Democratic Party decided to undertake a speaking tour in America to raise money for the party. The Avelings were invited along to accompany Liebknecht and to lend English support in what had become a crucial year for the socialists in America. On May 1, 1886, the Knights of Labor had organized a nationwide strike in favor of the eight-hour day. On May 4, the famous explosion had gone off in the Chicago Haymarket. The bombing was attributed to the anarchists, who had officially split away from the socialists, but to the public and the press, all "reds" were equally guilty. The eight-hour movement began to falter under the pressure of employers, and by the fall of 1886, when Liebknecht and the Avelings arrived, the whole movement in America was beleaguered, trying to recoup its losses by backing Henry George in the New York mayoralty campaign.

The Avelings spent four months in the United States, two in New York and the rest on a tour of the Midwest, meeting local labor leaders, giving speeches, and making such obligatory pilgrimages as a visit to the condemned Haymarket prisoners. The ostensible purpose of their tour was fund-raising for the German Social Democratic Party, but for Aveling it was also a chance to observe the "colonials" at close quarter. He later wrote a book, *An American Journey,* compiling his casual observations.

The Americans Aveling met were all, if we are to believe him, provincials—rude, vulgar, dirty, materialistic, and naive. When Tussy appeared in New York in a dress that was not the current fashion, a policeman said, "Say, what the blank is that?" Americans, he observed, used spittoons (which they often missed), wiped their noses without handkerchiefs, cleaned their nails in public, and never took cold baths. The women chewed gum and used snuff. Aveling spent hours trying to catch a woman "hiding" the snuff. What is extraordinary about Aveling's observations is that there is scarcely a mention of a workingman in the book. The closest he comes to the alleged purpose of his trip is to cleverly argue that cowboys are the true proletarians of the United States. As for the rest, he is his usual witty self.

He met a stranger in Fort Lee:

> Now, nothing would convince my young man that I was not an actor. Perhaps it was my close-shaven face; perhaps it was because of the striking likeness to Henry Irving, Wilson Burrett, and Beerbohm Tree that I possess in common with so many marquises and linen-drapers' assistants.

He was critical of the hypocrisy of prohibition, and did not allow himself to be inconvenienced. When thirsty in a dry state, he summoned a lackey: "In ten minutes a bottle of Heidseick was before us, and soon after, within." He visited the theater in every town, and criticized every performance (with the exception of Buffalo Bill, who "produced the effect of only two other men"—Charles Darwin and Henry Irving). He always stayed in the best hotels—the Adams in Boston, the Sherman in Chicago—all were inadequate, like the trains that took him from place to place. Indeed, the only praise he could offer for anything American was for the card catalogue of the Harvard College Library, a dream to any regular user of the British Museum.

Aveling complained of the materialism of the Americans ("New York is over-eager to get rich" is a constant refrain), but never did he seem to notice the poverty as much as the consumption. Only Tussy, on the boat going over, noted that the rich Americans returning from their holidays in Europe "could laughingly look at the poor emigrants lying on the deck in their wretched clothes . . . without the least sign of sympathy."

At the end of their tour the Avelings got themselves involved in a brouhaha with the executives of the American Socialist Labor Party by speaking out against the German character of the leadership. "The movement, if it were to succeed," they said, "must become American and pass from the hands of the German over to those of the English-speaking people." This point, which was repeated in their book *The Working Class in America,* did not make them much of a hit with the party's German leadership. But that speech was only the beginning of the troubles that were to develop from the American journey.

By the time the couple returned to England, a member of the executive of the Socialist Labor Party had leaked certain details of their visit to the press. Sensational accounts soon appeared in both the New York and London papers. The New York Socialists, a London paper reported, were determined "nevermore to import a professional agitator from the effete monarchies of Europe. The luxury is too expensive." In subsequent articles the papers reveled in the stories.

For thirteen weeks of lecturing the Avelings had charged thirteen hundred dollars. It was pointed out to Aveling that the sum was "rather stiff for a Socialist who professed to have the welfare of the poor at heart." Aveling replied, "Well, it's English, you know, quite English," intimating that another bill of six hundred dollars was coming. The accounting submitted included twenty-five dollars for "corsage bouquets" for Tussy, fifty dollars for cigars for Aveling and cigarettes for Tussy, and a two-days' wine bill at one hotel of forty-two dollars. Further, although Aveling got free admission into New York theaters by posing as the drama critic of the *Saturday Review,* the expense for playgoing was listed at one hundred dollars—"a nice round sum." Altogether, the paper concluded, "delivering lectures on Socialism seems a lucrative business."

Aveling answered with a circular to various sections of the Socialist Labor Party, in which he argued that the differences between him and the executive of the party were political, and that the expenses of his trip were a red herring that had been dragged out to obscure the political questions. The charges, he asserted, constituted a trial by adverse publicity. "If this is the kind of judicial procedure to be introduced into the Socialistic Labor Party, I for my part, should ask to be tried before a Chicago jury."

The scandal became so outrageous that Engels had to rally to the Avelings' defense. "I have known Aveling for four years," he wrote in a letter to an American leader. Chronicling the sacrifices Edward had made to his convictions, Engels rejected with anger and scorn the assertion that he had tried to swindle the party.

> How could he do that during all his tour without his wife being cognizant of it? And in that case the charge includes her too. And then it becomes utterly absurd, in my eyes at least. Her I have known from a child, and for the last seventeen years she has been constantly about me. And more than that, I have inherited from Marx the obligation to stand by his children as he would have done himself, and to see, as far as lies in my power, that

they are not wronged. And that I shall do, in spite of fifteen Executives.
The daughter of Marx swindling the working class—too rich indeed.

Engels' denial has the ring of innocence by association, a position that he
could persuade upon few in America or England. Later, Engels was willing
to admit that Aveling's poetic inclinations were a weakness: "The youngster
has brought it all on himself through his complete ignorance of life, people,
and business, and through his weakness for poetic dreaming. But I have
given him a good shaking-up, and Tussy will do the rest. He is very gifted
and useful, and thoroughly honest, but as gushing as a boy, and always
inclined to some absurdity. Well, I still remember the time when I was just
such a noodle.''

Engels was Aveling's only steady backer. When scandals arose, or when
other London socialists would boycott Aveling or an organization to which
he belonged, Engels was always there to stand up for Marx's son-in-law.
Whether from loyalty to Tussy and Marx or from a fondness for the free
spirit that Aveling sometimes seemed, Engels was constant in his support.
The Avelings were always welcome at the convivial Sunday night gatherings
at Engels' spacious home on Regent's Park Road, where a group of Engels'
friends would drink his fine Bordeaux wines and imported beers, and eat the
huge feasts prepared by Helene Demuth or by ''Pumps,'' a niece of Lizzy
Burns. The regular visitors included comrades from Germany, France, Russia or America who happened to be in London.

To Engels' chagrin, many of the English socialists would not attend these
gatherings. The reason was Edward Aveling. Many simply could not overcome their first, negative impressions. ''When we run down Marxism,'' said
Sidney Webb, ''we mean Aveling.''

The scandals were sometimes too egregious even for Engels to defend. In
America the Avelings had made a strong appeal on behalf of the convicted
Haymarket bombers, and when they returned to England Aveling organized
a collection to cable the governor of Illinois. A substantial sum was raised,
but the telegram was never sent. As everyone guessed, Aveling had pocketed the funds.

Even those who would associate with the Avelings kept a distance. When
Eduard Bernstein first came to know the various English socialists, he often
spoke of the Avelings. ''There was suddenly a suspiciously unanimous
chorus of praise of them,'' he wrote. '' 'Oh, the Avelings are very clever
people.' 'Oh, everybody must admit that they have been of great service to
the movement,' and so forth, in the same key, so that it was at once clear to
me that there was something in the air. I diverted the conversation to politics. But a judge of human nature might have blurted out the question:
'What's the truth about them, really? Have they murdered their children, or
what?' ''

52

The Socialist League was an organization in which they were still accepted, but even there dissent broke out. Mme. Gertrude Guillaume-Schack, a leader of the women's movement in Germany and one of the energetic workers in the League, finally wrote Engels to announce that she would no longer visit him. The reason she gave was that she could not bear meeting Aveling again, as he had committed unmentionable acts far more serious than his conduct in America, and had slandered his own wife.

In time the Avelings quit the Socialist League, allegedly as a protest against the anarchist faction that was beginning to dominate the politics of the League. In fact, it was again a case of Aveling being ostracized and Eleanor following. When Eduard Bernstein investigated the matter, the Secretary of the League began with the usual polite disclaimer, protesting that he had "the greatest respect for Dr. Aveling's talents and knowledge." Bernstein pressed, and finally got a vague but honest explanation: "Well, I will tell you. The reason given was not the real reason. The matter is simply this, that we don't want to have anything more to do with the fellow."

The publication of the English edition of *Capital* in 1887 should have done much for their reputations. Aveling was listed as a cotranslator on the title page, and it was well-known that Eleanor had participated in the translation of her father's book. But reviews were few, and most were unfriendly. Not even the Avelings' friends had many kind words for the book. Shaw, now well ensconced among the Fabians and recovered from his initial enthusiasm for the book, made some cutting remarks in public. In a letter to Aveling he wondered how he was going to face Tussy after his "blasphemy." "Remember," he added, "that Newton was wrong about light— that Goethe was wrong about colors—that Darwin clearly overstressed natural selection, and then ask yourself whether it isn't at least possible that Marx was wrong about value. Even I had erred in my time." The first printing of five hundred copies sold out, but on the whole it was as a social historian with documentation of factory legislation that Marx was read, not as a theoretician of socialism. Aveling's name on the title page probably did not hurt sales, but it did not help Aveling's reputation.

Scandals and the snubs of their former colleagues isolated the Avelings from the socialist movement in England. Although they could still claim some influence because of Engels' support, they had no forum from which to speak, no journal in which to write, and no organized followers. "I shall be glad to get any work I am capable of doing," Tussy wrote to Havelock Ellis. "I need work much, and find it very difficult to get. 'Respectable' people won't employ me."

Shortly after their return from America the Avelings moved to a flat on Chancery Lane, and in the summer of 1887 they found that for two shillings a week they could rent a tiny cottage at Dodwell ("pronounced 'Dad'll' by the natives," wrote Tussy), not far from Stratford-upon-Avon. Two or three times a week they would walk over to the Shakespeare birthplace, and by special permission they were allowed to work in the library.

The spirit of the bard seemed to bless their endeavors. Tussy translated short stories by Alexander Kielland from the Norwegian, and Aveling wrote "no end of things," dreaming of the days when, as he put it, "the plays begin acting & royalties roll in."

There was not long to wait. In November a play by Aveling, *By the Sea,* was performed in Landbroke Hall. An adaptation of a French piece based on the old Scottish ballad "Auld Robin Gray," it was the story of a young woman, Jeannie, who thinks she has lost her lover, a sailor, in a shipwreck, and marries an elderly suitor, Robin Gray. The sailor eventually returns, and a struggle ensues between Jeannie's youthful passion and her loyalty as a wife. Loyalty wins out in the end and the sailor agrees to leave the country. Tussy played the lead; the conflict between passion and family duty was one she knew well.

Unfortunately, the critics did not take to her portrayal. The play was called "a pretty little drama." Eleanor did not fare as well.

> Miss Eleanor Marx [wrote the critic in the *Dramatic Review*] is said to be a pupil of Mr. Herman Vexin, and it must be admitted that some of her elocution was worthy of her distinguished tutor. But small though the theatre was, she was frequently inaudible, even close to the stage, and never for a moment seemed to understand that she ought to be heard by anybody more than a few feet off. Some of her lines were prettily spoken, but she did not rise to the height either of the repentent wife, who grieves to have offended against her husband even in thought, or the loyal wife who repulses the still-loved lover of her childhood. . . .

To add a final insult, Herman Vexin wrote to the *Review* to deny that Tussy had ever been his pupil. (She had in fact studied with Mrs. Vexin.)

The notice dashed any hopes Tussy might still have entertained about the stage. Indeed, her choices were rapidly narrowing. She was politically isolated, cut off from the movement identified with her father's (and her own) name. Her dramatic career had been short-lived and unsuccessful. Her friends virtually all cut her. ". . . I am getting so used to being boycotted that it is no longer a novelty," she wrote to G.B.S. Her name, coupled always with that of Edward Aveling, had been dragged through scandal after scandal. Many of Aveling's enemies were careful to distinguish his own calumnies from her innocence, but as long as she lived with him and called herself Eleanor Marx-Aveling, she shared his infamy.

What was remarkable was that Tussy never seemed to question her "free union" with Aveling. Most of her troubles, with the exception of the failure as an actress, were troubles she inherited from Aveling's disrepute and his continued scandalous behavior. Theirs was supposed to be a mutual relationship between two free souls, each independent, each respected by the other, each free to live a full life. But in every case Tussy seemed to be dragged by Aveling's whims and fortunes and pushed to and fro by his reputation.

What held them together? Shaw thought it was sexual attraction that held Tussy; Hyndman thought it a mysterious hypnotic subjugation; still others believed that Tussy had inherited some Jewish trait of reverence for the marriage bond. Was she perhaps proving she could be as loyal as her mother had been? Or compensating for her lapse of loyalty to her dying father? Was Aveling, as a socialist, so identified with her father's mission that fidelity to one was fidelity to the other?

In fact, Tussy would say, it was love that held them together. And by love she meant that sense of duty that made marriage—even a "free marriage"—an almost indissoluble bond for the Victorians. Tussy had been intrigued by Aveling's blithe disregard for his own marriage, but she treated their free union as a firm bond, made all the stronger because it had not been falsely sanctified by a registrar at Somerset House. Where she had once painfully weighed the choice between her loyalty to a man and her dreams of independence, that choice now was long behind her. It was a different man now, Edward Aveling instead of her father, but the question of independence seemed closed, and that made her even more dependent upon Aveling. Her life was his life, just as much as if they had been married in a church. She shared his name, his fame, and his shame.

Tussy had been lonely when she met Aveling. Within the space of two years, her mother, sister and father had died. Aveling was not only a lover, but a companion. He shared Tussy's love of socialism and the stage, and together they could pursue their course as revolutionary gadflys, regardless of his notoriety.

The premiere of Aveling's play, though, augured a change. She had been a flop, he was a success. Soon he got a booking in Torquay, taking a traveling company with him. For weeks at a time, he went on the road with the production, leaving Tussy alone in the flat. To fight off loneliness she wrote letters. For the first time, it seems, she began to know Aveling. ". . . I am alone," she wrote to Olive Schreiner,

> and while in some sense I am relieved to be alone, it is also very terrible. I can't help thinking and remembering, and then the solitude is more than I can bear. . . . The *constant* strain of appearing the same when nothing *is* the same, the constant effort not to break down, sometimes become intolerable. How natures like Edward's (i.e., pure Irish and French) are to be envied, who in an hour completely forget anything. If you had seen him, for example, to-day, going about like a happy child with never a sorrow or

55

sin in his life, you would have marvelled. Yet apart even from all the other troubles, we have mere money troubles enough to worry an ordinary man or woman into the grave. I often don't know where to turn or what to do. It is almost impossible for me now to get work that is even decently paid for, and Edward gets little enough. And while I feel utterly desperate, he is perfectly unconcerned! It is a continual source of wonder to me. I do not grow used to it, but always feel equally astounded at his absolute incapacity to feel anything unless he is personally much incommoded by it—for twenty-four consecutive hours. I said just now how such natures were to be envied, and there are moments when I think it. But only moments. We, into whose hearts joy and sorrow sink more deeply, are better off after all. With all the pain and sorrow (and not even you, my Olive, know quite how unhappy I am), it is better to have these stronger feelings than to have practically no feelings at all.

Tussy wrote letters to fight off despair. When there was no one left to write, sometime in 1887, Tussy attempted suicide by taking an overdose of opium. Havelock Ellis discovered her. By administering strong coffee and making her walk up and down the room, he worked off the drug's effects. "I never knew what special event in her domestic life it was which led to this attempt," he wrote. "Her friends were grieved; they were scarcely surprised."

VII

You want to know what we're doing [Tussy wrote to Laura]. Well, we're hard at it, as usual. Edward writes plays & newspaper articles, books on botany & essays & "pomes." He goes to theatres to criticize other folk's plays; he occasionally travels for a Railway paper; He keeps Bax in order; teaches and sometimes lectures. He harbours, I believe, a private ambition to train as an "homme forte." He seems well and happy withal.

The state of Tussy's spirits coincided with the boom and bust cycle of Edward's work. Not long after her suicide attempt, Aveling began to succeed astoundingly with his writings. Six of his plays were produced, some in the provinces, some he produced himself in London. "If he has now one marked success in London," wrote Engels, "he is a made man in this line and will soon be out of all difficulties. And I don't see why he should not, he seems to have a remarkable knack of giving to London what London requires."

Aveling's best-known play, an adaptation of *The Scarlet Letter,* drew praise even from G.B.S.: ". . . this is the power that makes me remember, out of dozens of forgotten matinées, 'The Scarlet Letter' as I remember the

Bayreuth performance of 'Tristan & Isolde.' '' Aveling was also turning out a series of textbooks for students preparing for exams at London University. *Darwin Made Easy* and *The Student's Marx* were never best-sellers, but the royalties allowed him to continue his playwriting.

Tussy also got back to work. ''In all of us,'' she wrote, ''there are certain hidden nooks and corners & I don't think many people know what our literary nooks and corners are. I only know them dimly—as in a glass darkly— from old remembrances, but still I do know.'' Her writing, she admitted, was chiefly ''hacking,'' but as she kept busy with translations, including Ibsen's *Enemy of the People,* the dark days of the suicide attempt receded. From Havelock Ellis she got the job of editing an Elizabethan play, *A Warning to Fair Women,* for the Mermaid series that he was commissioned to compile. Enchanted by its social documentation, she shocked A. H. Bullen, the Elizabethan scholar, by the casualness with which she referred in conversation to ''the less decorous aspects'' of her subject. Unfortunately, her labors were wasted, as the publisher of the series was prosecuted for issuing Zola's ''obscene'' novels, his business was ruined, and the Mermaid series slipped out of Ellis' hands.

In 1888, the Avelings returned to America, this time to accompany Engels. They made no socialist speeches, but Edward was going to try to make his name on that American stage he had criticized so sharply two years before. Everyone had a good time on the trip, which included a visit to Niagara Falls, but nothing came of the performances of Aveling's plays which were scheduled for New York, Chicago, and another town.

Undaunted by his failure in the colonies, Aveling continued to write for the London stage. By 1890, ''Alec Nelson and E.M.A.'' were writing drama criticism for *Time,* a weekly edited by their old friend Belfort Bax.

By then a performance of an unaltered version of *A Doll's House* on a London stage had again raised the volatile question of Ibsen. The London theater world was ringing with the allegations of both the Ibsenites, who argued that their master was the only true advocate of women's emancipation and honest morality, and the anti-Ibsenites, who regarded Ibsen as the devil incarnate, the enemy of all that was decent and proper and right. The battles took place in newspapers, in the drama reviews, and in fervent public meetings. Shaw gave the lectures that were to become *The Quintessence of Ibsenism* at the Fabian Society. Edward Aveling offered his voice as a weapon by giving several enthusiastic defenses of Ibsen at meetings at the Playgoer's Club. G.B.S. attended two of the meetings with Tussy. ''. . . An assemblage of barloafing front-row-of-the-pit-on-a-first-night dilettanti,'' he called them. ''Mrs. Aveling and I,'' he wrote, ''being of course seasoned socialist mob orators, were much in the position of a pair of terriers dropped into a pit of rats.''

But even Ibsen was no longer strong enough for the Avelings. In *Time* they expounded a new dramatic manifesto, concealed in a review: "The only essential modern lines along which a dramatist can work are the economic, the religious, the sexual, i.e., from our point of view, as the greater includes the lesser, the economic only. The really great modern play, when it comes, will deal not with the struggle in two human lives only, but with that class-struggle which is the epic of the nineteenth century also. And thus far, even Ibsen has failed us." Aveling's plays certainly would not have met the criteria. Indeed, the only drama that could measure up was the working class movement itself—a struggle which heightened in the 1890s, as the cast grew, and the European audience became aware of the dramatic possibilities in the confrontation of workers, police, employers, and governments. Ostracism from the socialist organizations in England excluded Tussy and Edward from regular parts in the production, but as the stage grew larger in the 1890s, there was nothing that could keep them out in the wings.

Unlike the leaders of the groups that shunned them, Tussy and Edward were experienced in publicly addressing the English workers. From the days of their first performances and readings to workers, and their participation in the great demonstrations in Hyde Park or Trafalgar Square, they had developed a sense of the language the workingmen and -women wanted to hear. The labor movements of England had changed too, as the older unions that had descended from the guilds gave way to unions that sought to organize and campaign across whole industries. When the new unions of the 1890s began to agitate for the eight-hour day and increased wages, the Avelings joined the fracas.

Tussy was willing to assume the drudgery of keeping accounts and preparing reports for the Gasworkers Union, the first of the militant new unions. She became a close and trusted associate of its leader, Will Thorne, and it is said that she taught him to read and write. When she appeared on the podium with him, the gas workers called her "Good Old Stoker." After helping to organize the great dock strike of 1889, Tussy also became a regular with the Dockers Union. She served on the union council, and in time the members called her "Our Mother"—a mixed but well-intentioned compliment.

Because of her ability with words, Tussy was entrusted with writing the regulations and constitutions of many of the unions she worked with. She made sure they included not only the language of contemporary Marxism ("marching steadily and invincibly forward to the ultimate goal—the Emancipation of the Working Class"), but clauses demanding equal pay for women. She personally organized groups of women in the tailoring industry and "the unhappy human machines," the new typists.

Her speaking tours ultimately took her to the Jewish communities of the East End, and she learned Yiddish so she could speak to the unassimilated Jewish workers. She was a bold political speaker, unafraid of using the language of the streets. Many a Sunday evening she would spend on the corner of Dod Street, Limehouse, or another Whitechapel locale, coaxing and urging men and women who were terrified of their employers and even more so of the typical union leaders. (There is a story that G.B.S., bored by one of her speeches, but admiring her ankles, passed her a note asking her to stop talking and stand on her head. Shaw hotly denied this, declaring that Tussy was incapable of making a dull speech and that she wore skirts too long to reveal her ankles anyway.)

With Engels' blessings, Tussy and Edward were delegates in Paris for the founding of the Second International in 1889. Hyndman was also there, representing the SDF. The acrimony between the Avelings and Hyndman exacerbated the record-breaking heat of that sweltering Paris July. The Avelings joined one congress, with the powerful German Social Democratic Party and the French Marxists, while Hyndman went along with another congress that had attracted the anarchists, the syndicalists, and what the French called "possibilists." The Marxist group ended up as the Second International; the congress Hyndman had joined became a mere footnote in the history of socialism.

The first act of the Second International was to call for an international work stoppage on May Day as a tactic in the struggle for the eight-hour working day. The Avelings became the leading sponsors for the May Day celebration in London. The size of the demonstrations in Trafalgar Square shocked the public and police alike with the growth and the visibility of the working class. This demonstration, and the prestige of backing from the German Social Democrats, gave a real boost to the Avelings in their role in the working-class movement. Hyndman, jealous of their increasing prestige, watched their every move.

In January 1891, Aveling was asked to stand as a Labour candidate in a by-election for a Northhampton seat vacated, ironically, by the death of Charles Bradlaugh. Hyndman denounced Aveling as unfit to serve as a socialist candidate, and finally posed five questions to the prospective candidate in the press:

1. Why was he forced to leave the National Secular Society?
2. What were the proceedings in regard to his classes in Newman School, Oxford Street, which occasioned so much talk?
3. What sort of bills did he run up for Mrs. Eleanor Marx Aveling and himself when the Socialist workers of the United States (all poor men) paid the expenses of his tour? . . .
4. What did he do in relation to the money collected to send a cable despatch . . . to the Governor of Illinois, when the fate of the Chicago anarchists were trembling in the balance?
5. What was his action in regard to a certain family whose children he undertook to educate?

It was a perfect smear campaign, for there was enough truth in each insinuation to damn any explanation Aveling might offer. Forced to withdraw, Aveling gave as his excuse some question about the provenance of the funding of the campaign.

Despite Hyndman, the Avelings' efforts to organize the trade unions proved ever more successful. What Engels called "the rush towards Socialism in the provinces" carried enough momentum for the couple to use the Legal Eight Hours and International Labour League that Edward had founded as a springboard toward founding an Independent Labour Party. They joined forces here with Keir Hardie, a Scot and the first Labour M.P. ever elected. (He showed up to take his seat with a band playing, and wearing a tweed workman's cap.) Hardie had organized much of the New Union strength in the North that was to be the party's backbone. Hyndman, jealous of Hardie, boycotted the new party, leaving Aveling as its sole London representative. The latter participated in drafting a constitution, and while the party was no more than a loose coalition of unions and organizations, the constitution contained some firmly socialist clauses that drew praise even from Engels and the German socialists.

Aveling hoped to use the London District Council as his base to dominate the ILP. But again, his successes were short-lived. After less than a year, he was expelled by the Council. ". . . In my absence, without my being heard, without my witnesses being heard, without the names of my accusers being given to me," he protested. To maintain the party's good reputation, the reasons for the expulsion were never made public, but Eduard Bernstein has suggested that they "would have sufficed to land him in prison." It was probably his customary peculation of funds.

Aveling's departure from the ILP led him into the strangest of situations. Hyndman, smarting at the rapid growth of the ILP that had eclipsed his own position in the English labor movement, began to look for new alliances. He wrote editorials in his magazine, *Justice,* about "letting bygones be bygones on both sides." Hyndman needed any support he could get, and the Avelings, if they were to remain in labor politics, needed some kind of base. The days of popular agitation had been obscured by the organization of the New Unions and the astounding growth of the ILP, leaving the Avelings, once again, in relative isolation. In 1895 the outsiders—Hyndman and the Avelings—began to come together, despite Engels' objections. Twelve years of labor agitation, with the scandals and the ups and downs, had brought the Avelings back to the only Marxist organization in England, Hyndman's SDF. It was as peripheral to the real concerns of workers as it had always been, and Hyndman still lacked the blessing of the Master, such that he would remain an "unauthorized" Marxist as long as his archenemy Engels was alive. The Avelings were still minor figures in the socialist movement to which they had devoted so much of their lives.

Tussy could see an optimistic side to their labors: "The 'movement' [she wrote to her old friend Ernest Radford] has a rapacious maw and swallows more work & time than most people would believe. The 'show' work of lectures and meetings is the least part of it. And then you know we are poor as the proverbial church mice, & I find earning a living no such easy matter.— Ah well, I suppose the work will result in something some day.'' Someday, perhaps. But for Tussy and Edward it seemed to lead nowhere. All their efforts in drama had come to almost naught. Tussy had failed in her great debut, and Edward's play never made the great hit in London he had hoped for. In politics they had made the round of organizations and even founded some of their own, but in the end they were where they had started—poor, with few prospects, few connections, and almost no achievements. By the mid 1890s, the cycle of ups and downs had reached another down.

VIII

In the midst of the infighting between the factions of the English labor movement, Hyndman referred to Tussy in one article as "Miss Marx." The name was probably meant to raise questions about her relationship with Aveling. Engels commented that it revealed "the degree of lowness" to which Hyndman had fallen. But in another way Hyndman was right. Tussy's relationship with Aveling was as much a marriage as any bond that had been made formally, and she might always insist on the name Mrs. Aveling or Eleanor Marx-Aveling, but to much of the world she was and would remain only Marx's daughter. The Avelings had not been involved in much beyond scandals that warranted or attracted attention. But as the daughter of Karl Marx, a man whose reputation was widening in the 1880s and 1890s, Tussy was a person to be noticed, courted, and reckoned with.

Engels spent much of his energy in the 1880s and early 1890s editing volumes II and III of *Das Kapital* out of the mountains of notes Marx had left behind. The remainder of Marx's manuscripts were pretty much untouched. His correspondence had not been published, no official biography had been written, his many unpublished studies had not been edited, and the published writings themselves had not been collected in new editions. By the 1890s, these were important tasks, for enormous political parties had come into being that considered Marx their prophet and ideological fount. The editing of his manuscripts would establish the canon of Marxism; a task rather like the scholars of the Middle Ages deciding on the correct texts for the Bible; every word or phrase that was included or excluded would or could have untold future consequences.

As long as Engels was alive, there was no question about what would happen to the Marxist legacy. He had been entrusted with the complete literary estate, and was widely believed to be the only person qualified to work through the mass of scribbled notes and marginal comments that constituted the manuscripts of *Das Kapital*. But even as Engels first showed signs of weakening health, in the early 1890s, the future epigoni of Marxism were carefully laying their claims to the rest of the estate. The German party, in particular, was interested in asserting both its doctrinal purity and its primacy in the Second International. It was widely known that Marx and Engels had always argued for the German character of socialism; the possession of the Marx *Nachlass* would assure that the German party was the true standard-bearer of the legacy of Marxism.

Engels had also inherited Helene Demuth from Marx. After Marx's death she came to live with and care for Engels. Although "Pumps"—the married niece of Lizzie Burns—was officially the queen of the household, Helene Demuth lived with Engels as his maidservant and as a kind of second mother to the Marx daughters until her death in 1890.

It was Pumps who presided over the Sunday evening bashes at the Engels household, although she and her husband had short patience with the Germans who came in such numbers to consult with Engels or to study in the British museum. One of those she could least bear was Karl Kautsky, an Austrian of Czech descent, who had spent considerable time in London. In 1888 he and his wife Luise left London together. Weeks later he met another Luise (Ronsperger) in the Salzburg Alps. He informed Luise Number One, and she set him free with a divorce. In 1890 he married Luise Number Two. Luise Number One, who still went by the name Luise Kautsky, moved to Vienna, set herself up as a midwife, and began working with the Austrian socialists. Victor Adler had built up the Austrian party and its newspaper, the *Arbeiterzeitung*, and his wife Emma was putting together a women's weekly, the *Arbeiterinnenzeitung*, to which Luise was invited to contribute. In the meantime, Victor Adler and August Bebel, the leader of the German socialists, came up with another idea. Since the death of Helene Demuth, they reasoned, Engels probably needed someone to take care of him. Luise, with her experience as a midwife, was perfect. She went to London with the two schemers to celebrate Engels' seventy-eighth birthday, and when the party was over, Engels asked her to stay. Two weeks later an arrangement had been worked out.

> Luise Kautsky remains here for good. [wrote Engels] So my troubles are settled. She seems to like it better after all than settling other people's children into this world. And we get on capitally. She superintends the house and does my secretary's work which saves my eyes and enables me to make it worth her while to give up her profession, at least for the present.

Bebel and Adler had undoubtedly been concerned about Engels' comfort. Yet there was another reason for the dispatch of Luise Kautsky. Shortly after his return from London, Bebel wrote Adler to announce that the Marx papers could not be published, since they were "not at Luise's disposal," but that he had advised her to "come openly and frankly to an understanding with Engels."

Luise played her role carefully. First she had a contest with Pumps, whose role as queen of the household was threatened. There were agitated discussions about who would sit at the head of the table and other such trivia, until Pumps finally learned who was boss. She got drunk one night and confided to Luise that she "knew she had to behave to her, or she'd get cut out of the will."

Tussy still had no suspicions. Indeed, she thought only of the sacrifice Luise was making: "It hardly seems fair to her. She was getting on so well at Vienna & to sacrifice her whole career is no trivial matter.—No one would ask a *man* to do that."

In 1893, Adler and Bebel went one step further in their plan. Adler, himself a physician, sent a young Viennese physician, Dr. Ludwig Freyberger, to care for the aging Engels. Freyberger soon became a trusted attendant to Engels, and when Engels drew up his will, Freyberger was one of the witnesses. The manuscripts and letters, together with Engels' library (which included Marx's books) and their copyrights were to be given to Bebel and Bernstein for the German party. Only the manuscripts in Marx's hand (generally the least important, since the important materials had been worked through by Engels and transcribed by various assistants) and the letters written or addressed by him were to be returned to Tussy. Luise was to inherit Engels' house and its contents and a fourth of the residuals of the estate. The other three-fourths were to be divided between Tussy, Laura, and the children of their dead sister Jenny.

Tussy did not know the details of the will, but she became mildly suspicious when Luise asked her "to sign a paper making *her* [Luise] the responsible owner of the papers for fear Pumps should get hold of them." Bebel then assured Tussy that she need not worry about her father's papers as "*he* knew it was all right." Tussy put *her* and *he* together and saw a plot. Her concern for Luise turned rapidly into open rancor, and when Luise and Freyberger got married in 1894, she added another conspirator to the plot and another hatred to her relationships in Engels' household.

The dispute quickly escalated. Luise made slurs about Tussy's relationship with Aveling: ". . . *no* society would tolerate a friendship between a man and woman without sneers and comments." The Freybergers took Engels with them on their honeymoon, and with triumph Luise announced that she and Freyberger would remain with Engels afterward. In a series of "battle reports" to her sister, Tussy chronicled "the latest news from the menage of Regent's Park Road (Oh! for a Balzac to paint it!)."

In time the Freybergers made it impossible for Tussy ever to be alone with Engels. They convinced him that Tussy and Laura mistrusted him, that somehow Marx's daughters were conspiring to deprive everyone else of their rightful shares in the Marxian legacy. When Tussy heard of Engels' suspicions, she wrote him, "taking the tone of the offended party":

> As to the general MSS. of Mohr, you surely must know that Laura & I are sure *you* would deal with them as Mohr himself would have done. But you can equally understand that we should not like the letters & papers (many of a personal nature) to fall into other hands than *yours* or ours. . . . I should be blind indeed if I had not seen the efforts to set you against us. . . . If you had not been very much poisoned against us you could never have thought so meanly of Mohr's children as to think they could mistrust *you*.

The letter was effective. A few days later, on Christmas Day 1894, Engels had a private talk with Tussy, as an appetizer for the festive meal. He promised her that all of Marx's papers would be returned to her and Laura. For the first time in many years, the Christmas dinner at Engels' home was a pleasant party—plum pudding, dunking for apples, and stirring the punch in an atmosphere of peace.

The truce was short-lived. By midsummer, Engels had drawn a codicil to the will, changing some of the money bequests, and stipulating that all letters between Marx and himself were to be regarded as his own manuscripts and consequently handed over to the Germans, rather than to Tussy. Then Luise began to spread a rumor that Tussy considered the final blow.

Before Tussy was born, Helene Demuth had given birth to a son, christened Frederick Demuth and given as a foster child to a working-class family. In the 1890s, Freddy had begun appearing regularly at the festivities in the Engels home, and Tussy took this as confirmation of what she had always been led to believe—that Freddy was Engels' son, and that his presence at the home was Engels' way of admitting his paternity. Luise told a different story. The father, she suggested, was not Engels, but Marx. "Freddy looks comically like Marx and, with that really Jewish face and thick black hair, it was really only blind prejudice that could see in him any likeness to General." Utter defamation, answered Tussy, and they agreed to put the question to Engels.

"Tussy wants to make an idol of her father," said Engels.

Tussy was so upset that she came straight to Engels to ask him in person. By this time the cancer in his throat was so advanced that he could communicate only by writing on a little slate. Tussy asked, and Engels wrote out the answer: Freddy was Marx's son. "Tussy left the room so shattered," wrote Luise, "that she forgot all the hate she had for me and wept bitterly on my neck."

The next day, August 5, 1895, Engels died. His remains were cremated, and the urn was sunk six miles out to sea from the Eastbourne beach he had loved so much. It was a futile last revenge, but only Tussy, Edward, Eduard Bernstein, and Engels' old friend Ferdinand Lessner were in the little two-oared boat.

The vultures were quick. At probate Engels' estate was over twenty-five thousand pounds, of which Tussy inherited several thousand. Even this was too much, as far as the Germans were concerned. "A reduction in the amount of money which goes to private hands," wrote Bebel to Adler, "would have done no wrong. With the exception of what Luise receives, the money in the other hands will be squandered quite soon, and with this money will be created as little benefit for mankind as with the many thousand pounds that have already flowed into the same hands." Tussy too grew bitter as she watched the heirs grab at their portions of the estate. The Freybergers, who had received the lion's share, incensed her. "The Duke and Duchess are 'launching out' in grand style," she wrote in a final battle report. "They have—or *say* they have, spent £3000 on new furniture, and speak only with contempt of what they made the poor old General buy."

The Marx manuscripts—the sacred Scriptures for the Marxists—were divided. Neither Tussy nor the Germans had enough material for a biography of Marx, although after what Engels had revealed on his deathbed a biography became even more important. The secret of Freddy's fatherhood was perhaps the most damaging news. But what other secrets lurked in those private papers? To Tussy and her sisters, and to the world, Marx had always been presented as the incorruptible. Only from an impeccable position could he write what he had written and make the accusations he made. Only if he did not share any of the petty crimes of which he had accused others could he be a worthy prophet for a new religion. Now he had fathered a bastard. What else? "After all," wrote Tussy, "Marx the 'Politiker' & 'Denker' can take his chance, while Marx the *man*—the mere man . . . is less likely to fare well."

Tussy wrote a collection of notes on Marx for the Austrian Workers Calendar of 1895, and edited a few manuscripts that were among the papers left to her. None of these was an important book, and even after she had made peace with Hyndman and the SDF, he refused to review her long edition of *The Eastern Question,* which he considered unworthy of its author. "She was very angry," he wrote, ". . . and declared my refusal was due partly to laziness and partly to incapacity to appreciate the book. I admired her filial devotion so much that I allowed her to have the last word, which, in any case, feminine fashion, she would have taken without my consent."

Yet filial devotion could not make up for the absence of documentation. Even after Tussy and Laura instituted a blanket solicitation for letters to and from their father, they had nowhere near enough material to compile a biography. Nor, of course, did the Germans, until Franz Mehring obtained permission to use the papers which Laura then controlled. His biography, the first, and despite its official tone still in many ways the best, did not appear until 1918. The canonization of Marx was a slow process.

IX

In his lifetime Engels had been the financial savior of Karl Marx. In death he was the savior of Tussy and Edward Aveling. All their years of exertion in drama and journalism had never made a decent living for the Avelings. They had lived from day to day, moving from one drabby flat to another, making do on small royalties. Aveling's fiscal shenanigans had never contributed to their assets; his high life squandered every penny he had gotten. With thousands of pounds inherited in one lump from the Engels estate, the days of penury were over. Tussy started house-hunting, and soon found a pleasant two-storey house, with all the luxuries (separate studies, electric and gas lighting, wine cellar, garden) she had never known in their transient flats. Most of all Tussy liked the location: "The house (Edward swears this is my only reason for wanting it) is in *JEWS* Walk, Sydenham. . . ." The address fascinated her. Two weeks later, she had already named the house "The Den," and begun decorating. "I am Jewishly proud of my house in Jew's Walk," she wrote. (In part it was all a joke, but Tussy seems to have been the only one of the Marxes to take any pride in the Jewish part of their ancestry. Tussy often proclaimed, "I am a Jewess," although even those statements were usually tinged with sarcasm.)

Aveling's wife had died intestate in 1892. With characteristic luck and aplomb he inherited one hundred twenty-six pounds, which he and Tussy used to furnish The Den. The house was soon a cozy retreat. "Her face would beam with pleasure," wrote Eduard Bernstein, "as she welcomed her friends to the 'Den.'" For the first time, she and Edward could live a secure life, free from constant financial tension. ". . . Home life ceases to be free and beautiful directly its foundations are borrowing and debts" was the line from Ibsen that had haunted them. Now, the golden age of their free union could come forth. With the death of Aveling's wife, they could have got married. They chose not to. That their union would continue without the false security of a legal ceremony was the proof of its purity. The only touch of legality was the drawing up of wills at Edward's insistence. Tussy drew up hers shortly after Engels' death, leaving everything to Aveling except the royalties on her father's works, which were left to the children of her sister Jenny. A year later Aveling demanded and got a codicil, giving the royalties to him in his lifetime.

One thing was missing from this little scene of marital bliss. "A house is so different that rings with a child's laugh," Tussy wrote to Laura. "But I suppose le père would not give me one." The silence became unbearable on occasions that brought to mind her childhood, and she contrasted the warmth of the big Marx family with the loneliness of her life with Aveling.

> I am writing to you on Christmas Eve [she wrote to Laura]. I remember times when you and Jenny dressed dolls for me & times when there were Xmas trees. This is a stupid & sad time when there are no children. I sometimes wonder is it worse to have had a lot [of] little ones or never to have had them?

Activity was the way to make the morose times pass. The security of the little house meant that Tussy and Edward could take yet another plunge into politics and drama, and their efforts—removed from money worries—could be as pure as their personal union. Engels' death had also removed the last obstacle to their renewed association with Hyndman. The 1896 Congress of the Second International was scheduled for London, and the tours intended to trump up support for the congress gave Tussy and Edward a chance to combine politics and drama, by giving entertainments and speeches for the workers. Tussy gave propaganda talks all over England and Scotland, and Edward wrote a poem for recitation:

> Tramp, tramp, tramp—how they tramp along,
> Thousands marching, an army strong,
> Led by Generals Dire Distress,
> Cold and Hunger and Nakedness.
> . . .
> Sound the loudest, as is most meet,
> Is the sound of the workers' feet
> Keeping step as they march along,
> Till their march is a psalm and song.
> . . .
> Workers all! To the fight, the fight!
> Length and breadth of the world unite!
> What to lose but a galling chain?
> What to win? Why a world to gain!

Tussy recited the "Pied Piper," and with Edward gave another reading of *By the Sea.* For some of these benefit performances Aveling put together a small troop of professionals who were willing to donate their services, including a gay and charming young actress called Lillian Richardson. As the star of Avelings' *In the Train* she made a hit. One critic called her a character with whom "any traveling companion might certainly be pardoned for falling in love."

The production traveled, and it seems that Miss Richardson's traveling companion indeed fell in love with her. The company put on other Aveling plays, such as *Judith Shakespeare* and *Hundred Years Ago,* and after the Congress of the Second International Aveling found other causes for his benefits, including a series of performances to raise money for science classes sponsored by the SDF. The only change in the production for the London stages was a little name-swapping. Aveling concealed his notoriety under his usual stage name, Alec Nelson, and Miss Richardson dropped her pseudonym for her real name, Eva Frye.

Aveling gave science classes for the new venture on Wednesday evenings, and Tussy gave language classes on Fridays. For a while, at least, it was easy enough for him to maintain a double life, commuting between his affair with Eva Frye and his married life with Tussy. But in time the young Miss Frye grew impatient with the logistic inconvenience and the unending commitments of his work with the socialists. Finally, in late August 1897, Aveling too grew restless. Apparently without warning, he took everything in The Den that could be sold and left. Tussy was given no forwarding address, and told only that she could write to him through a certain actor, "M."

Tussy had defended Aveling so often to so many people that there was no one to whom she could turn for consolation. In desperation, she called upon a soul as alone as she was—her half-brother Freddy Demuth. Freddy never learned who his father was. Tussy and Laura and the whole warm family that he had met so often at Engels' home were "cousins," friends of his mother who were willing to treat him with warmth and friendship. He was a workingman, only half-educated, and the political talk of this family was perhaps strange to him. Yet he could and would react when called upon for understanding.

> I wrote once more to Edward this morning [wrote Tussy to Freddy shortly after Aveling had left]. No doubt it is weak, but one *can't* wipe out 14 years of one's life as if they had not been. I think anyone with the least sense of honour, not to mention any feeling of kindness and gratitude, would answer that letter. Will he? I almost fear that he will not. . . . Tomorrow evening is the Executive of the S[DF]. I *can't* go—because if he is not there I *can't* explain. I hate to give you all this trouble, but could you go? . . . You could ask, if he had been. . . .

Two days later Tussy got a note from Edward: "Have returned. Shall be home early to-morrow." Then a telegram: "Home for good, 1:30." Tussy described the reunion in a letter to Freddy:

I was working—for even with all the heartbreak one has to work—in my room—and Edward seemed surprised and quite ''offended'' I did not rush into his arms. He has so far made no apology and offered no explanation. I have—after waiting for him to begin—therefore said one *must* consider the business position—and that I should never forget the treatment I had been subjected to. He has said nothing.

Later that evening Aveling was willing to talk ''business.'' There was still a good deal of the Engels inheritance left, and his demands were stiff. The next morning Tussy sent an urgent message to Freddy: ''Come, if you possibly can, this evening. It is a shame to trouble you; but I am so alone, and I am face to face with a most horrible position: *utter* ruin—everything, *to the last penny,* or utter, open disgrace. It is awful; worse than even I fancied it was. . . . I am heartbroken.

Freddy hurried to The Den. When he got there Tussy had already lost her nerve. She had made some settlement with Aveling, probably involving a payment of hush money to Eva Frye. Aveling, for his part, was already playing the role of repentant husband. Never again, he probably promised her; from now on he would be true, their love would be pure.

X

Two weeks later the Avelings left for Draveil, outside Paris, to visit Laura and her husband, Paul Lafargue. For years, Tussy had not been close to her sister. The reasons are obscure, but one factor may have been the long-standing bitterness between Lissagaray and the Lafargues. Not a word of the temporary separation was leaked to the latter.

Paul Lafargue had been born in Cuba, of French and Creole parents, then moved to Bordeaux as a young man. He was thoroughly French in upbringing, but was dark enough in coloring and fluent enough in Spanish to pass for a Spaniard if necessary. He had been a medical student in Paris in the 1860s, when his political activities earned him exile. He retreated to London to finish his studies, and there fell into the circle that gathered at the Marx house. He shifted his theoretical masters from Proudhon to Marx, married Laura Marx, and returned to Paris. After the Commune he went to Spain as a gray eminence for Marx, leading the propaganda battles for the Marxists against the Bakuninist anarchists. His reports from Spain were all optimistic, but it was Bakunin's allies who triumphed, leading ultimately to the breakup of the First International.

The death of their two children from the hardships of exile in Spain made the Lafargues skeptical of medicine, and when they moved to London in the

1870s Lafargue worked at a whole spate of jobs, in photoengraving, insurance, and journalism. He failed at all of them. ("If Paul 'had been born a hatter,' " wrote Laura, quoting Bulwer-Lytton's *Money,* " 'little boys would have come into the world without heads.' ") Through the 1870s and 1880s, the Lafargues were supported by modest weekly stipends from Engels.

After an amnesty was granted to the Communards in the 1880s, the Lafargues went to Paris, and there Lafargue tried to combine the incompatible goals of socialist leader and country gentleman. He sold some land he had inherited in New Orleans, and bought a small country house outside Paris, using money from Engels to stock the wine cellar. He wrote witty socialist tracts, like *The Right to Be Lazy,* but cleverness did not make up for lack of theoretical content, and his aloofness prevented him from exercising much influence among the French workers. His one moment of fame came in 1891, when, after he gave a propaganda speech in Fourmies, a glassmaking town in the Nord, the workers held a demonstration and were fired upon by government troops. Nine workers were killed, among them women and children. The authorities reacted by jailing Lafargue for inciting the riot. He used his trial for further proselytizing, was convicted, and from jail he campaigned for and was elected to the *Chambre des députés.* In the *Chambre* his tendentious speeches managed to alienate even his supporters. He retired to his country estate, where he tried to support himself as a journalist. Laura made translations and wrote poetry. They were still subsidized by Engels.

After Engels' death, the Lafargues used their inheritance to buy a truly palatial villa. It included a house with thirty rooms, apart from outhouses; a smaller house for the gardener; billiard rooms; studio; orangerie; and greenhouses. The grounds were more a park than a garden, with a profusion of flowers, vegetables, fruits, and game. All around was the Forest of Senard, and while the journey to Paris was difficult, it hardly mattered, for the socialists of Paris were so put off by this ostentatious show of wealth that Lafargue's already tenuous ties to the party were all but broken. Occasionally he would go to the Sorbonne for a debate or a lecture, but otherwise he remained out of touch with the socialists.

To Tussy the whole show was simply too much. "I don't think I would exchange my little Den with this palace," she wrote from Draveil. After two weeks she and Aveling went home. They had put on a good act abroad, but a week later a casual acquaintance, William Collison, saw "the faded beauty of her face and hopeless eyes and the grief inscribed in deep drawn lines about the mouth."

Aveling resumed his science instruction, started a series of drama and elocution classes, and, we may presume, returned to his private instruction of Miss Frye. His classes met occasionally at the SDF Hall, more often at a coffeehouse nearby, and from there he revived his old practice of borrowing any and everywhere. Aveling even tried to put the squeeze on poor Freddy Demuth. But his credit everywhere had so dried up that only Tussy would fund him. For this he played the repentant husband.

Edward and Tussy went on a propaganda tour to Manchester in the midst of a real Lancashire winter. ". . . Certainly if Dante could have dreamed of a Lancashire factory town in bad weather," wrote Tussy, "he would have added half a dozen circles to his hell, & to his 'lowest depth, a lower deep.' " Aveling, already physically weakened from an overactive life, saw his influenza develop into pneumonia. The illness entailed considerable expense and a full-time nursing job for Tussy. The doctor told her that at any moment Edward might "take a turn for the worse," and that she ought to contact his relatives at once. It was touch and go for a couple of weeks, until he was finally well enough to go off to Hastings for a rest, alone. ". . . I really could not go with him," wrote Tussy. "These four weeks have cost too much to make this possible."

Ill as he was, Aveling still noticed "a fair-haired, blue-eyed girl" at the beach. He met her at the post office, "and invented a telegram that I might stick on a stamp her hands had touched. She was as easy and frank as she was beautiful."

Alone again, Tussy was as gloomy as the winter weather. "Yes," she wrote, "I sometimes feel like you, Freddy, that *nothing* ever goes well with us. I mean you and me. Of course, poor Jenny had her full share of sorrow and of trouble, and Laura lost her children. But Jenny was fortunate enough to die, and sad as that was for her children, there are times when I think it fortunate. I would not have wished Jenny to have lived through what I have done. I don't think you and I have been very wicked people—and yet, dear Freddy, it does seem as if we get all the punishment."

Two weeks of sun cleared up Aveling's lungs, but in the meantime an old abscess in his side had ulcerated and developed into a fistula twice the size of a fist. He came back to The Den, then left immediately to see his physician. "He *would not let me go with him!*" wrote Tussy. "That is mere *cruelty, and* there are things he does not want to tell me. Dear Freddy . . . I have nothing; and I see nothing worth living for."

Aveling returned that day and told her the prognosis was not good. He needed a major operation, chances of success were slim, and there was little hope for ultimate recovery.

Tussy reacted with a burst of compassion. This was the explanation she had sought for all that Aveling had done: He was not evil, but sick.

> I don't think you quite understand [she wrote to Freddy]—I am only *beginning* to. But I do see more and more that wrongdoing is just a moral disease, and the morally healthy (like yourself) are not fit judges of the morally diseased; just as the physically healthy person can hardly realize the condition of the physically diseased. In some a certain *moral* sense is

wanting, just as some are deaf or have bad sight, or are otherwise un-
healthy. And I begin to understand that one has no more right to blame the
one disease than the other.

Two days later it was even clearer. "There is a French saying that to *understand* is to *forgive*. Much suffering has taught me to understand—and so
I have no need to forgive. I can only love."

The operation was arranged for University College Hospital. As a fellow
of the college, Edward was placed under the special care of the famed
surgeon Christopher Heath, and given every possible attention. Tussy took a
room nearby, and paced the halls during the operation. There she met Mrs.
Hyndman, who had come to see Edward, and as they walked up and down
the corridor, Tussy poured out her whole depressing story of misery and humiliation. Mrs. Hyndman begged her to leave Edward as soon as he was out
of danger, and Tussy said she would gladly do so. The Hyndmans thought
Tussy's "martyrdom" was near an end.

The operation proved a success, and soon Tussy could take Edward home
in a carriage. The doctors suggested Margate for recuperation, and so to
Margate they went. Because Edward was too weak to walk, Tussy would
take him out in a bath chair and read to him. In the evening she had to dress
the open wound, which meant inserting a syringe, squeezing the open
wound from all sides, then forcing a plug into the wound with sinus forceps.
"You can think what pain this is to Edward, & how awful it is to have to do
this. If *I* could bear the pain how gladly I would!"

The whole scene was a rerun. Exactly fifteen years earlier Tussy had been
at the same beach, caring for an invalid patient—her father. Then, too, she
had been torn between freedom and duty, between what she knew she
should do and what she felt she had to do. And then, too, she had elected
her duty to a man over her dreams of independence.

In a way it was Tussy who was sick, afflicted with the Victorian disease
of duty. The symptoms were loss of self and moral blindness.

Even in despair, Tussy could not give up the impossible dream of socialism and drama. From Margate she followed the developing Dreyfus Affair,
bemoaning the fact that it was Zola and not the socialists who had protested
the injustice done the poor man. She worried about Eduard Bernstein's new
articles that were challenging some of the most basic assumptions of Marxism and raising questions about the organization and effectiveness of the
great German Social Democratic Party. She read the original of Georg Bran-
des' *Shakespeare,* and thought it "a re-hash—& not a good one."

On March 27, 1898, the Avelings returned to The Den. Aveling had
regained his strength sufficiently to get around with help. If the moral disease responded as well, Tussy hoped, the future was all theirs. She invited
guests to The Den for April, and accepted dinner engagements for May.

72

Early on the morning of March 31 Tussy received an unexpected letter. It was subsequently destroyed by Edward Aveling, so we cannot know the author or the exact contents, only that, in the words of a subsequent reader, it threw "a very discreditable light on a certain person."

What the letter, or a clipping enclosed in the letter, probably disclosed was that on June 8, 1897, Alec Nelson and Eva Frye had been married.

Tussy's world collapsed. For nine months, Aveling had been committing legalized adultery. His marriage had made a mockery of the free union with Tussy: What had been sacred was now degraded to another convenience to Edward Aveling. Tussy, like the poor souls who had loaned money to Aveling, had been used and abused; from others Aveling had taken money, from Tussy he took love. For the first time, Tussy truly understood. This time, to understand was not to forgive.

If Ibsen had written the script, it was time for Tussy to leave, to walk out even as Edward protested, letting him plead like Helmer of *A Doll's House* until the famed voice echoed alone in an empty house. But it was too late for Ibsen. Until that letter arrived Aveling had written the script, as her father had written an earlier script; Tussy had played the scenes they wrote. She determined now to add her own ending.

They must end their lives together, she said. He agreed. The maid was sent to a nearby chemist with a visiting card engraved "Dr. Aveling" and a note which said: "Please give bearer chloroform and small quantity prussic acid for dog, E.A." A few minutes later the maid appeared with a small white parcel containing two ounces of chloroform and one drachm of prussic acid—the usual dose for a dog and enough to kill several humans. The maid also brought a book which purchasers of poison were required to sign. Tussy took the book to the front room and signed in Aveling's presence.

Aveling then said that he had to go up to town on business. Tussy protested, but Aveling left quickly, despite the fact that only the day before he was so weak that he had to be wheeled around in a bath chair.

After he left, Tussy went upstairs and wrote two notes. The first, to her solicitor, she enclosed in an envelope with the unexpected letter. The second was to Aveling: "Dear, it will soon be all over now. My last word to you is the same that I have said during all these long, sad years—love."

The maid found her at eleven o'clock, unconscious on the bed. A doctor was summoned, but by the time he arrived Tussy was dead.

The end, like the life itself, had not been written by Tussy. Her old heroine, Emma Bovary, disillusioned after two love affairs, returns home and tells the chemist that she wants poison for the rats that keep her awake at night. She takes the arsenic, writes a note to her husband, and lies down on the bed. When she is found, her husband insists that she be dressed completely in white. The only difference was that Edward Aveling was no Charles Bovary: Tussy had dressed herself in white.

73

Aveling had gone to the office of the SDF, and pointedly called attention to the time of his arrival. He did not return to The Den until late afternoon. The maid alerted him to the news, and he ran upstairs to destroy the letter. A constable prevented him.

At the coroner's inquest, Aveling insisted that he had known nothing about the tragedy until his return.

> CORONER: Was the deceased your wife?
>
> AVELING: Legally or not, do you mean?
>
> CORONER: You are a most difficult man to deal with. Were you married to the deceased?
>
> AVELING: Not legally.
>
> CORONER: Had you any idea that she would destroy herself?
>
> AVELING: She had threatened to do it several times.
>
> CORONER: Did you consider that the threats used were intentional?
>
> AVELING: I regarded them as idle, because they were so frequently repeated.
>
> CORONER: Had you any quarrel before you left in the morning?
>
> AVELING: None whatever.

The coroner censured the chemist for assuming that Aveling was a physician, then returned a verdict of "suicide whilst in a state of temporary insanity." The two letters were given to Aveling, who destroyed them.

Many people attended the funeral, more friends than Tussy had ever known in life. Will Thorne, crying "like a child," spoke until his voice was inaudible. People in the crowd whispered that Aveling had gone to a football game the day before, and the gossip did not die down when he went to a pub with Paul Lafargue after the rites. He did deliver a short, theatrical speech, but his real obituary for Tussy had been written years before, in the magazine which chronicled their courtship.

> My wife's in her room that looks to the south,
> Her eyes are aflame, and a-quiver her mouth,
>   But I am alone with my ale-can.
>
> A step, heavy-light, I hear from the south,
> And all of my life is an ache and a drouth.
>   For I am alone with my ale-can.
>
> He creeps up the stairs, takes the last at a bound;
> The waft of a door, and then not a sound.
>   I am alone with my ale-can.

A silence has followed the step on the stairs
Just so many times—Can you count grey hairs?
  I am alone with my ale-can.

And fair to the eye is the eager face,
And each is the child of an ancient race.
  While I am alone with my ale-can.

Here is the dagger I sharpen again.
It mirrors the stars that are dulled by the rain.
  I am alone with my ale-can.

Shall I spare or smite? Do I hate or love?
A ripple of laughter faint from below.
  And I am alone with my ale-can.

Ah! The secret door! 'Tis a rare device!
A stab in the dark—is it once or twice?
  Hush! I am alone with my ale-can.

Parted the lips of the corpse on the floor;
My wife is at rest and will love no more;
  And I am alone with my ale-can.

"Poor Tussy! . . . No doubt the scamp has driven her to her death." Almost everyone had the same reaction as Victor Adler, though few were as callous as he and the Germans. "But the main thing," he continued in his letter to August Bebel, "—what will happen to the *Nachlass?* She had, I believe, many of Marx's letters in her hands."

Tussy's closest friends wanted to do something, if only to write a short notice of her in a monthly review. But even Olive Schreiner could not bring herself to reveal all she knew. "I felt [that] as I could not speak the truth about him I could not write of her. It would have hurt her to have him blamed. . . ." A few colleagues from the socialist movement considered the possibility of incriminating Aveling, until a lawyer advised them not to proceed for want of evidence. As a gesture, they expelled him from the SDF.

Probate of the will was granted to Aveling without challenge, and he inherited an estate valued at almost two thousand pounds—most of it in property. By that time he had already moved almost everything of value to Eva Frye's flat. She also inherited the burden of nursing Aveling. There was some rumor about a sojourn in New Zealand for his health, but they managed no more than a brief trip to Ireland. When Aveling returned to London, the wound in his side reopened, and grave complications set in. On August 2, 1898, only four months after Tussy's death, while he sat in his bath chair overlooking Battersea Park, Aveling put down the book he had been perusing and died.

His epitaph was written by G.B.S. *The Doctor's Dilemma,* an attack on the wave of appendectomies which had become so fashionable after Edward VII's operation on the eve of his coronation, has a central character based on Aveling. In the play, Aveling has become the poet Louis Dubedat:

> . . . He is as natural as a cat; he moves among men as most men move among things, though he is intentionally making himself agreeable to them on this occasion. Like all people who can be depended upon to take care of themselves, he is welcome company; and his artist's power of appealing to the imagination gains him credit for all sorts of qualities and powers, whether he possesses them or not.

Jennifer Dubedat, his wife, is the only woman in all of Shaw's plays who loves with complete passion. If she lost faith in Dubedat, she says, "it would mean the wreck and failure of my life." Although Shaw mercifully allows Dubedat to predecease his wife, Dubedat is no less a scoundrel than Aveling. He even cites Shavian scripture in his defense: "All your moralizings have no value for me. I don't believe in morality. I'm a disciple of Bernard Shaw . . . the most advanced man now living." (This passage is usually omitted from acting versions of the play.)

Dubedat dies with a circle of physicians standing around him. The scene is Shaw's final snicker at Aveling.

> SIR PATRICK: Aye! that is how the wicked die.
> For there are no bands in their death;
> But their strength is firm:
> They are not in trouble as other men.
> No matter: it's not for us to judge. He's in another world now.
> WALPOLE: Borrowing his first five-pound note there, probably.

Laura Lafargue had been so overcome with grief that she could not attend her sister's funeral. She and her husband took seriously the importance of their role as the survivors of Marx and the bearers of the heritage, but they were so alienated from the socialist movement that all Laura could do was rail against the Germans who were publishing more and more of Marx's manuscripts. Lafargue had been the most able of the French socialists, at least in his grasp of Marxist theory, but he was so taken with the life of the country squire that he rarely took time for work in the movement. And despite his wealth, he had the reputation of being a miser; the French socialists called him *le petit épicier.*

Their home at Draveil was a required pilgrimage for important socialists on their way through Paris, and on these tours the Lafargues were often the object of awe. "I was actually walking with the daughter of Karl Marx!" thought Krupskaya in wonderment as she visited with Lenin in 1910. When Lenin and Krupskaya were about to leave, Laura said of her husband, "He will soon prove the sincerity of his philosophical convictions." Lenin had no idea what she was talking about.

On November 25, 1911, the Lafargues dressed up and spent the day on the town in Paris. They went to one of the new cinemas and ate fancy cakes. When they came home at nine-thirty in the evening, they took a promenade around the estate, then retired to the library. The gardener found them there later in the evening, dead in their armchairs.

A note, in Lafargue's handwriting, explained that they had committed suicide so they would not be a burden upon others in their old age, and so they would not suffer the agony of progressive senility. "During the years," Lafargue explained in the clear prose that always characterized his writing, "I promised myself to not surpass seventy years of age, I decided the time of year for my departure from this life, and I prepared the mode of execution for my resolution, a hypodermic injection of prussic acid."

Socialists everywhere were shocked, except Lenin, who remembered a chance remark in the garden at Draveil.

R O S A
LUXEMBURG

In April 1898, a young couple were married at the civil marriage registry in Basel, Switzerland. The bride was a short woman, dressed simply but carefully—though no more fashionably for her wedding than for any other occasion. She wore her hair swooped up to compensate for her shortness, and chose a dress that would conceal a hip defect that dated from a childhood disease. The groom was Gustav Lübeck, a serious but petty man, so incompetent in dealing with his personal affairs that his mother, who had set up the marriage, found friends to handle the details that Lübeck was certain to bungle. He had protested the match as a compromise to his dignity. His mother prevailed by arguing that it was much better than anything he was likely to achieve on his own account. After the ceremony, the bride and the groom shook hands on the steps of the registry office and parted company. They would never live together, and would only rarely, by chance, see one another.

The bride was Rosa Luxemburg. Her marriage was a sham, arranged solely to permit her to move to Germany. She had no feeling for her new husband. In letters and conversation she used "typical Lübeck" as a synonym for carelessness, unreliability, and incompetence. The formalities of this marriage ceremony were only a minor inconvenience she would willingly endure to attain the important goal of working in the German socialist movement.

Rosa had always been in pursuit of an elusive life that was somewhere else: "Life is playing an everlasting game of hide-and-seek with me [she wrote in a letter]. I always have the feeling that life is not within me, not wherever I happen to be, but somewhere else, far away." As a child of seven, Rosa would sneak to the window in the earliest hours of the morning (it was forbidden to arise before her father did) and look out into the courtyard where the old servant was awakening with a loud yawn to begin his day of work.

> At that time I had the firm conviction that "life," "real," life was somewhere far away, beyond the roofs. Since then I have been travelling to find

80

it. But it always hides behind some roof or the other. Was it, after all, nothing but a hallucination, and has real life remained right here in the court . . . ?

I

Rosa Luxemburg was a very private person. She made frequent public speeches and wrote many articles, pamphlets and books; but she kept no diaries, wrote no autobiography, and rarely discussed her private life with any but her very closest friends. What details we have of her personal life, like the memory of her childhood dreams of "real life," are glimpses that she has carefully, perhaps artfully, leaked into her letters.

Of her childhood, we know almost nothing. She was born in 1871, the fifth of five children, in Zamosc, a provincial town in Russian Poland. Her father was a timber merchant, an assimilated Jew who spoke Polish and German at home, and read widely in German literature. Her family life was a model of trust and respect, a tiny familial ghetto of humanized civilization amid the rampant racism and nationalism of Russian Poland. As Jews, and as heirs of the enlightenment, her family—in common with many Jewish families of Central Europe—held an almost naïve contempt for ethnic and social distinctions. They were the descendants of Nathan the Wise. Although no one in her family shared her views on socialism, Rosa never broke with her parents, brothers, or sister—even when her growing interest in revolutionary politics split the family along a clear ideological line. Only a tinge of rebellious contempt in her attitude suggests the gap between them; when someone asked Rosa why she considered Schiller a second-rate poet, she answered, "Well, perhaps I took an instinctive dislike to him because my mother was so crazy about him. By that very fact he was labelled old-fashioned and sentimental as far as I was concerned."

When Rosa was only two and a half, the family moved to Warsaw. Better schools and business opportunities were the ostensible reasons, although her father admitted that "he could not stand life with the Jews" in Zamosc. She attended one of the best girls' high schools, a remarkable feat in light of her Polish and Jewish background. The schools favored Russian students, and all classes were conducted in Russian; even among themselves children were forbidden to speak Polish.

By the time she was in high school, Rosa was politically active and probably in contact with a group of illegal revolutionaries. In her last year, she qualified for a gold medal in academic achievement, but the medal was withheld "on account of her rebellious attitude towards the authorities." Soon after she left school, in 1887, she became a member of the revolutionary socialist party *Proletariat* and began to read the works of Marx and Engels.

Since the partition of Poland in the eighteenth century, the nation had existed only in language, culture, and the minds of revolutionary schemers. Over and over again the rallying cry of Polish independence had brought together revolutionaries who spanned an entire political spectrum, from monarchists who longed for a revival of the Napoleonic Grand Duchy of Warsaw to anarchists who sought to destroy the domination of Russia, Prussia, Austria, and any other government. Between the nationalistic outbursts, the revolutionaries were forced either to join forces with their dominators or to try to subsist as tiny, isolated, and ineffective splinters. The Leftists generally allied themselves with the various revolutionary groups of Russia. Thus the rise and fall of revolutionary activity in Russia was paralleled in Russian Poland.

The 1880s marked a caesura in the life of the revolutionary movements in Poland. In Russia, the *Narodniki,* populists who believed that through a kind of agrarian utopianism Russia could avoid the horrors of an era of capitalism, were on the decline after their radical organization, the *Narodnaya Volya* (Peoples' Will) had successfully assassinated Czar Alexander II in 1881. The works of Georgi Plekhanov, which were to introduce Marxism into Russia, were not published until 1883 and 1885, and for about ten years they had little influence. This hiatus between populism and Marxism meant a general apathy toward the revolutionary movement, and when *Proletariat* tried to fill the gap by organizing strikes, it managed to do enough to get itself destroyed by the police, though not enough to arouse the working class in Russian Poland.

As the police closed in on the activities of *Proletariat,* Rosa got her first taste of the conspiratorial politics that characterized the socialist movements in Russia and Poland. By 1889 the Russian authorities had her name, and she was scheduled for arrest. She faced two choices: Siberia or exile abroad. With the encouragement of her comrades in *Proletariat,* Rosa chose exile. It was not a reluctant choice. To become a full-fledged Marxist, it was essential to study capitalist society and modern political and economic thought, since Marxism required a firm knowledge of the great texts and commentaries. As a woman and a Jew, Rosa was forbidden to attend a university in the Russian empire. Exile would provide the opportunity for her to attend a university in Western Europe.

In order to cross the border, Rosa and a comrade had to convince a village priest that she was a Jewish girl who wished to be baptized in order to marry her lover, "but owing to the violent opposition of her family, could only do so abroad." The priest had her hidden under the straw in a peasant's cart. Toward the end of 1889 she finally arrived in Zurich and enrolled in the university.

82

Rosa registered under the faculty of philosophy, and took courses in the natural sciences and mathematics. Botany and zoology were to become avocations of her life. In moments of political frustration she would lament that society did not follow the laws of nature in the elegant fashion of animals and plants. Mathematics was a *violon d'Ingres* at which she was extremely proficient. Later in life she would protest that whatever ability she had in economics was only an extension of her ease with mathematics. Yet her passion for the natural sciences ultimately had to give way to the necessities of political training, and in 1892 she transferred to the faculty of law. Studying with Julius Wolf, the professor of political economy, she mastered the classics of economics—Adam Smith, Ricardo, Marx. She was a brilliant student, his ablest, as he recalls in his autobiography. He had the good humor to put up with the malicious games that Rosa and her colleagues would play with him. One of her friends would innocently ask a loaded question. The professor would get himself hopelessly entangled, and Rosa would then get up and expose his incompetence point by point. She delighted in the quick repartee and in rhetorical questions.

The university constituted only a small segment of Rosa's life in Zurich. Switzerland was the center for Russian and Polish revolutionary exiles, and Rosa, who arrived well-armed with introductions from her comrades in *Proletariat,* soon fell in with the émigrés in various Swiss cities. She met the pope of Russian Marxism, Plekhanov, who in the 1880s conceived the brilliant idea that Russia was headed not for a utopian, agrarian revolution, but a variation of the feudal-capitalist-socialist pattern of development that Marx had predicted for the industrialized states of Europe. Plekhanov expounded the theory in what became the first book of Russian Marxism, then settled in exile as a resident theorist, ruling a vast revolutionary family from his throne in Geneva.

In 1890, in Zurich, Rosa met the person who was to be the most important in her life, Leo Jogiches. He had been born in Vilna in 1867, to a prosperous, assimilated Jewish family. By the age of eighteen he had already been arrested and imprisoned twice for revolutionary activities; both times he escaped. He had organized workers and even soldiers in the town and had formed a revolutionary circle. In Lithuania he enjoyed enormous prestige as a radical leader, and especially as a master of clandestine conspiratorial techniques. Finally, to escape military service (in a penal batallion where his organizational talents would be wasted), he joined the emigration of revolutionaries to Switzerland.

Jogiches was like a fish out of water in Switzerland. His forte was conspiracy, secret groups with pseudonyms and complicated strategic plans; he was accustomed to working behind the scenes, directing, infiltrating, slipping away from detection by the police, then striking again. He came to Switzerland with an established reputation and his arrogance and tenacity only increased the distance between him and the great names of Russian socialism in exile. The latter had no need for secrecy, and to Plekhanov and others who spent their hours in theoretical arguments over the correct tactics for the distant overthrow of capitalistic society, the antics of Jogiches were so many childish games. "A miniature version of Nechaieff," Plekhanov once called him, in a demeaning comparison to Bakunin's most disreputable anarchist disciple.

Jogiches came to Switzerland with a considerable sum of money, a combination of his own and party funds, which he intended to use to publish classic Marxist literature—Marx, Engels, Bebel, Plekhanov—to be smuggled into Russia. He went straightaway to Plekhanov and proposed a joint venture: his money and pipeline, Plekhanov's copyrights and prestige. On what basis? Plekhanov asked. When Jogiches haughtily proposed fifty-fifty, he was shown the door. Their private difference soon became a public dispute, made notorious in letters and socialist newspapers. The consequence was that Jogiches was effectively cut off from the exile movement. He would have to await revolution and return to Russia before his considerable talents would be brought back into the struggle.

By the time of his break with Plekhanov, Jogiches had already fallen in love with Rosa Luxemburg, and she with him. They were both reluctant to reveal their emotions. Neither had ever loved before, and neither would ever really love anyone else. Theirs was an age convinced that love strikes only once, and while they might endorse every Marxist argument about the liberation of women and the wretchedness of the bourgeois conventions of marriage as another act of materialistic exploitation, they were unable to escape the ethos of their epoch.

In one respect, though, Rosa and Leo did hold ideas about the role of women which differed from their contemporaries', and had he not shared these ideas with her their love would have been difficult or impossible. As Clara Zetkin, the leader of the women's socialist movement in Germany and an on-again, off-again friend of Rosa put it, "He was one of those men who can tolerate a great personality in the woman by his side, working with him in loyal and happy comradeship, without feeling her growth and development as a limitation on his own personality." There were times when Rosa's fame eclipsed whatever reputation Leo established, when he was thought of only as "Rosa's man"; yet he had the self-assurance to accept and even nurture that situation. He was content to work from behind the lines while Rosa enjoyed the publicity of the front.

Their love and dependency were mutual. When Jogiches broke with Plekhanov, Rosa tried to mediate, or at least to moderate Leo's obstinacy. She failed and within a few years she too was at odds with the "old man," as they called Plekhanov. The result was that Rosa and Leo, the two talented and young revolutionaries, in exile from Poland and Russia, were excluded from the émigré organizations. They had no party, no comrades, and except for the spy network that Jogiches could feed with publications—as long as his money held out—they had no means to work in the revolutionary movement to which they had dedicated their lives.

II

In 1892, leaders from all sectors of the Polish socialist movement formed a new united party, the Polish Socialist Party (PPS). Its program was Marxist, but it also incorporated significant concessions to the nationalism that had been the great rallying cause for Polish revolutionaries throughout the nineteenth century. To attract a large following, the party was willing to make its appeal a compromise among the various revolutionary groups and their sometimes contradictory demands.

The program was extremely important for an exile party, for while the legal or quasi-legal parties of Western Europe could concentrate on tactics and organization, the exiled parties of Russia and Poland had, in effect, no organization and no opportunities to utilize tactics. Theirs was a world of patient preparation, a world in which the program became a sacred document, like a book of prophecy. To question the program, once it had been agreed upon, was to question the very existence of the movement.

Within a few months of foundation of the PPS, a new socialist paper, *Sprawa Robotnicza (The Worker's Cause)*, appeared in Paris, and in the first issue questioned the goals of the new Polish party. The PPS had called for "liberation from Russian tutelage." *The Workers' Cause* argued that the only viable and truly Marxist course for the working classes of Poland was to work in closest cooperation with the working classes of Russia. Further, the newspaper contained not a mention of the holy of Polish holies—independence from Russia. It was thus a direct challenge to the PPS program.

The new newspaper was the production of Rosa Luxemburg and Leo Jogiches. He was responsible for the finances and organization, she for the writing. They had timed their challenge carefully so as to coincide with the opening of the Third Congress of the Socialist International in Zurich in August of 1893. With a legitimate newspaper established, Rosa and Leo and the small group around them could present a claim to be represented at the Congress as rival representatives of the working classes of Poland. Rosa and a few colleagues appeared at the Congress, defending their right to mandates with a written statement and speeches by Rosa.

Her first appearance before the world of international socialism made a striking impression on at least one old-timer:

> Rosa, 23 years old at the time, was quite unknown outside one or two Socialist groups in Germany and Poland . . . but her opponents had their

hands full to hold their ground against her. . . . She rose from among the delegates at the back and stood on a chair to make herself better heard. Small and looking very frail in a summer dress . . . she advocated her cause with such magnetism and such appealing words that she won the majority of the Congress at once and they raised their hands in favor of the acceptance of her mandate.

Emile Vandervelde, the Belgium socialist leader who wrote the description, was deceived by either memory or chivalry; in fact, Rosa lost the vote and was forced to leave the hall with a group of anarchists who had also been refused mandates.

The dispute at Zurich was a declaration of war, and with war declared, the break in the ranks of Polish social democracy became permanent. Rosa's group, though wary of formal organizations, formed themselves into a separate party, The Social Democracy of the Kingdom of Poland (SDKP). The little newspaper became their doctrinal organ. The cause of Polish independence was formally dismissed—in Rosa Luxemburg's phrase, as "a utopian mirage, a delusion of the workers to detract them from their class struggle"—and what had been a minimal Marxist program in the PPS was strengthened to a set of sharp, "maximum" demands.

The rivlary of the two groups polarized their positions until what had been vague commitments became crystallized programs. The new party expressed the self-conscious assertion of a group of younger revolutionaries; its existence was due as much to a generation gap between Rosa, Leo, and their colleagues, and the older generation of Polish leaders, as to any theoretical differences. The SDKP leadership formed what Peter Nettl, Rosa Luxemburg's biographer, has identified as a "peer group," a circle of contemporaries who were able to work together closely because they saw themselves as equals. Besides Rosa Luxemburg and Leo Jogiches, the nucleus included Julian Marchlewski and Adolf Warszawski, as well as other Poles and Lithuanians of their generation who floated in and out of the group.

Rosa was from the beginning the fount of policy ideas. Her command of Marxist theory and of political economy was already extraordinary, and it was she who articulated the group's positions in the journal and in the papers and speeches presented at subsequent meetings of the Second International. Jogiches remained the behind-the-scene administrator of the group. The main outlines of policy were probably set by him. Everything Rosa wrote was certainly discussed with and reviewed by him, and it was he who decided who were to be the allies and the enemies of the new party. Although Rosa was the public figure most closely associated with the SDKP, Plekhanov and some of his contemporaries considered Rosa to be nothing more than Jogiches' mouthpiece.

What was remarkable about the membership was that their similar backgrounds, their mutual regard, and their exclusiveness enabled them to function through a kind of established consensus unknown to most revolutionary movements. Their values, ideals, and personalities differed. They bickered on dozens of tactical points. But they were able to agree on major issues, and were quick to rally to a common defense against attacks from outsiders. Their unity was not the common front of a vast organization with its inertial bureaucracy, like the Western socialist parties, nor the enforced loyalty of the conspiratorial groups of Russia, where a breach of subscription to policies set by the leadership would lead to immediate expulsion. Hierarchy, loyalty oaths, any distinction between decision-making and execution were unknown. Proceedings were informal, but so effective that party congresses were unnecessary.

In Poland the SDKP made little impact. With its leadership centered in Zurich, and few copies of its newspapers smuggled into Poland, it could count on having almost no rank-and-file following. Yet its very illegality, and the adversity against which it struggled, was something of an advantage. Since the newspaper was outlawed in Poland, and by its language ignored by authorities in the West, those who wrote for it had little reason to temper or circumscribe their writings. In the case of legal socialist newspapers, everything printed had to be carefully couched in language that would escape or deceive the eyes of the censor. Rosa and her colleagues had no such fears. They wrote of the activities of various socialist parties with an easy cross-reference between countries and movements that added much to the paper's internationalism.

Her writing for this newspaper, as much as her study of politics and economics that culminated in a dissertation on the industrial development of Poland, made up Rosa Luxemburg's political education. The paper survived only a few years, until 1895. Those few years were long enough to gain her international recognition for her contributions. She was later invited to work for the prestigious *Neue Zeit,* a journal read by most European socialist intellectuals. Rosa used the columns of *Neue Zeit* to expand her attack on Polish nationalism into a general organizational and strategic study, involving the German and Austrian parties, and piquing the socialists of both parties.

At the London congress of the Second International, in 1896, her radical position was again voted down, but only after she had defended it publicly. The defeat was not as important as the fact that some of the most distinguished socialists, including Kautsky, Plekhanov, Victor Adler and Wilhelm Liebknecht, had considered her views worthy of refutation.

By questioning both the orthodoxy and textual accuracy of the pronouncements of Kautsky and Plekhanov, who saw themselves as the high priests of Marxism, Rosa had become very much the upstart youngster. The Germans, on the whole, had inherited their views on Poles and Russians from Marx, who had little more than contempt for the "barbarians" of the East. For Rosa, a Pole, still in her twenties, and a woman, to challenge the self-appointed keepers of the tradition, was the very essence of audacity. To

Rosa, the battle was exhilarating, an opportunity to take on the greats in the same way she had taken on her professors at the University of Zurich. Yet as she enjoyed the polemics, her comrades in the SDKP grew anxious about the exposure that her solos produced. Jogiches, especially, questioned her loyalty to the group, and he was right. Rosa remained faithful to the idea of the SDKP, as a collaboration of equals, but she was growing impatient with the narrow confines of the Polish émigré movement. That elusive life, somewhere else, was calling. For a few months in 1896 and 1897 she lived in France but for someone as involved in socialism as she was, somewhere else could be only Germany.

Germany was the land of the mighty German Social Democratic Party (usually abbreviated SPD, for *Socialdemokratische Partei Deutschlands*), a party so carefully organized and disciplined that it formed a separate state within the German state. August Bebel, the grand old man of the German working class, rang out the challenge of total defiance in his uncompromising statements: "Not a man nor a farthing for this system!" "I am and always will be the mortal enemy of existing society." The smallest children of socialist families could quote Bebel's words, and for many of them the institutions of the party and the trade unions were more familiar even than the ubiquitous symbols of imperial German might.

To the socialist world, the SPD was the very symbol of Marxist might and right. Their parliamentary delegation would vote with absolute discipline on every issue. Their theoreticians were at the forefront of the debates which sought to evolve a policy and body of theory to cope with the changing world of politics and society in the closing years of the century; their every pronouncement in *Neue Zeit* was a new orthodoxy. Compared to this the French socialists were a mélange of bickering factions. Most of the other parties were so small, so divided, and so remote from the possibility of exercising power, that they stood back in awe of the Germans, unable to argue or challenge in the face of such organized and disciplined power. Socialism was international, but its language was German, and the rules of the game had been written by Germans.

To work in this party, in 1898 Rosa married Gustav Lübeck and moved to Berlin.

III

It was not easy to leave Jogiches and the comfortable circle of the SDKP for Germany.

My soul is bruised and it is difficult to explain exactly how I feel [she wrote in a first letter to Jogiches]. Last night in bed in the middle of a strange city, I completely lost heart and asked myself the frankest question: would I not be happier instead of looking for adventure to live with you somewhere in Switzerland quietly and closely, to take advantage of our youth and to enjoy ourselves. . . . In fact I have a cursed longing for happiness and am ready to haggle for my daily portion of happiness with all the stubbornness of a mule.

In Germany, Rosa introduced herself at SPD headquarters. To her surprise, her name was known. Her articles had already given her the reputation of a gadfly. She offered to take on any assignment, even suggesting the murky task of campaigning for the Reichstag elections among the Poles of Silesia. Though nervous about her accent and her ability to speak directly to the workers, she found herself an immediate success.

Yet speechmaking in the Polish areas of Silesia was not the reason Rosa Luxemburg had come to Germany and the SPD. In the years of working within the exclusive circle of the SDKP, she had developed ideas about socialism and the development of society, and she wanted those ideas heard. For Rosa, Marxism was more than a systematic economic and historical theory. It was a key to understanding the world, a tool which if used properly could come very close to approximating the "real" life she had sought since childhood. By proper application of the Marxist dialectic, the secrets of "life" could be unlocked, and Rosa—a young, Jewish, Polish woman—could be the one to unlock those secrets. She faced an uphill fight:

> Why should they trust a person whose only claim to existence is a few articles, albeit first-class [she wrote to Jogiches]? A person moreover who does not belong to the ruling clique, who won't rely on anyone's support but uses nothing but her own elbows, a person feared for the future not only by obvious opponents . . . but even by allies . . . a person best kept at arm's length because she may grow several heads too tall? . . . I take all this with great calm, I always knew it could not be otherwise. . . . In a year or two, no intrigue, fears or obstacles will help them and I shall occupy one of the foremost positions in the party.

The program of the SPD, drawn up at Erfurt in 1891 as a compromise between Marxist determinism and other trends in the German socialist movement, foresaw the inevitable collapse of the capitalist society within a distant but foreseeable future. In deference to the laws of the Empire, which were particularly harsh in such areas as subversion and lese majesty, it contained no mention of revolution, but the collapse of capitalist society was discussed as a concrete and inevitable millenium. The rhetoric was strong enough to provide ideological unity for the party, and a firm distinction dividing the socialists from the rest of German society.

At the same time, the SPD was also a large and complex institution which sought to preserve and strengthen itself. Its hierarchy paralleled the bureaucracy of the German state, from local officials up to an executive committee, and at almost every level it had an organization or activity which could substitute for the institutions of the state. Socialist children attended public schools, but they participated in after-school activities sponsored by the party. On weekends or on holidays, workers went to party functions. Workers were encouraged to follow party activities, from proclamations and demonstrations to the annual congresses which publicly defined and celebrated their unity and might. In their homes, workers were more likely to hang portraits of Wilhelm Liebknecht and August Bebel, the co-chairmen of the SPD executive, than the portrait of the Emperor which hung in bourgeois homes.

To the rest of society, from the Emperor down, the socialists were pariahs, enemies of the state who could in no way be considered ''official'' opposition. Although the party was legal after 1890 and suffered no special restrictions, the fact that it subscribed to a program that awaited the collapse of capitalism led the state to label the socialists as irresponsible, subversive, and undesirable. In the bourgeois press, in the Reichstag where they filled the left side of the hall, and in bourgeois homes, they were the ''reds''— sworn enemies of the state and of everything that had made the German Empire the world's most powerful state. This pariah status was important, as it provided external reinforcement for the unity and exclusiveness of the party. The more sharply the line between the SPD and the state was drawn, the less the party had to worry about losing membership or votes. The state and the party unconsciously were allies in making an either/or choice out of membership or voting for the SPD. In the Reichstag, the SPD delegation voted resolutely as a bloc—always against any measure that the state proposed.

Yet the party was far from revolutionary in practice. Marxism, as Kautsky and the other party theorists interpreted it, saw history as a vast human drama, played out by actors according to an unvarying script. The action could perhaps be slowed down or speeded up by the actors' improvisations, but the acts of the drama, each of which represented some stage of the inevitable struggle between the classes, would follow one another inexorably. And, since the drama would eventually play itself out, since the collapse of capitalism and the triumph of the proletariat was the inescapable ending of the play, the players could easily excuse inaction for tactical reasons. In this way the SPD often avoided exposing itself to the risk of repressive measures by the state. May Day work stoppages and parades were a subject of constant debates in Germany, although socialist parties elsewhere followed the injunctions of the International in holding them as demonstrations of working-class solidarity. The reason for such caution in Germany, argued the party leaders, was to avoid antagonizing the state and jeopardizing party organization. The latter had to be kept intact and at the ready for revolution and the seizure of power when capitalism and the German state collapsed. In fact, the party had become its own reason for existence; the doctrine of Marxism was used to rationalize or justify that existence. Thousands of officials held positions in the SPD or trade union organizations, and hundreds of thousands of workers had a sense of belonging that the state could never provide them.

Thus, while the rhetoric of the official program spoke of the inevitable collapse of bourgeois society, the party members complacently enjoyed their outings, clubs, reading groups—all mirrors of the activities of the capitalistic society which would disappear in the inevitable millennium. That contradiction was well hidden behind the stirring rhetoric and solidarity of the party. When August Bebel could shout "Not a man and not a farthing to this system!" and could refuse to attend a court function because he would not cowtow to bourgeois custom; when a party parade could attract thousands or hundreds of thousands of marching workers; when as many as one out of three votes cast in the Reichstag elections went to SPD candidates—few would question the actual readiness of the party for the coming revolution.

The SPD's complacency was shattered in 1898 by a series of articles written by Eduard Bernstein. He had been one of the figures who had kept the German socialist movement alive during the years of its semi-illegality, from 1878 to 1890. Working from Switzerland and later from London, he had edited the central journal of the party, and visited Marx and Engels to negotiate tactical points of the SPD program.

When the party regained legal status in the 1890s, he remained in London, watching the activities of the SPD from some distance. What he saw was a pattern of development that to him seemed to diverge from the progressive weakening and ultimate collapse of capitalism that Marxism had predicted.

Extrapolating from the tensions he saw in the capitalist society of his own time, Marx had written a powerful epic of class struggle, in which classes were variously predestined, through the workings of the dialectic of history, to move inexorably toward inevitable triumph or defeat. As the drama of capitalist development played out its run, the peasantry would decline into a set of agricultural wage laborers—rural proletarians. The middle classes, by which Marx meant the petty bourgeoisie of shop owners and small merchants, would be squeezed out of their unprofitable position, falling into the working classes, as society split into two warring camps, the bourgeoisie and the proletariat. Misery and a kind of economic serfdom would increase, and at the same time the proletariat would become conscious of its position and its historical destiny. The increased "class consciousness" would lead to increased class solidarity, which would enable the proletariat, with growing courage, to take advantage of the increased frequency and depth of the crises that would beset capitalist society.

In a series of articles in *Neue Zeit,* and later in a book, *The Underlying Assumptions of Socialism and the Tasks of Social Democracy,* Bernstein noted that although Marx's predictions were rigorously logical, history had not followed the predictions. The essence of Bernstein's observations were summarized in a few notes to himself that he once scribbled on an envelope:

> Peasants do not sink; middle class does not disappear; crises do not grow ever larger; misery and serfdom do not increase. There *is* increase in insecurity, dependence, social distance, social character of production, functional superfluity of property owners.

His observations were accurate. In late nineteenth-century Europe, the peasantry did not "sink." If anything, they were more numerous, and more conscious of their own goals as a class; instead of declining into the proletariat, they were supporting their own cooperatives and political parties. The middle classes had also failed to disappear. Indeed, with the expanded production of the great factories of Germany, England, and France, the middle classes were larger than ever, as they filled the great demand for means to distribute the goods produced in those factories. Misery and serfdom were not on the rise, but on the decline; governments had gone out of their way to pass measures like factory inspection bills, health and disability insurance for the workers, and restrictions on the length of the working day or on factory conditions. Rather than a step on a down staircase, the wretched condition of the workers while Marx was writing, from the 1840s to the 1860s, had been a nadir; in the intervening decades the workers of every country had experienced gains in real wages, working conditions, and living conditions. Finally, the great periodic crises of capitalism, such as the depression of the 1870s, which were supposed to become ever more frequent and more disastrous, seemed to be quite the opposite. As one of Bernstein's allies put it, "Capitalist economy is far more viable than you think."

Bernstein's commentaries were originally intended as footnotes to Marxist theory. He had no intention of creating a new, systematic philosophy to replace Marxism, and he considered himself a very loyal Marxist. Nor did he abandon the aim of socialism. Its goal, he argued, was its moral content, the important task of redistributing income and opportunity within society. Yet, as a good Marxist, Bernstein had to frame his observations within a historical and dialectic context, and the only conclusion he could thereby draw was that certain fundamental faults in the Marxist theory had been guiding the socialist movement of his time. If the crises of society were not sliding ever closer to an inevitable collapse, it made little sense for the socialists to maintain a utopian hope for some millennial overthrow of the society. Rather, the only realistic and progressive course of action was to place constant pressure on and within capitalist society, using cooperatives of producers and consumers, and the trade unions, to expand the reforms and advantages the working classes had already won. The party should not be preparing for a revolution in the vague future, but should use its electoral strength to press unrelentingly for political reforms and for social legislation.

What Bernstein demanded was in fact what the SPD was already doing. All he asked was that the party "dare to appear as what it actually was; a democratic socialist party of reform." Yet that was an impossible call for the party to meet. If the leadership were to admit that they were seeking only reforms, then the SPD would no longer remain outside the political spectrum of Germany. The socialists would no longer be pariahs, and they would no longer retain the advantages of their exclusiveness, their relative isolation from the rest of society, and their reputation as the intractable enemies of capitalist society. The leaders and the rank-and-file of the SPD could no longer proclaim the glorious rhetoric about the inexorable march of history and the inevitable collapse of capitalism.

Thus, what Bernstein did was to point out the inherent contradiction within the SPD between a revolutionary theoretical program and reformist tactical goals. And what began as a series of observations on the development of capitalist society provoked an identity crisis for the party that could be resolved only through the difficult process of critical self-examination.

It was this crisis of revisionism that provided Rosa Luxemburg her entry into the "real world" of socialism.

Rosa Luxemburg attacked Bernstein's contentions as soon as his first article appeared in *Neue Zeit,* at a time when his views still seemed inoffensive to most of the socialist world. She used every opportunity to dismember his writings—speeches at party congresses, articles in any newspaper or journal that would print them. When he put his theory into a book, she answered with a pamphlet, *Social Reform or Revolution,* which collected her critique of revisionism. Her tools were the same as those Marx had used to good effect against his intellectual opponents—biting sarcasm and a razor-sharp critical style. Like Marx, she did not so much answer her opponent as dissect him, pulling out each and every part of his arguments and holding them up so any reader could see how diseased and rotten it all was. The effect was electrifying, and while many other participants later entered into the debate on revisionism, it is Rosa Luxemburg's criticisms which were and are the most influential.

Rosa questioned both the assumptions (the theory) upon which revisionism rested, and the tactics that it proposed as a result of that theory.

The theory, argued Rosa, was really a rejection of scientific socialism. Marxism, above all, was scientific; the inevitable coming of socialism was not argued on moral grounds but as a demonstrable consequence of the working of the dialectic. Bernstein, Rosa pointed out, had treated Marx's law of value as an "abstraction" of equal validity with other convenient abstractions. But, she wrote, "Bernstein has quite forgotten that this Marxist abstraction is not an invention but a discovery. It exists not in Marx's head but in our commodity economy." Similarly, if the anarchy of capitalism is discounted, and "adaptability" and "viability" are stressed, then the most basic Marxist tenet of the "objective necessity" for socialism is abandoned. With scorn, Rosa compared Bernstein with Wilhelm Weitling, who in the 1840s had also argued for a socialism based on "justice" and "fair distribution."

> With how much more force, more spirit and more fire did Weitling advocate this sort of socialism fifty years ago! Of course, Weitling, the ingenious tailor, was not then acquainted with scientific socialism. If today, half a century later, the conception torn to shreds by Marx and Engels is happily patched up and offered to the German proletariat as the last word in science, that too is the art of a tailor—but not an ingenious one.

Bernstein and his supporters, she pointed out, believed that one need only put the label "socialism" onto a set of policies to justify them: "They only forget that, as Engels once said, if you classify a clothes brush as a mammal, it won't grow breasts for quite a while."

Rosa used Bernstein's own arguments against him. He had cited the increase and internationalization of credit as evidence of capitalist stability; in reality, she demonstrated, it would contribute to the downfall of capitalism by further separating methods of production from property relations. Cartels and trusts, far from stabilizing capitalism, are symptoms of the final stages of capitalism, in which vast properties are controlled by the few. The relative prosperity of the 1890s could neither hide the shadows of convulsions yet to come, nor conceal the fact that the preconditions for the ultimate contradiction between production and exchange (read: "proletariat and bourgeoisie") already exist.

Ironically, Rosa pointed to Bernstein's admission that capitalism does show "a little" anarchy: "He is—to use Marx's illustration—like the foolish virgin that had a child 'who was only very small.' " Even partial crises in the capitalist economy would inevitably lead to world crises of unlimited dimension, and ultimately to the downfall of capitalism.

The revisionists, and Bernstein in particular, had tried to dissociate their theoretical observations from the practical, tactical consequences that the theory would have for the party. "This is quite understandable," wrote Rosa,

> for our "theory," i.e., the principles of scientific socialism, imposes clearly marked limitations to practical activity—concerning the *aims* of this

activity, the *means* of the struggle applied, and the *method* of struggle. It is thus natural for those who only run after practical results to want to free their hands, i.e., to split our practice from "theory," to make it independent of theory.

Rosa was as merciless with the revisionist tactics as she was with the theory. Bernstein had advocated a program of trade union and cooperative pressure, social reforms, and gradual democratization of the state. All three, argued Rosa, would fail. The trade unions could not destroy Marx's law of wages, could not abolish exploitation, could not gain for the workers any influence over production policy, and could not affect either the size or the output of technical methods. Therefore they could not fill an aggressive role, but could only be looked upon as "the defense of labor power against the attacks of profit, as the defense of the working class against the depressive tendency of capitalist economy." This simple and absolute consequence of the objective nature of capitalist society transformed the functions of the trade union struggle into "a sort of labor of Sisyphus." The striking analogy to the hopeless efforts of Sisyphus, pushing his great stone up the hill, only to have it roll down again, was later to get Rosa into much trouble.

Social reform and democratization, too, she argued, were illusions. Capitalist society would permit as much reform as was in its interest because those reforms "are not an interference with capitalist exploitation; they lend order and regularity to this exploitation." Democracy exists only as long as the goals of the society as a whole are identical with those of the capitalists. When they are not, as in the case of tariffs or militarism (the former to protect powerful industrialists against the consumer and the latter to protect the capitalists of one country against the capitalists of another), the illusory democracy is scuttled and in its place the state introduces its measures by deceit or naked power.

Rosa's critique was a virtuoso performance. A brief summary fails to do justice to the dialectic technique or the Talmudic subtleties of her argument. Revisionism raised the most basic issues of Marxism, and this gave Rosa the chance to explore raw concepts instead of tactical questions. She had shown the philosophical bases of revisionism to be nothing but "vulgar bourgeois economics," the same vulgar bourgeois economics for which she had taken her professors at Zurich to task. The tactics of revisionism she had shown to be a false rationalization of hollow and faulty strategies, which would not achieve the same goal more slowly and more gradually, but would abandon that goal in favor of insignificant modifications in the existing order. Revisionism, in other words, was nothing but opportunism by a different name, and the SPD would be well rid of it.

The battles over revisionism in 1898 and 1899 were fought to a draw, for while Rosa's critique was persuasive and incisive, it was not until party policy was discussed that revisionism would be settled as an issue. In 1901 and 1903, the party made the absolute condemnation of revisionism part of their program—not because they accepted the validity of Rosa's arguments, but because they were anxious to preserve the isolation of the party as a caste. In practice, as we have seen, the SPD *was* revisionist. But to support revisionism in word would be to invalidate the very reason for the existence and the independence of the party.

In 1904 the debate erupted again, this time on an international scale. The French socialists had the possibility of getting one of their number, Alexandre Millerand, into a bourgeois government. Jean Jaurès argued passionately that in the more open political conditions of France, this radical new method was a potential key to socialist advances. But participation in a bourgeois government was a "revisionist" tactic and Rosa, unwilling to admit exceptions to the universal validity of Marxist orthodoxy, dismissed Jaurès as an eloquent but outdated revisionist.

The dispute was settled at the Amsterdam Congress of the Second International, in 1904. Rosa attended as a member of the German delegation—in the official photograph she stands out as the only woman among the mostly bearded high priests she once called "the Fathers." On the surface, the congress was all internationalism and cooperation. When Jaurès made a speech to a group of Germans, Rosa translated his French into equally passionate German, although she disagreed with his every line. It was the sort of gesture that reassured every member of the International of their solidarity and international unity.

Yet when it came time to settle the question of the proposed new tactics of the French party, the German leadership and their allies in the French party, led by Jules Guesde, had already prepared a script. A motion was introduced to condemn Millerand's participation in a government. After a monumental debate between Bebel and Jaurès, the motion was voted in, over Jaurès's protests. He rose in an especially eloquent denunciation of the SPD as a cowering monument of rhetoric, but was forced to yield. Revisionism as a theory was officially drummed out of the socialist movement.

Rosa Luxemburg's participation in the revisionism debates earned her instant fame and notoriety. Her spirited and brilliant defense of Marxist orthodoxy had propelled her into the front ranks of the party intellectuals. Even those whom she had once offended as the upstart from Poland could only be impressed by her clever and forceful arguments against Bernstein.

At the same time, her criticism of revisionist tactics and her reference to trade union activities as "the labors of Sisyphus" had raised the hackles of both the unionists and those South German leaders who had been the chief advocates of what in effect was revisionism. Her sharp language fueled their anger; in one speech she had referred to the "crazy" notions of a comrade, changing the term to "mistaken" only when a chorus of boos censured her breach of party etiquette. To the old-timers of the working-class struggle, she was a firebrand, an outsider interfering in matters beyond her ken.

As Rosa increased the tempo of her attacks on revisionism all stops were pulled by her opponents. Her statements were called tactless, and her attackers stooped to the level of her Polish critics, one of whom had called her "an hysterical and quarrelsome female." One wrote, "I am especially annoyed that she proved herself too much of a woman and not sufficiently a party comrade." Another spoke of the "unpleasant tone in the party press produced by the male and female immigration from the East." In a debate, Georg von Vollmar, a supporter of Bernstein, countered her arguments with condescension: "You greenhorn, I could be your grandfather."

IV

For many revolutionaries, the loneliness of exile and separation from a loved one is filled by the friendships and camaraderie of a party. Certainly for the members of the SDKP, exiled in Switzerland, the activities of the group compensated for the isolation in language and culture they had felt. But Rosa Luxemburg could never find that camaraderie in the SPD. Even as she became a prestigious party intellectual, she was never accepted as one of the hierarchy. She sought to influence the party, but only because she shared its ultimate goals. Bernstein's most famous line had been: "The final goal, whatever it may be, is nothing to me; the movement is everything." "No," answered Rosa, "on the contrary, without relating the movement to the final goal, the movement as an end in itself is nothing to me, the final goal is everything."

The movement was nothing; the men in the movement were never more than foes or allies. None of them possessed the ego and temper of Russian manliness that she associated with Jogiches. He was a man of action and passion, who knew how to do and how to suffer, who could fight with tenacity and pride. Next to him the German socialist luminaries were a clique of gossips. She once wrote that she preferred Graf Westarp, a German conservative leader, to all the German socialists "because," as she put it, "he is a *man*."

The only genuine friendships Rosa formed in Germany were with women, such as Clara Zetkin, the leader of the socialist women's movement. Clara Zetkin had little talent for theory, but she instinctively took a Left stand on all issues, with the result that she and Rosa could take politics for granted. They could also agree on the question of women. "I am of the opinion," wrote Clara, "that just as we are physically, so we are also emotionally and intellectually different. . . . But different does not mean lesser and . . . we feel just this being different as an advantage in regard to the completion of man and the enrichment of society." Rosa would share the analysis, and agree in shouting *vive la petite différence*.

Rosa constantly voiced that little difference with the self-consciousness of a woman who is still unsure about the complex matter of male and female roles. When she carelessly forgot to mention something in a letter to Luise Kautsky, her next letter began, "This genuine representative of the fair sex of course does not remember until she climbs the stairs as she returns home, that she has forgotten the main point. . . ." Rosa's letters are filled with these half-snide, half-ironic comments, on the fine line between embarrassment and militant consciousness.

But to Rosa the struggle for the rights of women could not be separated from the general struggle for a revolutionary solution. "Both phenomena," she explained in a speech, "—the instrument of heaven as the leading political power, and woman, demure by the fireside, unconcerned with the storms of political life, with politics and class struggle—both phenomena have their roots in the rotten circumstances of the past, in the times of serfdom in the country and guilds in the towns." The enslavement of women was simply one of "the most important tools of the ruling class." Female subjugation could be abolished only when capitalism was abolished.

To work directly for the women's movement would be to admit a certain inferiority; it would be to settle for petty politics instead of the great struggle. So, despite the harsh reception she felt she had received because she was a woman (on speaking tours, the men sent to pick her up at the train would often blanch to find that their speaker was a diminutive woman), Rosa insisted on concentrating her activity in the theoretical and tactical struggles of the SPD. She spoke about women's causes on one or two occasions, but she played no significant role in the women's movement.

Another friend was Luise Kautsky, the second wife of Karl Kautsky. Because Rosa and Kautsky both attacked revisionism—though for different reasons—they were colleagues. The friendship with Luise was to survive even after she had broken with Kautsky over an unbridgeable theoretical disagreement. Like Clara Zetkin, Luise was a source of comfort to the intellectual and emotional injuries Rosa suffered. "When I am with you again," she wrote after one long separation, "you will, as usual, take me on your lap in your large, deep chair. I shall bury my head in your shoulder, and Hans will play us the Moonlight Sonata or the second movement from the Pathetique. Then everything will be all right."

Besides Clara Zetkin and Luise Kautsky, Rosa had few friends in Germany. She had acquaintanceships, most based on political alliances, but as an individual she was so compulsively private that friendships were difficult. When comrades called on her, the visits were invariably formal. Everyone sat on the edge of the chairs, nibbling cake and talking in polite clichés about the party or its personalities.

Only with Jogiches, whom she loved, would Rosa be open and honest. Love, for Rosa, was a kind of brutal frankness—the corollary of her privacy with all whom she did not love. To Jogiches, she poured out everything. Sometimes she was romantic and poetic; at other times she described the tortured dreams of frustration.

> I am living here like somebody without air; if you were here, if we were living together, my life would be normal and I would like Berlin and I would find pleasure in walking in the Tiergarten. Now it is dark; not a single pleasant impression. It makes no difference to me whether it rains or whether the sun shines. When I walk about I do not pay the slightest attention to shop windows or people. At home I only think of what I have to write and I go to bed with just the same indifference with which I got up. To cut the story short, all this has one basic cause—you are not here.

Rosa and Jogiches argued at times. He thought her open engagement with SPD policy was wasted effort, advising instead that she concentrate her energies in personal, behind-the-scenes manipulation. Not understanding her insistence on public positions, he called her an idealist. "You are an ass," she answered. ". . . To you everything depends on 'pushing'; this person has to be pushed, that one has to be pushed, a third one has to be made a bit more attractive, etc. I held the same view till my last visit to Kautsky and Bebel. Now I see that it is all rubbish. Nothing can be done artificially. One has to concentrate on one's work, that is the secret and nothing can be done by puppetry behind the scenes."

Even as they argued, Rosa counted the days until Jogiches could perhaps come to Germany, and they could live out her dream of "our own little room, our own furniture, a library of our own, quiet regular work, walks together, an opera from time to time, a small—very small—circle of intimate friends. . . . And perhaps even a little, a very little baby?"

Although she had craved the approval of the world of socialism, enough so to "marry" Gustav Lübeck and to put up with the inhospitality of Berlin, in a way Rosa had done all for the man she loved. "My dear," she wrote in one letter,

> how you delighted me with your letter. I have read it six times from beginning to end. So you are really pleased with me. You write that perhaps I only know inside me that somewhere there is a man that belongs to me! Don't you know that everything I do is always done with you in mind; when I write an article my first thought is—this will cause you pleasure—and when I have days when I doubt my own strength and cannot work, my only fear is what effect this will have on you, that it might disappoint you. When I have proof of success, like a letter from Kautsky, this is

99

simply my homage to you. I give you my word, as I loved my mother, that I am personally quite indifferent to what Kautsky writes. I was only pleased with it because I wrote it with your eyes and felt how much pleasure it would give you.

Jogiches occasionally visited Rosa in Germany, but he was always uncomfortable there. Berlin was *her* city, the triumph there was *hers*. Jogiches, even when he came for a year in 1900, was an outsider, torn away from the plotting he knew well. The SDKP, expanded by an alliance with groups in Lithuania to a new name, The Social Democracy of the Kingdom of Poland and Lithuania, or SDKPiL, was still a moribund institution. The leadership had been forced into exile, and Jogiches was as restless as a general without troops—especially when he contrasted his own bitter position with Rosa's successes. He spent some time in Algeria, where a brother was dying of tuberculosis in a sanitorium, then vacillated between cities where his revolutionary roots had never quite taken hold.

When Jogiches was in Berlin, Rosa withdrew from any regular contacts with party people. She gradually realized that personal participation in the party's cliquish politics would never be productive for her, that she could never adjust to what she felt was false comaraderie. And dimly, she began to perceive what her own contribution would be:

Something in me stirs and wants to come to the surface—naturally something intellectual, something to write. Don't worry, it is not poems or novels again. No, my dear, something in the brain. The fact is that I have not used a tenth, a hundredth part of my real strength. I am already very fed up with what I am writing. I already feel that I have risen above it. I feel in a word the need, as Heine would say, "to say something great." It is the form of writing that displeases me, I feel that within me there is maturing a completely new and original form which dispenses with the usual formulas and patterns and breaks them down, and which will convince people—naturally through force of mind and conviction, and not just propaganda. I badly need to write in such a way as to act on people like a thunderclap, to grip them by the head—not of course through declamation, but by the breadth of outlook, the power of conviction and the strong impressions that I make on them. But how, what, where? I don't know yet. But I tell you that I feel with utter certainty that something is there, that something will be born.

V

In the midst of the great SPD controversies, Rosa carved out time to keep abreast of socialist activities in Poland, and periodically to participate in the convulsions of the Polish and Russian parties. After 1899, in one of those mysterious, periodic revivals that come upon revolutionary movements, the many groups and factions of socialists in Russia and Poland were reorganizing. Although scattered in exile, the leaders of the SDKPiL followed these new developments closely. They were witnesses to and participants in the founding of the Russian Social Democratic party. They also watched as the newly united party was split by Lenin into the Bolsheviks and Mensheviks.

The leaders of the German movement never realized the extent of Rosa's involvement with the Poles and the Russians. Still, on account of her origins and her linguistic abilities, she was trusted as the Russian expert in the SPD. To the Germans, the squabbles of the Russians were of minimal importance and maximal incomprehensibility. It was thus the perfect chore to assign to the newcomer and outsider. In the course of investigating the issues involved in the break-up of the Russian party, Rosa came upon Lenin's pamphlet *What Is to Be Done?* Her criticism of that essay, though hardly acknowledged at the time, was to be more responsible than anything else for her posthumous fame.

There was something very similar in Lenin and Rosa Luxemburg. Both were individualistic, determined, single-minded; both rose to fame on the strength of their ideas and the forcefulness of their presentations of those ideas. Both were unafraid of a fight and tenacious over points and issues that sometimes seemed silly pedantic principles to others.

Yet there was a real difference. Lenin was an obsessed and forceful conspirator and organizer like Jogiches. The same qualities that drew Rosa to Jogiches may also have drawn her to Lenin. Perhaps because of this respect for him as a man, Rosa felt sharper ideological and temperamental antagonism toward Lenin than toward almost any other thinker in the socialist movement. In her disputes with him, she never hesitated to use arguments that even she would have deemed sophistic in German party politics.

In his organizational ideas, and in the insistent tactics that forced the split in the Russian movement, Lenin followed the program he had drawn up in *What Is to Be Done?* It was a prescient and novel conception for the organization of a revolutionary party. Almost no one in the West realized its significance.

Left to its own devices and development, argued Lenin, the working class was incapable of developing any conception of the "historic mission" assigned to it in Marxist thought. "The *spontaneous* development of the workers' movement leads precisely to its subordination to bourgeois ideology . . . the ideological enslavement of the workers to the bourgeoisie." In other words, the workers care only about their wages and working hours, and will never develop on their own the "socialist consciousness" requisite to their historic mission.

This socialist consciousness, Lenin continues, can be brought to the working class only from a party of guardians, a self-constituted vanguard for the working class. This vanguard will be drawn from all classes, but mainly from declassed revolutionary intellectuals who have made revolution their profession. Only this vanguard can be expected to understand and use "the teachings of socialism [which] have grown out of the philosophical, historical, economic theories which were worked out by the educated representatives of the possessing classes." Even in countries where the working class is backward and weak, according to Lenin, the vanguard could appear and begin to inject the proper consciousness into the working class.

The "party of a new type" that Lenin proposed would also require a new type of organization. The model was to be an army, with unquestioning military discipline, centralized authority, and power residing exclusively in a "general staff" or Central Committee: The workers, schooled by life in the factories and barracks, would take naturally to the new organization, for they have no time for "the toy forms of democracy." They will look forward to having a highly centralized party organization as the "dictator of the program," even as the party moves toward the eventual dictatorship of the proletariat.

It was exactly this program that Lenin followed in his organization of the Bolshevik faction of the Russian socialist movement.

Rosa sided with Lenin in the disputes within the Russian party, agreeing that its mission should be revolution rather than insignificant, incremental reforms. But the important aspect of Lenin's program was the centralized party led by a vanguard of professional revolutionaries, with authoritarian control of the working-class movement. It was precisely this that Rosa Luxemburg attacked. Instead of an all-powerful central committee whose writ ran "from Geneva to Liège and from Tomsk to Irkutsk, the role of the director must go to the collective ego of the working class," she wrote. ". . . The working class demands the right to make its mistakes and learn in the dialectic of history. Let us speak plainly. Historically, the errors committed by a truly revolutionary movement are infinitely more fruitful than the infallibility of the cleverest Central Committee."

In the context of Russia, Rosa's optimistic pleas for broad popular participation were probably misplaced. Without firm direction the working classes in Russia might never have advanced to a level of organization beyond trade union activity. But it was not for the question of Russia that Rosa attacked Lenin. Rather, it was the whole conception of class consciousness in his program that she questioned. Lenin believed that class consciousness required a certain critical mass before it could "take off" on its own; only a rigorously and ruthlessly centralized party could bring the workers to the level of that critical mass. Rosa, much closer to Marx in her views, believed that class consciousness developed in direct proportion to the friction between the working class and the ruling bourgeois society: "The world-historical advance of the proletariat to its victory is a process whose particularity lies in the fact that here, for the first time in history, the masses of the

102

people themselves are expressing their will consciously and in opposition to all ruling classes. . . . Today the mass can only acquire and strengthen this will in the course of the day-to-day struggle against the existing social order—that is, within the limits of capitalist society.''

Rosa was affirming the most marvelous and perhaps the most appealing concept of Marxism—the idea that the revolutionary consciousness of the proletariat, and thus the motive force for social change, develops of its own accord from the inexorable forces of history. The class consciousness of the proletariat, which would lead them to play their role in the great drama of class struggle, was a direct consequence of their appreciation of the contradictions in the social order. They needed no leaders to form that consciousness, no generals to lead them as a revolutionary army. All that leaders could do, in fact, was help history along, by directing the fantastic energy that would emerge spontaneously from the very forces of dialectic contradiction between the bourgeoisie and the class they had unwittingly and inevitably created as their own gravediggers.

Later, as Rosa began to develop her ideas, this idea would be the kernel of her great contributions to socialist thought. For the present, it was buried, inchoate, in a review with the scarcely exciting title of ''Organizational Questions of Russian Social Democracy.'' The article had almost no impact. Criticism might sting Lenin, but it would not change his policies. And to the rest of the socialist world, the issue seemed to involve little more than the tiresome quibbling of the disorganized and divisive Russian social democrats.

Rosa had become so involved with her role in the movement from 1900 to 1905 that much of the levity and frivolity of her youth had given way to an earnest concentration on party affairs. When she first arrived in Germany she had treated the German leaders as she had treated her professors at Zurich: they were the victims of harmless practical jokes and puns. She would leave scurrilously funny notes in the shoes that August Bebel and other party leaders placed outside hotel doors at night.

Now all was serious business. In her seriousness, Rosa also straightened out her personal affairs. In 1903 she obtained a divorce from Gustav Lübeck, since as a permanent resident she could live in Germany. There had been no feeling in the marriage; there was no bitterness in the divorce. ''Typical Lübeck,'' she wrote, ''. . . naturally he will not have to pay a penny.''

In July 1904 Rosa was sentenced to three month's imprisonment. The authorities had taken offense to a remark in one of her speeches that ''a man who talks about the security and good living of the German workers has no idea of the real facts.'' The man she referred to was the Emperor, Wilhelm

II, who prided himself in his inspired capacity to understand the workers better than any social democrat. Rosa was convicted of lese majesty, and began serving her sentence in August, just after the Amsterdam congress of the International.

Rosa enjoyed the stay in prison. "Rest quite easy about me," she wrote. "Everything is all right—air, sun, books, and good fellowship on the part of fellow human beings." In fact, she was angry when a general amnesty in October, on the occasion of the coronation of King Friedrich August of Saxony, limited her stay in prison to only six weeks. It was not the loss of prison comforts that annoyed her, but a principle: She did not want to accept any form of royal grace or favor.

While Rosa was in prison, the prologue to a revolution was playing out in the East. For a year, Russia and Japan had been on the verge of war because of Russian expansion in the Far East. When hostilities finally broke out in 1904, the Russians awaited a quick and easy victory. A string of unexpected disastrous defeats in the fall of 1904 all but discredited the government and fed popular insistence on governmental reforms that had been seething since before the turn of the century. The clamor for reforms culminated in the strange demonstration of January 22, 1905, which came to be known as Bloody Sunday. Led by Father Gapon, an inspired Tolstoyan priest, a crowd estimated at over two hundred thousand converged in procession on the Winter Palace in St. Petersburg. In one day, indeed a few brief hours, that crowd spanned the chasm from the Middle Ages to the twentieth century. They had come in a time-honored fashion to lay their troubles at the feet of the Dear Father Czar. Many carried icons as they marched. Singing "God save the Czar," they presented their pleas on a great scroll, as peasants had done for hundreds of years:

> Do not refuse assistance to Thy people. Give their destiny into their own hands. Cast away from them the intolerable oppression of the officials. Destroy the wall between Thyself and Thy people, and let them rule the country together with Thyself. . . .

Yet the crowd's demands were the demands of a modern industrial society: a representative assembly, an eight-hour working day, a minimum wage.

The Czar was not there. He had fled in haste, leaving behind officials and troops, who surrounded the crowd and opened fire at close range. When the firing stopped, the snow was crimson. Hundreds were killed, thousands wounded. The greatest casualty was the Old Russia of the Dear Father Czar, for in the revolution that followed the masses of Russia would turn not to the protection of a benevolent autocrat, but to the doctrines and teachings of republican socialist intellectuals.

The revolution took the West by surprise. As the waves of strikes crescendoed for months and months after Bloody Sunday, the few observers who attached any importance to Russian affairs had to modify or at least reconsider their theories to account for the strange and unscheduled outbreak in the backward reaches of Europe. Nothing Marx had written could account for this revolution, no interpretation of the dialectic could explain this spontaneous uprising against autocracy by a mass of peasants and workers.

Later, with hindsight, Rosa would connect the events of 1905 with the waves of strikes that had swept Russia in the later years of the nineteenth century. But her immediate task was to interpret the events in Russia in the light of socialist theory, to explain correctly whatever significance that uprising might have for the German and the international socialist movement. An immediate enthusiasm for the Russians sprang up in Germany, amidst a general climate of support for workers anywhere who had risen against oppression. But only a few intellectuals in the party saw the revolution in Russia as holding more than fraternal interest for Germans and for the SPD.

The most important lesson for Rosa was the significance of the strikes. The events in Russia demonstrated how effective a mass strike could be. Germany too had seen a wave of strikes, and, by analogy, Rosa argued that the mass strike was a key revolutionary tactic that could and should be used in Germany. The idea was elegant in its simplicity. If thousands of unorganized workers and peasants could disrupt and all but topple the Czarist autocracy by a single massive strike, how easy it ought to be for the organized workers of Germany, led by the trade unions and the SPD, to coerce the government by similar methods. Moreover, the very experience of the strike, even if unsuccessful, provided that friction with the ruling society that would develop the all-important revolutionary consciousness of the working classes.

The mass strike had been discussed in Germany, and had been opposed by the trade unions as a potential threat to their organizations. The time was not ripe for such experimentation, they said. Their usual response was a litany they chanted during debates: "General strike is general nonsense." Rosa, as the chief advocate of the general strike, became the personal butt of many of their arguments. The trade unionists, smarting from the beating she had dealt them in the revisionist debates, were always anxious to send home the Polish woman:

> In Russia the struggle for liberty has been raging almost a year. We have always wondered why our experts on the "general strike theory" don't take themselves off speedily to Russia, to get practical experience, to join in the battle. In Russia the workers are paying with their lives; why don't all those theoreticians who anyhow come from Poland and Russia and now sit in Germany, France, and Switzerland scribbling "revolutionary" articles, get themselves on to the battlefield? High time for all those with such an excess of revolutionary zeal to take a practical part in the Russian battle for freedom, instead of carrying on mass-strike discussions from summer holiday resorts. Trying is better than lying, so off with you to the Russian front, you class-war theoreticians.

Other sarcastic gibes reviled her as an imitation Joan of Arc. The liberal press, delighted by the splits among the socialists, started what was to become rather regular coverage of "Red Rosa."

Very few intellectuals in the party sided with her. Yet in the disputes with the trade unions she began to see that the real issue before the SPD was not the theoretical issue of revisionism, but the question of action versus inaction. The unions were on the side of inaction, of waiting passively for power to fall into their hands. Rosa's pleas became more desperate:

> Are we really living in the year of the glorious Russian revolution, or are we in fact ten years previous to it? (*Shouts:* Quite right!) Day by day we are reading news of revolution in the papers, we are reading the despatches, but it seems that some of us don't have eyes to see or ears to hear.

"What do you know about the mass strike?" she shouted at Bernstein, who interrupted one of her speeches. She answered for him, "Nothing." Those who took issue with the mass strike she saw as cowards, hiding behind a myth of preserving their organization.

> Surely we can see in history that all revolutions have been paid for with the blood of the people. The only difference is that up till now this blood has been spilled for and on behalf of the ruling classes, and now when we are within sight of the possibility that they might shed their blood for their own class interests, at once there appear cautious so-called Social Democrats who say no, that blood is too precious. . . . When will you finally learn from the Russian Revolution? There the masses were driven into the revolution; not a trace of union organization, and step by step they built and strengthened their organizations in the course of the struggle.

She finished with a flourish:

> . . . We have to say to ourselves that the last words of the *Communist Manifesto* are not a series of pretty phrases for use only in public meetings, but that we are in deadly earnest when we call to the masses: "The workers have nothing to lose but their chains but have the whole world to gain."

The reaction to Rosa's fiery speech was sarcasm. Bebel said, "I have attended every congress except during those years when I was the guest of the government, but a debate with so much talk of blood and revolution I have never listened to." That line got a good laugh and he went on. "Listening to all this I cannot help glancing occasionally at my boots to see if these weren't in fact already wading in blood."

The trade unionists used irony as their weapon: "Look, Comrade Luxemburg, I am a mason by trade. I didn't go to high school and cannot cope with these razor-sharp ideas. We all know that our knowledge doesn't reach up to the rarefied level of Comrade Luxemburg. . . . We all know that our knowledge doesn't match up to that of people who in their own youth had a good education and were never hungry.'' Already the socialist movement had a touch of that proletarian one-upmanship which has marked politics in the Soviet Union.

Sarcasm was a poor answer to the gauntlet Rosa had thrown down, but when no one would listen she had no choice but to retort in kind. After one of Bebel's speeches, she answered angrily, ''I wanted to say a few words with regard to his speech, but I am not certain that I have understood it correctly, because I sat on the left, and today he spoke strictly towards the right.'' The crack brought great amusement to the meeting, but did not alter Rosa's situation of increasing alienation and isolation.

The debates over the mass strike took place in November and December 1905, the very months of the preparations of the Moscow rising, the general strike in St. Petersburg, and the parallel events in Warsaw. Various right-wing leaders in the Reichstag began to call for the expulsion of the sympathizer with revolution, that homeless purveyor of hatred, Rosa Luxemburg. Other Russians in exile had already beat a hasty return to various Russian cities, where they became active in the formation of the soviets or in expounding theory and tactics. Jogiches was in Warsaw, taking command in the natural way that he had longed for since the beginning of his exile. When Rosa heard how many of the exiles had gone to Russia she wrote to Jogiches: ''[The news] agitates me; my heart is gripped by a sense of isolation and I long to get away from the misery and purgatory of *Vorwärts* and to escape somewhere, anywhere. How I envy them.''

Once more, Rosa was seized by that recurrent conviction: Real life was somewhere else. She wanted to go to Poland and the revolution.

Friends, especially the Kautskys, tried to dissuade her. Their warnings—that as a woman and an intellectual she belonged in the safety of Germany—only convinced her that she would have to go. She took a week to arrange formalities and to get a signal to Jogiches. December 28, 1905, she set off by train for Warsaw, borrowing the papers and thus the identity of a woman named Anna Matschke. After some transfers and a close call, she made her entrance into Russian Poland on a troop train, the only woman and the only civilian. Thinking perhaps of the Trojan Horse, she called the journey ''a joke of history.''

VI

Like the rest of her generation in the socialist movement, Rosa had learned about revolution from books. The last rising in Europe that had earned the title of revolution was the Commune in Paris in 1871, and even for the old-timers in the socialist movement that was a distant memory. For the most part, the reality of revolution to these socialists was what they had read in various histories of the French Revolution, in Marx and Engels' classic accounts of 1848, and in Lissagaray's history of the Commune. Marx and Engels—especially *Class Struggles in France,* the *Eighteenth Brumaire of Louis Bonaparte,* and *Germany: Revolution and Counter-Revolution*—were read almost as chapbooks; Rosa and others could and did quote whole sections from memory.

Yet, as brilliant and memorable as Marx and Engels or other historians of revolution are, as much as they might succeed in conveying the immediacy of a revolutionary situation, there is something very deceptive in any history of a revolution. Even a history written by an on-the-spot observer, like Lissagaray's history of the Commune or Engels' history of the German revolution of 1848, conveys a false sense of time. In a narrative, events are telescoped such that they seem to cascade one upon another. The historian groups, edits, and selects to give his story force and sweep. In the process he gives to the revolution a sense of inevitable flow that the participants rarely feel. As readers, we forget that revolutions do not consume twenty-four hours of every day—that people still eat, sleep, read, talk, visit. We also overlook the horrible hiatuses, those calms that sometimes forebode a terrible storm and at other times seem an anticlimactic ending. No historian can capture the dread and frustration that the periods of waiting convey. To the historian and his reader, the revolution is an orderly progression of events; to the participant it is filled with apprehension about the unknown—an alternation of incredible excitement with periods when nothing seems to happen and the movement of people and events seems permanently stalled.

Rosa arrived in a Warsaw that was under one of those terrible palls of anxiety. "The city is practically dead," she wrote in her first letter. "General strikes, soldiers wherever you go, but the work is going well, and I begin today." The work was writing, translating the broad theoretical concepts of her thinking into strategies and tactics for the leadership and for the movement itself. Rosa wrote for small newspapers and journals that had sprung up in the course of the revolution; they were funded by the revolutionary parties, and her audience was, on the whole, the party's young intellectuals. They expected and she gave a dialectical analysis of the very process of revolution, written even as the events unfolded. Never before and perhaps never again would Rosa be so consumed by any activity: The immediate juxtaposition of perception, analysis and exposition with the more mundane but necessary editing, printing, and distribution. Her journalism appeared almost daily, and she was soon swept into half-believing the flow and continuity that her reporting lent to events. For an intellectual, this was the supreme experience of revolution, an all-stops-pulled crescendo of excitement, enthusiasm, and the inevitable optimism.

The revolution of 1905 was a catalyst to Rosa's thinking. Just as the poverty of those first years in London infused Marx's writing with a sense of reality and human drama that had been wanting in his earlier philosophical works, so, too, the revolution brought Rosa's theoretical arguments down to the level of action. The question was no longer, What is the correct policy for the party to follow in preparing for the inevitable but eternally distant revolution? but, What now? When she perceived a failure of tactics, it had to be rationalized, the theory had to be refined, and the action brought into line with a correct theory. In a word, she was face to face with the line engraved on Marx's tomb: "Other philosophers have interpreted the world; our task is to change it."

Her program for the revolution was textbook Marx, rewritten in the context of conditions in Poland and Russia. Because it was a program for revolution, it could not be tempered by the cool skepticism of her letters to comrades. The failure of the general strike that she noted in a letter to Germany had to be explained, placed within an evolving dynamic of the revolution. "The reason for all this," she wrote, "is simply that a *mere general strike by itself* has ceased to play the role it once did. Now nothing but a general uprising on the streets can bring about a decision, though for this the right moment must be prepared very carefully."

The central questions for her program, and, by extension, for her whole idea of revolution were: How could a general rising be brought about? When was the right moment? How would the rising be signaled and led? In answering those questions she translated the arguments she had made in her struggle against revisionism and against Lenin's centralism into a theory of revolution, expanding from piecemeal arguments into a coherent and complete script.

As in her critique of *What Is to Be Done?*, Rosa agreed with the Bolsheviks up to a point: In the backward Czarist autocracy an autonomous advance-guard action by the proletariat would first have to secure what was essentially a bourgeois revolution; the proletarians would then maintain their supremacy lest a cowardly and fearful bourgeoisie—the actual beneficiaries of the revolution—allow things to slip back to autocracy. Throughout, the proletariat would act as the mover of history, but would not claim exclusive benefits of the revolution; it would make its revolution for all of society.

Here Rosa parted ways with the Bolsheviks. In her analysis there was no mention of a dictatorship of the proletariat, either in words or by implication. Rather, the achievements of the working class would provide the class pride that could develop into class consciousness. In the next stage of revolution, the proletariat and the bourgeoisie would confront one another—as in Germany—and in that confrontation the proletariat would gain the political maturity and consciousness that would enable them ultimately to seize power in their own behalf.

Rosa saw the soviets, which had spontaneously arisen in several Russian cities, as means in the struggle, but of no institutional significance. Similarly, she did not follow or support Trotsky's attempts to rectify the obvious problems of following a lock-step dialectic, with its necessity for a lengthy capitalist "pause" on the road to socialism.

The slow and precise articulation of Rosa's revolutionary ideas, in pamphlets and articles, took place amid the internecine fighting of the various revolutionary parties. The SDKPiL still considered its old enemy the PPS as much an opponent as the forces of the Czar or the bourgeoisie. The climate of strikes and demonstrations of 1905 brought other opposition parties out into the fracas as well. Thus the development of a program had to take place within the context of political infighting. This was the kind of maneuvering at which Jogiches excelled. Once again, the two worked together—Rosa writing and Jogiches maneuvering—and their partnership was an important component of Rosa's exaltation and revolutionary ecstasy.

In Germany, when disillusioned or depressed, Rosa would share her skepticism with Jogiches in long, brutally frank letters. With both of them working for the revolution in Warsaw, she could not vent her cynicism on him, so she turned instead to the Kautskys, in Berlin. Even as she wrote her dialectical analyses in Poland, long letters to the Kautskys proffered a sober estimate of the revolution: "To characterize the situation in two words (but this is only for your ears), the general strike has just about *failed*. . . . People everywhere are hesitant and waiting." The cool objectivity of these letters stood in marked contrast to the passionate enthusiasm of her Polish and Russian articles, in which she would exhort, urge, cajole—anything to keep up the revolution's motion.

The skepticism proved well-founded. By the first three months of 1906, the revolutionaries had fallen behind the popular movement. The strikes and the militant spirit of 1905 were waning. Manifestos and exhortations could not bring out workers who were already feeling the pressures of a Czarist counteroffensive. In March 1906, the police were sweeping the major cities with waves of arrests and summary executions that no SDKPiL resolutions on the imminence of a resumption of the revolution could halt. The Liberals, with their promises of compromise, concession, and consolidation of benefits gained, began to attract massive worker support. The revolution had indeed failed.

Admitting a setback, if not total defeat, in February 1906 Rosa began to make plans for a return to Germany. She was too late. On March 4 a police raid caught the German journalist named Anna Matschke in bed. A raid on Rosa's sisters' home uncovered photographs that were sufficient to break the alias: Anna Matschke was the notorious Rosa Luxemburg. She was thrown into a cell designed in normal times for one:

> . . . It now contains fourteen guests, fortunately all of them political cases [she wrote in a letter smuggled out]. . . . We are all sleeping like kings on

110

boards on top of each other, next to each other, packed like herrings, but we manage nicely—except for the extra music provided; for instance yesterday we got a new colleague, a mad Jewess, who kept us breathless for 24 hours with her lamentations . . . and who made a number of politicals break out into hysterical sobs. Today we finally got rid of her and there are only three quiet *meshuggene* left. . . . My own spirits are as always excellent.

When there was a principle to be served and quiet to think and write, Rosa did not mind a brief stay in prison. But little principle was served in a Czarist prison, and fourteen to a cell did not allow much pondering of the subtleties of the dialectic. Even before she was transferred from the jail cell in the town hall to another prison and finally to the notorious Pavilion X of the Warsaw Citadel—the bastion where particularly dangerous public enemies were incarcerated—she initiated efforts to get herself released. The charges against her were very serious and no one in the SDKPiL could risk helping her.

Her family visited her and immediately set to work on an appeal for clemency to Count Witte, the Russian premier. Rosa, out of principle, refused to authorize a petition to a state which she did not recognize as legitimate. The family then attempted other means, including bail money, which the Czarist government was willing to collect, with little hope of her returning, as a kind of bribe and fine combined. Rosa's brother made a trip to Germany to raise the sum required (3,000 rubles), almost certainly from the SPD executive. No one in the family sympathized with Rosa's politics, but nothing had diminished their extraordinary closeness.

To supplement the bribe, the SDKPiL leadership issued an unofficial threat of reprisal, suggesting that if anything happened to Rosa, unnamed prominent officials would pay.

Prison doctors justified the release of the prisoner on the grounds of ill health. Indeed, the months of frantic activity had taken their toll: Rosa's hair had begun to turn gray, and a medical commission reported that she was suffering from "anemia, hysterical and neurasthenic symptoms, catarrh of the stomach and dilation of the liver." In July 1906, after four months in prison, she was released.

She went directly to Finland, where the Russians and Poles were holding a socialist gathering of the clans. From Kuokkala, the revolutionaries could stealthily visit St. Petersburg during the day, where, according to their various diagnoses, they either monitored a terminal patient or conducted an autopsy on the corpse of the revolution. At night they would return to the sleepy Finnish city for long talk sessions in the proverbial smoke-filled rooms.

Rosa visited with all of the Russian and Polish revolutionaries, but spent most of her time with Lenin. They had met only once before. Now, after polemics and distant dislike, they got to know and soon admired one another. Mutual intellectual respect, together with the attraction Rosa felt for assertive (she would say *masculine*) men, created a kind of personal sympathy between them. And despite polemics, they found that their agreements outnumbered their disagreements. Years later, when they got into another ideological dispute, there was sufficient personal respect on Lenin's part to spare Rosa the personal abuse he heaped on most of his political enemies.

Much of Rosa's time in Finland was spent writing a pamphlet on the Russian revolution and the mass strike for a German audience. Once again she carefully separated the two halves of her life: The Russians did not know that she was again active in German affairs, and the Germans had no idea of her continued involvement with the Russians. The compartmentalization was important for party affairs, since the Russians and the Germans distrusted one another. It was also important for Rosa, who insisted in her politics as in her personal life that every matter be carefully and precisely pigeonholed.

Among the Russians, the postmortems and recriminations concerning the revolution would go on for years. But for Rosa the revolution was over and it was time to analyze the lessons it taught. The revolution was probably the most important catalyst in Rosa's thinking. Her experiences those few months in Warsaw converted the vague dissatisfactions she had felt with the official policies of German social democracy into a doctrine of revolution. Russia had shown that it had what Germany lacked—the spontaneity and energy to move from preparation to action. At the same time, the failure of the revolution had proved that Russian "will" was no substitute for a class-conscious and militant proletariat, such as only Germany could boast. Russia had tried, but in Marxist terms only Germany was ready for a revolution.

The obvious conclusion for Rosa was that someone would have to create or at least identify the moment when the great German proletariat should move from the years of preparation and waiting to the actuality of revolution. As she summed it up, in what might be the real lesson she learned from the Russian experience: "The revolution is magnificient; everything else is rubbish."

VII

The lessons of the revolution were not so obvious to most of the German socialists. "The brief May flowering of the new revolutionary spirit is happily finished," wrote one journal, "and the party will again be devoting itself with all its strength to the positive exploitation and expansion of its parliamentary power." When Rosa spoke about the revolution and her old passion, the mass strike, her speeches were greeted with silence. She complained that no one seemed willing to learn from the experience of the Russians. "Quite right, we don't," were the shouts at one party meeting.

The mass strike issue had been settled. In a secret agreement with the trade unions, the party executive had offered to kill any further discussion of the mass strike in return for renewed and strengthened support of the SPD by the vast trade union membership in the upcoming Reichstag elections. Rosa sniffed out the arrangement: "I fear that the relationship of the trade unions to Social Democracy is developing like that of a peasant marriage contract, in which the woman says to the man: 'When we agree, your wishes will prevail, when we disagree, then my wishes will be carried out.' . . ."

Rather than being inspired or educated by the Russian revolution, the German party was convulsed with fear that revolutionary activity would disintegrate or demolish their carefully constructed bureaucracy. It was the classic and ultimately fatal paradox of the SPD: The goal of strengthening and preserving the organization meant that the party had to abstain from any participation in the one activity—revolution!—for which the whole movement had been created. To the outsider the paradox was enigmatic; to the insider, such as Rosa, determined the revolution should not be bypassed, it was the source of total frustration.

"Since my return from Russia," Rosa wrote to Clara Zetkin in March 1907,

I feel rather isolated . . . I feel the pettiness and the hesitancy of our party regime more clearly and more painfully than ever before . . . I see with depressing clarity that neither things nor people can be changed—until the whole situation has changed, and even then we shall just have to reckon with inevitable resistance if we want to lead the masses on. I have come to that conclusion after mature reflection. The plain truth is that August [Bebel], and still more so the others, have completely pledged themselves to parliament and parliamentarianism, and whenever anything happens which transcends the limits of parliamentary action they are hopeless—no, worse than hopeless, because they then do their utmost to force the movement back into parliamentary channels, and they will furiously defame as "an enemy of the people" anyone who dares to venture beyond their own limits . . . That's how I see matters, but the chief thing is to keep your chin up and not get too excited about it. Our job will take years.

Aware that she might have some sway with the party rank and file, Rosa made a number of public speeches. Her charismatic successes alienated her even further from the party executive, and her general hauteur did not help the situation. When Bebel offered her a moderate sum of money to set her on her feet again after her return from Poland, she refused it. "I will not be kept by the executive," she is alleged to have said. These barbs were not

113

appreciated, and Bebel never forgave her. In later years he would try to cover up their differences with his considerable gift of charm. But Rosa was not easily wooed. "Sugar sweet," she called it.

She resented efforts by Bebel or anyone else to treat her with special consideration, much preferring the rough-and-tumble of Lenin or the equality of the SDKPiL. On one occasion she and Clara Zetkin were on a morning walk and showed up late for a luncheon date with Bebel. He remarked that he had worried that they were lost. With a characteristic half-grin Rosa answered, "Yes, you can write our epitaph: 'Here lie the last two men of German Social Democracy.' " Remarks like that did not settle well with the dignified patriarchs of the SPD.

In time, Rosa even broke with Kautsky. Since the revisionism debates, he had been her closest German colleague. They worked together regularly on *Neue Zeit,* and she spent so many of her Sunday afternoons with the Kautskys that she jokingly called herself "The Sunday Supplement of *Neue Zeit.*" But by 1907 things had changed. When Rosa and Karl took a working holiday to Geneva, where they expected to work on the editorial policy for *Neue Zeit,* Rosa found Kautsky "heavy, dull, unimaginative, ponderous" and his ideas "cold, pedantic, doctrinaire." The lunch sessions at the Kautskys became a bore, and his writings worse. "Soon I shall be quite unable to read anything written by Karl Kautsky," she wrote in 1908. ". . . It is like a disgusting series of spider's webs . . . which can only be washed away by the mental bath of reading Marx himself. . . ." For Rosa, it was a final break with the SPD leadership. Before the Russian revolution she had been a dynamic if disloyal opposition; she now had little patience for men who preferred talk to revolution.

Yet there was more behind her complete break with everyone she had known and worked with in Germany. In the past she had also had deep political differences with the other Germans. Usually, her enthusiasm had been directly proportional to the adversity. This time, her isolation, and the cutting remarks she used to preserve that isolation, were of a different order. The answer is not in politics, but in that private world of feelings and love to which Rosa admitted almost no one.

Jogiches was arrested shortly after Rosa. He was still in jail when she left Poland for Finland, and for many months she was concerned about his health and his trial. The couple were scheduled to be tried together, but Rosa, of course, never returned. On the stand, Jogiches refused to plead or even speak in his own defense (mainly because he resented the condescending use of the familiar form of address by the court). He was convicted of high treason for his revolutionary activities, and of military desertion. The sentence was eight years of forced labor and lifelong residence in Siberia, a harsh sentence even for treason.

Like Trotsky, Parvus, and so many other Russian revolutionaries before him, Jogiches escaped just before he was sent off to Siberia, probably by bribing a policeman. He hid for a while in Warsaw, and then in Cracow, before traveling through Germany to a Russian party Congress in London in May 1907. While in hiding—a period of about six or eight weeks—he was aided and cared for by a woman comrade from the Polish party. Her name was Izolska, but little was known about their relationship, as Jogiches' conspiratorial skills were still quite effective.

Somehow, though, Rosa Luxemburg found out. Her reaction was to break off all relations with Jogiches immediately. As a man, he was dead. He had been the one person to whom Rosa had revealed herself. "I want you to see me as clearly as I can see you," she had written in one letter. What he had betrayed was not so much her fidelity as her vulnerability. With her love as with her ideology, Rosa had no room for pluralism or ambiguity.

Jogiches reacted—as Rosa interpreted it to other friends, much later—with jealousy and possessiveness. Rosa was his, had always been his, and, as he repeated to her again and again, she would never be free of him. Although the break between them was complete in personal terms, and they saw one another afterward only as party comrades, Jogiches was right: Rosa would never be free of him. Even as he lost his grip over her personal life, he tightened the party discipline of the SDKPiL, substituting what they had created together for the relationship that was no more.

They did not meet until the Russian party congress in London. They were invited to dinner at Rosa's brother's home in England, and as they walked in together Jogiches whispered, "As soon as this dinner is over I shall kill you." As Rosa remembered it, ". . . this terrible moment was instantly sponged away with laughter and handshakes all around, though not for me."

Rosa had learned of Jogiches' affair while sitting in her apartment in Berlin, probably from one of his own letters (he too, it seems, had her compulsion for absolute clarity). At the time, a young friend, Konstantin Zetkin, the twenty-two-year-old son of Clara Zetkin, was with her. Her friendship with Konstantin was probably encouraged by Clara—in the time-honored continental fashion of the conscientious mother hoping a close friend will introduce her son to the mysteries of life and love. By one of those coincidences of romantic novels, undoubtedly reinforced by her reading of Stendhal and George Sand, when Rosa finished reading the news from Jogiches she fell head over heels in love with Konstantin. Even Rosa described the relationship as straight out of *The Red and the Black*.

It was more than coincidence. Rosa was so private in her life that she desperately needed at all times one person with whom she could be open. This was what she called "love." And when Jogiches had broken her trust, someone had to fill the vacuum. Later in life it would be others. Now it was Konstantin Zetkin.

Clara Zetkin was Rosa's closest friend in the socialist movement, but the

115

relationship of the lovers proved more than she had expected. She interfered, somehow, and provoked Rosa's private ire: "My friends must keep their accounts clean and in order," Rosa wrote to another friend, "not only in their public but in their most private lives. To thunder magnificently in public about the 'freedom of the individual' and in private to enslave a human being out of mad passion—this I can neither understand nor pardon. . . ."

Clara's opposition was a minor impediment. When Jogiches found out about Konstantin Zetkin, his possessiveness turned to rage. Since he still had a key to her flat from the days when they had lived together in Berlin, he could call on Rosa at any time, a privilege he exercised capriciously. For the next two years, wherever Rosa traveled, Jogiches would follow—hoping, Rosa thought, to surprise her with her lover. In the fall of 1908, Rosa wrote: "The man is emotionally a wreck, he is abnormal and lives all the time with only one fixed idea in his mind—to kill me." Somehow she managed to continue her writing for the Polish party, but she was fearful enough of his threats to buy a revolver for self-protection.

By 1908, the Russian revolutionaries were beyond postmortems. Finland was no longer a safe refuge, and the exiles returned to Paris, London, and Switzerland. The SDKPiL fell apart as quickly as it had come together during the revolution. For several years Leo Jogiches personally held the remnants of the SDKPiL together. Rosa was hardly active in Russian and Polish affairs beyond the articles she wrote for *Przeglad Socjaldemokratyczny* (*Social Democratic Review*), the theoretical review of Polish socialism. Although the journal was ostensibly in Jogiches' hands, Rosa was not only the most important contributor, but through correspondence and unavoidable personal meetings, she acted as his main advisor on editorial policy. He was adept at using the pretexts of policy decisions to call on her unexpectedly. Even in 1909 she had to protest: "I simply cannot support this constant shoulder-rubbing."

The only political event in which Rosa participated directly during these years was the congress of the International at Stuttgart in August 1907. She held mandates from the Polish Social Democrats, which made her part of the Russian group, and enabled her to speak out very openly against the Germans, who not only hosted the congress in great style, as had become a tradition at meetings of the International, but dominated the content of every discussion or debate.

The chief issue was the debates on war, and on just what the socialists should do in case war broke out over one of the innumerable colonial disputes in which the European states so regularly embroiled themselves. The French, anxious to get the general strike incorporated into the policies of the International, suggested that a coordinated general strike was the one weapon that would bring all of the European states to their knees. Bebel, speaking for the Germans, answered that the general strike was nonsense, and that there was in reality little the socialists could do to prevent a war.

Rosa made only one speech in the debate, a sharp attack on the dilatory politics of the Germans. But the final statement on war, a scissors and paste job that incorporated somewhat contradictory passages from the various draft resolutions submitted by the different parties, also included a passage offered by Rosa and Lenin. As the two participants who had witnessed the interrelationship of war and revolution in Russia and Poland in 1905 to 1906, they were less concerned with the fine points of tactics and more interested in just what could be done with a situation created by a war. Their addition concluded the resolution:

> Should war break out in spite of all this, it is their [the socialists'] duty to intercede for its speedy end, and to strive with all their power to make use of the violent economic and political crisis brought about by the war to rouse the people, and thereby to hasten the abolition of capitalist class rule.

It was revolutionary language (the wording is probably Lenin's), but since it committed no one to any specific line of action, the resolution was grandly accepted by all parties—another gesture of that rhetorical unity that fired the International and faith of its members.

VIII

For months, almost years, Rosa floundered on the edges of the SPD, dreaming of going away, but with nowhere to go. "I would move instantly to the south and away from Germany if I had the slightest notion of how to earn a living," she wrote to one friend. She had romanticized Russia and Poland into a revolutionary Mecca, but with a sentence over her head she could not go to Russia or Poland. She also dreamed of the South, that vague, Goethean dream that comes upon Germans—infinitely promising because of its very vagueness and impossibility. This time the wanderlust ended not with a journey outside, but with a new direction within the party.

In 1906 the party had decided to establish a central party school in Berlin. It was to be an elite institution to train teachers and agitators. Like so many party structures, it was an imitation of a bourgeois establishment, in this case the famous German technical schools and universities. The project's organizers included a number of members of the party's left faction, such as Clara Zetkin and Franz Mehring, and the teaching staff included some of the most inflammatory SPD firebrands of the movement. As long as their activities were restricted to teaching instead of "doing," they met with no opposition from the party executive.

117

Rosa Luxemburg initially was not a participant in the venture. Her early reaction was distrust. "What is it? Who is behind it?" she wrote to the Kautskys. Her only contribution during the first session was to suggest to Clara Zetkin that the history of socialism be included in the curriculum. The idea caught on, and was incorporated in a course taught by Franz Mehring, who later published a history of socialism based in part on his lectures.

Rosa joined the school through the efforts of the most unlikely of agents, the Prussian police. Shortly before the second session opened, in October 1907, the police—who viewed the whole operation as a dangerous propaganda and agitation scheme—threatened two lecturers of foreign citizenship, Rudolf Hilferding and Anton Pannekoek, with expulsion from Germany. On short notice Rosa was invited to join the faculty as a substitute lecturer. Kautsky wrote her recommendation: "In Rosa Luxemburg you will be getting one of the best brains in Germany."

Rosa pretended diffidence. "The whole school interests me very little and I am not the type to act as a school ma'am." But the income proved "a magnetic attraction," as she put it, and she soon plunged into courses in political economy and economic history.

Teaching was an awakening. For two hours each morning she had a captive, ready and bright audience, who delighted in her natural talents as a teacher. She could explicate clearly the most complicated philosophical issues of Marxism, and her willingness to conduct individual tutorials after class made her very popular. Unlike the hardened officials of the party, her young students were willing and anxious to hear explanations of the revolution in Russia and the other ideas that stemmed from her broad and incisive interpretations of Marxism. Although they did not necessarily agree with her opinions, the openness of classroom discussions was a pleasant contrast to the implacable, settled character of official party debates. For almost seven years, until the outbreak of World War I, the school constituted Rosa's chief political activity. When critics attacked the school as elitist, she took the brunt of their attacks. When Kurt Eisner wrote that "the school should go to the masses, not an elite creamed off into the school in Berlin," Rosa used her answer as an opportunity to rearticulate her faith in Marx's concept of class consciousness:

> They have not the slightest conception of the fact that the working classes learn "their stuff" from their daily life, in fact absorb it better than Eisner does. What the masses need is general education, theory which gives them the chance of making a system out of the detail acquired from experience and which helps to forge a deadly weapon against our enemies. If nothing else has so far convinced me of the necessity for having a party school, of the need to spread socialist theory in our ranks, the criticism of Eisner has done it.

Karl Marx and Friedrich Engels with
Marx's daughters: Jenny, Tussy and
Laura

Karl Marx, taken in the 1850s, around
the time of Tussy's birth

Helene Demuth, Marx's housekeeper, Tussy's nurse and the mother
of Freddy Demuth, rumored to be
Marx's son

Tussy Marx as a young girl

Lissagaray, a member of the Commune, sometime activist in French
socialism, journalist and historian,
and the first man in Tussy's life

Tussy Marx, shortly before she began
her stage career

The last photograph taken of Karl
Marx before his death in 1883

Paul Lafargue, French socialist leader
and husband of Laura Marx

Rosa Luxemburg

Leo Jogiches, Polish socialist leader and Rosa's lover, taken around the time they met as revolutionaries in Switzerland in the early 1890s

Amsterdam Congress of the Second International in 1904. Rosa Luxemburg is in the center of the back row, with Victor Adler, the Austrian socialist leader, to her left, and Karl Kautsky, the high priest of German socialism, next to him.

Rosa Luxemburg during the World
War

Karl Liebknecht, son of one of the
founders of the German Social Democratic Party, and co-leader, with Rosa
Luxemburg, of the German left during the World War

Angelica Balabanoff, the Pollyanna
of international socialism

Angelica Balabanoff

As do many teachers, Rosa discovered the personal intellectual benefits deriving from her classes. "Only by sharpening the subject matter through teaching was I able to develop my ideas," she wrote. For years she struggled to compile her lectures in a book which would definitively synthesize the basic ideas of Marxist economics. The *Introduction to Political Economy* was only finished in prison during the World War, but in the meantime, a single facet of the problem, the study of imperialism, was expanded into the book for which Rosa Luxemburg is still best-known, *The Accumulation of Capital.*

The Accumulation of Capital is strange among Rosa Luxemburg's writings. Almost alone of her works it is apolitical. Social democracy as such is mentioned nowhere, nor are the political problems of imperialism, despite the subtitle, "A Contribution to the Economic Clarification of Imperialism." Rosa claimed that the book's real origin was her interest in "higher mathematics," that longstanding avocation dating from her university days. She completed the lengthy study—over four hundred fifty pages—in only four months.

What so captured Rosa's mind? When she began the project, she wrote to Konstantin Zetkin: "I want to find the cause of imperialism. I am following up the economic aspects of this concept. . . . It will be a strictly scientific explanation of imperialism and its consequences." In fact, the issue was even more basic. Marxism postulates the eventual collapse of capitalism under the weight of its economic contradictions. Recurrent and unavoidable crises are supposed to occur with ever-increasing frequency and severity until the entire capitalist structure itself implodes. In *Capital,* especially in volumes II and III, which Engels edited and published after the author's death, Marx provided empirical and mathematical "evidence" to prove this assertion. Rosa believed that the "evidence" did not warrant Marx's conclusions, and that some other explanation must be offered for the continued existence and growth of capitalism. The solution she found in the ability of capitalist societies to capture and incorporate precapitalist societies into their economic spheres. The collapse of capitalism, thus, would be postponed until imperialism had brought the entire earth into its web; then, and only then, would the true internal economic contradictions of capitalism lead to its collapse.

Rosa's analysis is incomplete and bewildering. Economic imperialism alone cannot account for capital accumulation, and her efforts to make the theory work led her to neglect both the rise in real wages that accompanies capitalist development and the internal inducement to invest that technical innovations can provide. Yet for all its shortcomings, Rosa's book is brilliant. It is perhaps the only treatise in the vast post-Marx bibliography that deserves comparison with *Capital,* after which Rosa's style is modeled. Like Marx, she alternates incredibly difficult theoretical chapters containing

119

confusing mathematical equations, with poignant descriptions of the torture of Negroes in South Africa or the militarism which necessarily must accompany imperialist ventures. And like Marx, she devotes much of her prose to demolishing the arguments of other economists, especially those who contradict or disprove her own basic tenets. Her stylistic tools are also Marx's tools: Sarcasm, overwhelming documentation, and subtle ridicule.

The reaction to the *Accumulation of Capital* was predictable. Most of the socialist world ignored it, both because it was so abstruse and because the *chutzpah* of "the Polish woman" tackling what Marx had left unfinished was more than they could accept. What probably rankled most of all was the self-consciousness with which Rosa coupled herself with Marx, in her constant references to *Capital* (which she had read more closely than most of the German socialists) and in defining a question that had been unanswered by Marx. The book's few reviewers were more interested in her errors than her logical argument. Lenin read the book in 1913, when they had fallen out again over some other matter. In the margins he noted his responses with terms like "nonsense" and "funny." More importantly, he branded her basic thesis a "fundamental error." Later Bukharin and other critics used that brand to characterize the special communist heresy of "Luxemburgism."

For Rosa, the *Accumulation of Capital* was exciting for the sheer mathematical elegance of its explanation of imperialism. It was, or it seemed, a nearly perfect extrapolation of the Marxist dialectic, and it appealed to her for the same reason that mathematics courses had at the university—there were no loose ends, no unexplained anomalies. Yet the theoretical explanation was only a stage of Rosa's thinking about imperialism. "As always in such cases, the exact theoretical understanding of the problem down to its very roots will give our practical policy in the struggle against imperialism that clearness of vision and that vigor which are essential for a successful proletariat policy." As she taught and wrote about the theory of imperialism, Rosa began to define for herself—and she hoped, for the party—a concept of imperialism as the key to political action for the social democrats.

As early as 1900, Rosa had been critical of the SPD's cowardly attitude toward such outrages as the Boxer expedition with Wilhelm II's exhortation to his troops to behave like the Huns. The whole first decade of the twentieth century was marked by a series of exploits of imperialist brinkmanship, as England, France, and Germany carefully carved up the few remaining potential colonies. Every time, the SPD, rather than opening an offensive against colonialism, would pusillanimously find some excuse why a campaign against imperialism at the time was inopportune. In 1911, when the second Morocco crisis exploded (after Wilhelm II dispatched the gunboat *Panther* to Agadir to "protect German interests"), the party again decided that inaction was the wisest discretion. Rosa lambasted the SPD in a newspaper article:

> That this attitude on the part of the German party could not have had an encouraging and stimulating effect on the socialist protest movements in other countries seems to us to be obvious. This makes it all the more interesting to know the reasons that have led to this attitude of our party. It sounds almost unbelievable, but these reasons are again consideration of the impending Reichstag elections.

The resultant criticism, ridicule, and isolation were nothing new for Rosa Luxemburg, and she continued independently to develop a politics of anti-imperialism which was to form the integrating element of her evolving Marxist ideology. For Rosa, imperialism was the primary characteristic of the era: "Militarism closely connected with colonialism, protectionism, and power politics as a whole . . . a world armament race . . . colonial robbery and the policy of 'spheres of influence' all over the world . . . in home and foreign affairs the very essence of a capitalist policy of national aggression." Rarely did she refer to specific imperialist episodes. What was important was not the phenomenon itself, but its effects, most importantly its effect on the socialist movement.

Indeed, to Rosa, the very strength of the current wave of imperialism was proof that capitalist society was on its last legs. In the *Accumulation of Capital* she had demonstrated, at least to her own satisfaction, that imperialism was the reflex of a capitalist society that could not otherwise survive. "Imperialism is simultaneously a way of prolonging the life of capitalism, and a way of very effectively limiting it." This was another of those marvelous paradoxes that made Marxism so appealing:

> The more violently capitalism liquidates the non-capitalist strata at home and abroad, and depresses the standards of living of all working people, the more the day to day history of international capital accumulation develops into a never-ending chain of political and social catastrophes and convulsions, which, taken together with periodically recurring economic upheavals in the shape of crises, will render the continuation of capital accumulation impossible, and make the rebellion of the international working class against capitalist dominance necessary even before capitalism has reached the natural self-created limits of its economic possibilities.

In elegant, dialectic simplicity she insisted that the strength of imperialism was proof of the strength of the social democratic movement that it would of necessity engender as one of its contradictions. Every imperialist venture would produce a quantum leap in the consciousness of the masses; imperialism, to use Marx's image, was producing its own gravediggers.

Imperialism further provided what she had been seeking in Germany—a sign of readiness for the German revolution. Russia had gone off half-cocked in 1905, lacking the vigilant preparedness of the SPD, which had been ever ready, but patiently waiting for the millennial moment. And while the masses waited, the party leadership had procrastinated and dallied, fearing for its own organization and its chances for success in the upcoming Reichstag elections.

Imperialism was not a tocsin. Although it was important for the Social Democratic party to help indoctrinate and lead the masses—a point Rosa never stopped stressing—there was no way in which it could blow a whistle or fire a cannon to signal the revolution. Revolution was a long, slow process—almost a continual process. This was the great bone of contention between Rosa and the other SPD leaders. They had always viewed revolution as a catalytic moment, a single instant when the temple would come tumbling down. Their visions were of barricades, with the workers on one side and the troops on the other, both locked in a do-or-die battle. Thus, they could comfortably wait, for a moment so great would surely be signaled by a loud and clear bang. Against this chiliasm, Rosa posed the idea that gradual and continual mass action *was* the revolution, and that the revolution itself was the process by which the masses acquire the class consciousness essential to the execution of their task. "Social Democracy," she wrote, "is the most enlightened and class-conscious section of the proletariat. It cannot and must not fold its arms and wait with fatalistic resignation for the arrival of a 'revolutionary situation', for a spontaneous mass action of the people to fall from the clouds." She had seen it happen in Russia, where the unprepared workers and peasants had been revolutionized and socialized by the events of 1905–06. Only by mass action against the imperialistic ventures of the German state, would the German working class translate its discipline and preparedness into a revolutionary class consciousness. Imperceptibly, inexorably, the mass actions would become the revolution.

Thus, with the addition of imperialism, Rosa's ideas on mass action and class consciousness added up to something close to a doctrine. Subsequently, through systematic misinterpretation, communist critics have accused her of advocating "spontaneity," the idea that the masses would conduct a revolution with no leadership at all from the party. Like so many heretical doctrines, while it is an idea that can perhaps be "documented" from her writings, it is not what she believed or advocated.

At the same time, Rosa placed an extraordinary faith in the masses. Although they were never specifically defined in her writings, it is obvious that they were more than mere ciphers and more too than a sum of the proletarians who "had nothing to lose but their chains." In fact, the masses in Rosa's doctrine are inseparable from their revolutionary actions: They are simply the great majority who fashion the revolution by their will and action.

It was this faith in the masses that more than anything else distinguished Rosa Luxemburg from other contemporary Marxist theorists. Most made the obligatory references to the rank and file or the fighting troops, but for Lenin or Kautsky or Bebel, these masses were passive troops, called upon only for their strength, discipline and bravery. To the Bolsheviks, in particular, the masses were an abstraction. They were led, and they followed. There was no admission of a possible contradiction between the consciousness or aims of the masses and the aims of the leadership.

For Rosa, as we have seen, the masses *are* the revolution. The revolution is complete only when the consciousness of the masses has developed to the point at which they have taken charge. Thus, while Rosa, like other Marxist theorists, never presumed to describe the form that government would take after the revolution, in her case the omission was deliberate, an assertion of positive faith in the ability of the masses to define their own theory and practice. When Lenin or Kautsky refrained from descriptions of postrevolutionary forms, the motive was only guarded caution, lest their activities as revolutionary leaders run counter to doctrine.

The evolution of Rosa's views had brought her very far indeed from official SPD doctrine. From her own experiences in Russia, from her reaction to the smug self-assuredness of Bebel, Kautsky, and the other SPD leaders, and from the intellectual challenge of presenting her ideas at the party school—she had conceived a view of socialism, or more particularly, of Marxism, which was the very antithesis of SPD practice. Her ideology was not so much a system as a critique of a system. She believed that Marxism was valid, and that it could be applied to the historical situation in Germany through an informed political action. Her role, as she saw it, was that of the gadfly to the SPD, criticizing the party's excessive preoccupation with itself. She did not propose an alternative, and the idea of creating a new Marxist party was unthinkable. Despite the ridicule with which she was regularly treated at party congresses and in the party press, Rosa as much as anyone believed in the essentiality of party unity: There was but one capitalist enemy, there must be but one organized arm of the socialist masses.

It was this "anti-system" component of Rosa Luxemburg's ideas that brought her into the sharpest conflict with figures like Karl Kautsky. At the very time that she was unsuccessfully clamoring against imperialism and for an active party policy, the sensation in party circles was a new book by Kautsky, *The Road to Power,* in which he contrasted the moral decay and scandals of imperial Germany with the doctrinal purity of the SPD. All that was required of the party, he argued, was that it maintain its readiness and doctrinal coherence. Although the book is thoroughly spiced with the word *revolution* (generally a rarity in SPD writings), it was the same old insistence on the importance of established institutions and structures that Kautsky had argued for years. What he really called for was a "strategy of attrition," with the expectation that a militant social democracy could survive when a chaotic capitalism disintegrated. The popularity of a book so

123

antithetical to her own views enraged Rosa, and her wrath was heightened by a personal rupture between her and Kautsky, or as she named him, "The Grand Inquisitor."

Although a mild and soft-spoken "rabbi" at party convocations, Kautsky was overbearing at home, so much so that Luise began to resent his domination. Perhaps as a reaction, she became very attached to his brother Hans, a painter of talent and sensitivity. Karl, unable to comprehend that his wife might feel some drive for independence, sought a scapegoat upon which to blame her errant relationship. He quickly concluded that Rosa, who spent a great deal of time with Luise and who was always suggesting holidays in Italy with her, was the nefarious meddler. "Karl hates my influence on Luise, who is increasingly emancipating herself from him in spirit," noted Rosa.

Kautsky was not really wrong. After the breakup of her own "marriage" to Jogiches in 1907, Rosa became increasingly more critical of and intolerant toward the marriages of her friends. In letters she urged Luise to acknowledge that her relationship with Karl was useless. In the case of domestic relations, as in her politics, Rosa was either/or: Either a relationship or an idea was perfect or it was no good. She could not understand the world of compromise that most people inhabit and accept.

Against this backdrop, Rosa began to see her former ally in the battle against revisionism as the worst of her enemies. When Kautsky closed the columns of *Neue Zeit* to an article of hers on the mass strike, she lashed out as she had never attacked anyone before: ". . . this coward who only has courage enough to attack others from behind, but I'll deal with him."

Of course, she had no way of effectively dealing with Kautsky, any more than she could deal with the SPD. The Italian sojourns with Luise never materialized, and Rosa discovered the South only on a trip by herself in 1909. Like generations of Germans before her, she emulated Goethe's route, and was as overwhelmed as he had been. Her letters home were filled with prosaic observations and clever patter: "First of all the frogs. As soon as the sun sets, frog concerts, such as I have never heard anywhere, begin on all sides. . . . Frogs—all right as far as I am concerned, but *such* frogs. . . . Secondly the bells. I love church bells, but to hear them ringing every quarter of an hour. . . . It is enough to drive anybody crazy." Whenever she could, she interpolated newly acquired phrases in Italian. She was being joyous, as the South required.

What made her letters ironic was that the gaiety was phony. As she described the joys of Italy to Luise Kautsky, she was painfully cutting Konstantin Zetkin loose from their relationship because she suspected that it was stifling him. But again, the compartments were watertight, and no one else would know about the private Rosa.

IX

War, like revolution, was unreal to the socialists of the Second International. Whenever the major powers rattled swords, the socialists made speeches and resolutions, routinely condemning the threatening actions in the colonies or the pacts and treaties in Europe. Each eloquent resolution—like the masterful hodgepodge of the Stuttgart Congress in 1907—was accompanied by symbolic and verbal tributes to the solidarity of workers of all countries. But care was taken, especially by the SPD, to see that the resolutions bound no party to any concerted action. The veiled threats contained in the resolutions were like the great programs the party periodically issued and ratified: a means of substituting rhetoric for action, pretending that verbal preparedness would itself thwart the possibility of war.

Even in 1912 and 1913, when the Balkan Wars brought open conflict to the edge of the European continent, few socialists were willing to speak out for specific steps to be taken in case of war. Jean Jaurès would make passionate pleas against war, calling for a mass strike to halt any general conflagration before the mobilization gained momentum. The socialists of the International heard him out with comradely courtesy, praised his eloquence, and ignored his pleas. In Austria, Friedrich Adler tried to point out the dangerous course the party was following; he was treated as an aberrant egghead by the rest of the party. In Germany, the alarm was rung by Rosa Luxemburg, who saw war as the inevitable product of rampant imperialism. By translating imperialism from a series of seemingly unrelated events into a theoretical abstraction that could be labeled as the enemy, Rosa believed she had a workable explanation for the ominous clouds of war that seemed to threaten Europe. When the party treated her theory as hysterical pratings, she tried to take her message to the masses in which she had so much faith.

At one public meeting in Bockenheim (near Frankfurt) in September 1913, during an inspired two-hour speech, she touched on the question of whether "we would permit ourselves to be dragged helplessly into a war." The crowd shouted "Never!" Allegedly, she responded, "If they think we are going to lift the weapons of murder against our French and other brethren, then we shall shout, 'We will not do it!' " That single sentence was enough to earn Rosa an indictment for inciting public disobedience to the laws.

The trial was held in February 1914. Conviction was certain. Following socialist tradition, Rosa used the opportunity to speak on her own behalf for neither self-defense nor an appeal for mitigation of sentence. Instead, the speech she gave, one of her greatest, was a sustained political attack on the prosecution and the society it represented. Mocking the prosecutor's caricature of her as "Red Rosa," she spoke out in the courtroom with the passion and clarity that had been burning in her for years, arguing with the courtroom audience as she had never been allowed to argue with her comrades in the SPD. Her harangue was a summary of the ideas she had been developing since the Russian revolution, presented with the forcefulness and precision of courtroom histrionics.

Throughout she spoke of the working class and the Social Democrats in the first person, plural tense—carefully concealing the fact that few in the party would join her in that use of "we."

The main point of the indictment had been her putative call to soldiers to disobey orders, to disregard the blind obedience which was so important to any military victory. She said:

> We are of the opinion that the great mass of working people does and must decide about the question of war and peace—that this is not a matter of commands from above and blind obedience from below. We think that wars can only come about so long as the working class either supports them enthusiastically because it considers them justified and necessary, or at least accepts them passively. But once the majority of the working people come to the conclusion—and it is precisely the task of Social Democracy to arouse this consciousness and bring them to this conclusion—when, as I say, the majority of people come to the conclusion that wars are nothing but a barbaric, unsocial, reactionary phenomenon, entirely against the interests of the people, then wars will have become impossible even if the soldiers obey their commanders. According to the concept of the prosecution it is the Army who makes war; according to us it is the entire population. . . .
>
> You will note that this is a clear expression of our idea of where the real center of political life lies: in the consciousness, the clearly expressed will and determination of the working masses. And we see the question of militarism in precisely the same way. Once the working classes determine not to let any more wars take place, then wars will indeed become impossible. . . .
>
> Ah, the mass strike, says the prosecution. It thinks it has caught me once more at my dangerous and seditious purposes. The prosecution today made great play with my mass-strike agitation in which it purports to see the grimmest evidence of my bloodthirstiness—the sort of fantasy that can only exist in the mind of a Prussian prosecutor. Sir, if you had the slightest capacity to absorb the Social-Democratic way of thought and its noble purpose in history, I would explain to you as I explained at that meeting that a mass strike can no more be "made" than a revolution can be made. Mass strikes are a stage in the class war, albeit an essential stage in present developments. Our role, that of Social Democracy, consists entirely in clarifying to the working classes these tendencies of social development, to enable the working class to be worthy of its tasks as a disciplined, adult, determined, and active mass of people.

Rosa was sentenced to one year. While appeals were pending, she made a triumphant whistle-stop tour through cities of major socialist strength. Party newspapers which had previously rejected her contributions and had condemned her as a disruptive element were now proud to hail the martyr who was attracting so much favorable socialist publicity. Wherever she went, her speeches attracted enormous crowds.

After protests from the right-wing parties (". . . the German people in so far as they do not paddle in the wake of the socialists, are unable to understand why an end is not put to the impertinent behavior of this female," read one resolution), the government also paid close attention to Rosa's new round of speeches. The Prussian Minister of the Interior instructed local authorities to be especially watchful at socialist meetings where "the agitator Luxemburg" was speaking. Subsequent addresses were carefully analyzed at the Public Prosecutor's office, and finally another indictment was sought "in the name of the entire corps of officers and noncommissioned officers of the German army," because Rosa had theoretically besmirched the army's honor by some allegation of mistreatment of soldiers. The second trial was ultimately adjourned indefinitely, but the publicity did even more to make Rosa's name, with differing prefixes, a household term in Germany.

Before the appeals on Rosa's first conviction were exhausted (all were rejected, of course) reality had impinged upon her little contest with the public prosecutor. On June 28, 1914, the assassin in Sarajevo fired his fateful shots, and the question of war suddenly became a very real question for the states of Europe and for the socialists.

The inexorable march toward war, through ultimatums, mobilizations, and countermobilizations, caught the socialists unprepared. An emergency meeting of the International in Brussels reflected the usual spectrum of viewpoints, from the resigned despair of the Austrian leaders—who assured everyone they could do nothing to stop their government—to the hopeful declarations of Jean Jaurès and Rosa Luxemburg, who declared in private meetings and at a mass rally that the socialists could and must use their unity and strength to stave off the war. The conference issued its customary resolution, strong on words and totally vague in specifics: "The International Socialist Bureau charges proletarians of all nations concerned not only to pursue but even to intensify their demonstrations against war. . . ."

Some spontaneous antiwar demonstrations took place in Germany, and the SPD newspapers ran stern editorials: "Not one drop of blood shall be sacrificed to the lust of power of the Austrian rulers and to the imperialist profit-interest." But these were more a reflex than an effective gesture. The party's real test came on August 4, 1914, when the SPD Reichstag delegation was called upon to vote on the question of war credits. To the surprise of almost everyone, they voted to the man in favor of the credits, thus introducing the policy of *Burgfrieden* or domestic peace in the face of war. The small dissenting minority in the Reichstag delegation, in the interest of party solidarity, agreed to vote with the majority.

The vote came as a shock to the socialist world. With the hindsight of communist historians who have viewed the party as diseased through and through, and Western historians who have explained the complex sociology that went into the vote, it is quite understandable. But to contemporaries it was a profound shock that the largest, most powerful and best disciplined socialist party in the world would support a world war. For some observers the only reaction was disbelief. A few foreign socialist newspapers declared the accounts of the vote to be a monstrous lie. Lenin believed the edition of *Vorwärts* reporting the vote was a forgery issued by the German General Staff. The reason given by the party—that a defeat by barbaric Russia was worse than the horrors of war—even sounded like General Staff propaganda.

For Rosa Luxemburg and the few individuals who considered themselves the "left" in the SPD, the vote was a signal for shame and despair. Clara Zetkin and Rosa both contemplated suicide. The vote initiated an open split between the left and the SPD regulars which released a pent-up flood of anger and vitriol on both sides. Many in the party had long been eager to disown the troublemakers of the left. Now, under the guise of patriotic unity, they branded the dissenters as traitors—a gesture they hoped would insure their standing in the influence politics of the German Empire. By voting for war credits, the party had given up its last pretense to being a "shadow party" awaiting its chance to seize power. Like the other parties in the Reichstag, it was now willing to proclaim and demonstrate its loyalty in a clamor for respectability.

The left, including Rosa, had chafed for years under its inability to influence policies they saw as officious, cowardly, and unfaithful to the Marxist doctrine the party was supposed to follow. Their protests had gone unheard and unheeded. Now, with the SPD openly supporting an imperialist, capitalist state, the left unleashed a campaign to discredit the party in the eyes of socialists and workers everywhere. The left policy was capsulized in a phrase of Karl Liebknecht: "The main enemy is at home." The stronger the party support for the war abroad, the stronger the left's attacks on the party. In true Marxist tradition, it was a dialectic response.

Although Rosa nearly suffered nervous prostration with news of the vote, she retained enough control of her emotions to call a meeting in her flat of her close friends and colleagues. Six people attended the meeting. Together with a few allies who responded sympathetically to the three hundred telegrams she sent in search of support, they were to form the nucleus of efforts to discredit the SPD and to oppose the war. The group gave formal notice of their existence to friendly newspapers in the neutral states.

Illegal handbills and clandestine meetings may have been good for the conscience, but they did little to attract mass support away from the SPD. Under wartime censorship, almost no avenue was open for antiwar propaganda. And in Germany, with its history of "respectable" SPD activity, except for the memories of the period of semi-illegality from 1878 to 1890, there were few traditions or mechanisms for clandestine printing and propaganda. The left was a haphazard organization; some of the adherents had worked together for years, others joined the group solely because they too— for whatever reason—opposed the war and the policy the SPD had taken in its support.

Rosa was the natural leader of the left. She was the most articulate spokesperson of their positions, with the longest tradition of opposition within the party, and the greatest experience at theoretical exposition of the trickier points of Marxism. Yet for those very reasons she could not be a public leader. The trial that had brought her so much publicity in socialist and working class circles had also labelled her a traitor. At any moment she was liable to be called to serve out her one-year sentence.

It was almost by default, then, that public leadership of the left fell to Karl Liebknecht. His was a famous name in socialist circles: His father had been, with August Bebel, one of the founders of the SPD. He was well-educated, a lawyer, and served as a deputy in both the Prussian Diet and the Reichstag. Yet he had never been popular in the party, on account of his radical proposals and his tendency to histrionic gesture that flouted the sober tradition of SPD debate.

It was Liebknecht's status as a Reichstag deputy that made him the focus of the opposition to the war and the SPD. In the second vote for war credits, in December 1914, he broke party discipline and voted "no." Although he had campaigned for supporters among the party, in the end he stood alone in his dissenting vote. This act immediately made him a symbol of the ideas and the people of the left.

Rosa had never got on very well with Liebknecht. A month after his dramatic Reichstag protest vote, she wrote, "He is an excellent chap, but. . . ." Yet personal differences could not be allowed to get in the way of the work to be done. The first task was to establish a theoretical journal, sufficiently erudite to escape censorship but hard-hitting enough to have broad impact on the faithful. Leo Jogiches popped up and his considerable talents at organizing behind-the-scenes were seized upon as plans were formulated.

Rosa's prison term was due to begin in December 1914. Because she was in the hospital at the time, suffering from a minor nervous breakdown, the start of the sentence was postponed to the end of March 1915. Suddenly, without warning, she was arrested by the criminal police in mid-February; the press reported that "the red Prima Donna" had been picked up for organizing illicit meetings.

Liebknecht protested her arrest in the Reichstag—the beginning of his long campaign to use his position to air his views. There was, of course, no response from the other deputies.

X

Six months earlier, Rosa had looked forward to prison as a respite and a marvelous publicity stunt for the cause. Now she saw it as the most unfortunate of interruptions at the most inopportune of moments. Prison was different this time. In the past, as a political prisoner during peacetime, she had never experienced the extreme degradation of prison life. She had enjoyed special privileges, even if—like solitary confinement—they were privileges that only she could appreciate. Now she was only a common criminal, and to her horror, she discovered that she was vulnerable:

> You mustn't get exaggerated ideas about my heroism, though, [she wrote] and I'll admit that when I had to undress and submit to a bodily examination for the second time that day the humiliation almost reduced me to tears. Of course, I was furious with myself at such weakness, and I still am when I think of it. But the first night the thing that made a deeper impression on me than the fact that I was once again in a prison cell, snatched from the land of the free was—Guess what it was? That I had to go to sleep without a nightdress and without being able to comb my hair.

Were it not for these occasional outbursts of candor, no one would have known how intensely Rosa felt and struggled as a woman and as a revolutionary.

In prison, she wrote letters incessantly. Some were smuggled out to allies or friends; others were written legally. She was determined not to disappear as a person—the fate the authorities expected of political prisoners. In bits and pieces, she would describe the diet, her cell, the regimen, details that would convey a sense of her existence. In part, no doubt, it was a way of reminding herself of the weird reality of life in a quiet prison while the world war was raging.

Before her arrest the first and only issue of the projected journal, *Die Internationale,* had been readied. She was confident in Jogiches' efforts to get it printed and distributed, and turned her own time to two different writing projects: the work on political economy that she was abstracting from her lectures at the party school, and what she called a "study of the war." The latter was not published until 1916, when it appeared under the title, *The Crisis of Social Democracy.* Just before it was printed, she was persuaded not to write under her own name; she chose the pseudonym "Junius," from the anonymous "Letters of Junius" that from 1769 to 1772 had taken George III and his ministers to task in the *Public Advertiser.*

The *Juniusbroschüre,* as the work is usually known, is neither journalism nor a theoretical tract, and while its subject is historical, it is not history. The argument throughout is curiously muted, perhaps to evade censorship.

Every line is carefully polished, with none of the hurried quality that dead-lines usually imposed on Rosa's style. Yet the power of this cry of anguish is unequaled anywhere in Rosa's writings, and perhaps in all writings on the war:

> Gone is the ecstasy. Gone are the patriotic street demonstrations, the chase after suspicious-looking automobiles, the false telegrams, the cholera-poisoned wells. Gone the mad stories of Russian students who hurl bombs from every bridge of Berlin, or of Frenchmen flying over Nürnberg; gone the excesses of a spy-hunting populace, the singing throngs, the coffee shops with their deafening patriotic songs; gone the violent mobs, ready to denounce, ready to mistreat women, ready to yell "Hurrah" and whip themselves into a delirious frenzy over every wild rumor; gone the atmo-sphere of ritual murder, the Kishinev air that left the policemen at the corner as the only remaining representative of human dignity.
>
> The show is over. The German sages, the vacillating spirits, have long since taken their leave. No more do trains filled with reservists pull out amid the joyous cries of enthusiastic maidens. We no longer see their laughing faces, smiling cheerily at the people from the train windows. They trot through the streets quietly, with their sacks on their shoulders. And the public, with a disturbed face, goes about its daily tasks.
>
> In the sober atmosphere of pale daylight there rings out a different chorus: the hoarse croak of the vultures and hyenas of the battlefield. Ten thousand tents, guaranteed according to specifications; 100,000 kilos of bacon, cocoa powder, coffee substitute—for immediate delivery, cash only! Grenades, lathes, ammunition pouches, marriage bureaus for war widows, leather belts, war orders—only serious propositions considered! And the patriotic cannon fodder that was loaded into the trains in August and September rots on the battlefields of Belgium and the Vosges, while profits are springing like weeds from the fields of the dead. The harvest must be brought quickly into the barns. From across the ocean a thousand greedy hands want to take part in the plunder.

The entire brochure is written in this negative tone. The party policy, the claims that Germany was fighting a defensive war, the whole specter of war and imperialism—each is torn down and destroyed. Nothing is offered as a replacement. Yet the *Broschüre* is not devoid of ideas. The poignant illustra-tions are stepping stones. From the horrors of the war, she carefully leads the reader to the larger assumption: "In the era of imperialism there can be no more national wars." And from the optimistic catalogue of prewar social democratic resolutions and proclamations, she leads up to "the unprece-dented, the incredible 4th of August, 1914." The *Broschüre* is an object les-son, like teaching a child that the stove will burn. In the end, the only posi-tive assertion is an undying faith in the masses and the process of the dialectic:

Thus we stand today, as Friedrich Engels prophesied more than a generation ago, before the choice: Either the triumph of imperialism and the destruction of all culture and, as in ancient Rome, depopulation, desolation, degeneration, a vast cemetery. Or, the victory of socialism, that is, the conscious struggle of the international proletariat against imperialism and its method: war. This is the dilemma of world history, an Either/Or whose scales are trembling in the balance, awaiting the decision of the class-conscious proletariat. The future of culture and humanity depends on whether the proletariat throws the sword of revolutionary struggle with manly decisiveness upon the scale.

The *Juniusbroschüre* was intended as an explanation of precisely what had happened and as a cry of pain on behalf of all who had been betrayed by the errant ways of the SPD and the other socialist parties who had supported the war. In *Die Internationale,* Rosa stated the problem in other terms:

The genuine International as well as a peace which really corresponds to the interests of the proletariat can only come from the self-criticism of that same proletarian conscience, by the conscious exercise of its own power of this sort—not paper resolutions—is simultaneously the way to peace and to the rebuilding of the International.

Her viewpoint was tenacious, perhaps simplistic, but it was certainly true to the most basic concepts of Marxism. Like all her ideas, it saw those basic concepts of consciousness and internationalism as an absolute solution.

Others in the socialist movement offered different interpretations of the collapse. For Lenin, once he got over the shock of the vote of August 4, the explanation was an indictment of the treacherous leaders of the SPD, and a vindication of his views on the organization of a party. Had it not been for the International's flabby organization, had there been an insistence on a controlled and disciplined unity administered from a powerful and centralized leadership, instead of only the amorphous rhetorical unity of its federal structure, the entire tragedy could have been avoided.

Lenin proposed a new International, joined only by those who accepted the necessity of a tight organization, a structured command, and the new revolutionary ideals. Where Rosa's vision of the future started with the masses and worked up to an organization that would follow, Lenin started at the top with a structure that would lead the passive masses.

When Lenin read and reviewed the *Juniusbroschüre*, he was unaware of the author's identity. Still, he was perceptive enough to identify the situation of its authorship all too accurately:

One senses the outsider who, like a lone wolf, has no comrades linked to him [sic] in an illegal organization, accustomed to thinking through revolutionary solutions right to the end and to educating the masses in that spirit. But these shortcomings—and it would be entirely wrong to forget it—are not the personal failures in Junius but the result of the weakness of the *entire* German Left, hemmed in on all sides by the infamous net of Kautskyite hypocrisy, pedantry, and all the "good will" of the opportunists.

He was right. The German left was hopelessly weak, bereft of any effective organization. On one pretext or another, most of its few members had been imprisoned or interned. Liebknecht was alone in his Reichstag protests, and the courageousness of these bordered on recklessness. He had been drafted into the army, and alternated his time between the front and the Reichstag. The left depended for administrative leadership on Jogiches, an outsider to German affairs.

The disarray of the left, and the solidarity of the SPD, changed only slowly. In a war credits vote of March 1915, a number of SPD deputies abstained instead of voting in favor, but they were careful to qualify their abstention as a denial of confidence in the government and not as an antiwar protest. By December 1915, twenty deputies voted against the war credits, and twenty-two more abstained. The trend was due to a general disenchantment with the war. When mobilization began, everyone expected the war to be short and easy. By the end of 1915, it had dragged on for seventeen months, and the German armies were everywhere bogged down, with victory nowhere in sight. With a decisive victory no longer assured, some party members thought they detected disillusion among the rank and file—the same rank and file who had passionately supported the war at the outset. Nothing fails like failure.

Yet the new dissenters were not willing to support the left in its call for a revolutionary break with the past. The new group was the Centrists, later to become the Independent Social Democratic Party or USPD. Although they were tenuously affiliated with the left, in fact, the center was in direct competition for the support of the masses with Rosa Luxemburg, Karl Liebknecht, and the left. And because the centrists were a greater threat to the party's authority and position than was the tiny if vocal left, the SPD moved even more dramatically against the center. In March 1916, the centrists were evicted from the party's Reichstag delegation, opening a bitter three-way struggle in German socialism.

The centrists took their cues from Karl Kautsky, who had written earlier during the war: "The International is not a weapon of peace." Their efforts were not so much to oppose the war or revolution, as to capture mass support and to work in whatever direction the masses inclined. On a local level, the centrists' organization, called the *Arbeitsgemeinschaft,* often appealed to and worked with the same people who were inclined toward the left. But to the leaders on either side, the commingling of centrists and left was anath-

133

ema. In an illegal pamphlet entitled "Either/Or," Rosa threw down the gauntlet with a quotation from the book of *Revelations:* "I would thou were cold or hot. So then because thou art lukewarm, and neither cold nor hot, I will spew thee out of my mouth."

The existence of the centrists made it even more important that the left establish an effective organization and program. Jogiches had established a small network of agents, despite the decimation of the numbers of the left by arrests and detention. On January 1, 1916, the survivors met in Liebknecht's law offices and drew up a program of twelve declarations and six propositions, based on a draft written by Rosa in December and smuggled out of her prison. The document was a careful reiteration of the sins of the "nationalist" socialist parties and a declaration of faith in internationalism, formulated to incorporate Rosa's unique ideas about imperialism and a call for the revival of the International as the voice and expression of socialist consciousness. The proclamation is a convenient dating point for the existence of the organized left. Extracts from the program headed *Spartakus-briefe* (*Spartacus Letters*), the periodic, illegal mimeograph sheets distributed by the left. The name of the legendary leader of a Roman slave uprising gradually attached itself to the group, as adherents and opponents alike made the name Spartacus infamous in Germany.

Rosa was released from prison in mid-January 1916. She was mobbed by well-wishers, until she was exhausted from shaking hands. Yet within days she came to feel a vacuum of friendship. The few people she had trusted or known well were either in prison or at the front. Although she took up a frantic schedule of work, she also began to spend the few moments not taken up with meetings or editorial work on walks with Karl Liebknecht, who was home on extended leave from his regiment. They established an effective working relationship, his emotional outbursts (he would perform handsprings or unpredictably sing in joy) balanced by Rosa's intensity of concentration. Rosa also developed a close and protective friendship with Liebknecht's young Russian-born wife, Sonia. Neither of the Liebknechts could supply the closeness that Rosa had always needed, but her friendship with them gave her life in the spring of 1916 a measure of normalcy she had not known since the start of the war.

Throughout this period, the fraternal battling between the SPD majority, the centrists, and Spartacus warmed with the weather. The majority had cleaned its house of what it considered disruptive elements. The dissenters reciprocated by breaking all ties with the SPD, including the important matter of paying dues:

> Subscriptions should not simply be withheld [wrote Rosa], but paid to the party and destined for their real purpose precisely by keeping them from the destructive, disloyal bureaucrats . . . usurpers. . . . All our strength

for the party, *for* socialism. But not a man, not a farthing for this system; instead, war to the knife.

The ironic quotation from Bebel, another stab at the SPD's treachery, angered the majority perhaps as much as the content of her new proposal.

"War to the knife" implied deeds more than words. To publicize their cause, and to attract or at least polarize the support of the working classes, the Spartacists decided on a concrete if futile gesture. They would call a demonstration for May 1 in the very center of Berlin. Open meetings were, of course, forbidden under wartime regulations, and May Day demonstrations had always been limited in Germany on account of SPD fear of authorities. Yet every worker in Germany knew the symbolism of May Day as the international celebration of worker solidarity. The defiance explicit in holding a public demonstration was a slap at both the state's authority and the SPD's cowardice.

Although the clandestine advertisements and publicity produced a crowd of only a few hundreds, even that was enough to bring out the police in force. At eight o'clock sharp, Karl Liebknecht's voice rang out: "Down with the government, down with the war." He was arrested immediately. The news of his detention provoked a larger demonstration, and as the police reinforcements arrived, the crowd increased. The protest was generally peaceful but the left had accomplished their purpose: The struggle was now out in the open.

The Reichstag, without delay, lifted Liebknecht's immunity. A majority of the socialists in the Reichstag voted with the government in doing so; one SPD spokesman contrasted his "pathological instability with our clearheaded and sensible calm. . . ." A court sentenced him to two and one-half years at hard labor. In due course, the higher military courts reviewed the sentence and increased it to four years, one month.

With Liebknecht out of the way, a few centrists made overtures of cooperation to Rosa. She responded with what she called "a well deserved kick in the pants," redoubling her speaking and writing efforts for *Spartacus,* drawing even sharper the line of distinction between left and the center. But her activity was short-lived. On July 10, she was arrested, taken first to the women's prison, and then to the interrogation cells of the infamous Alexanderplatz. She spent six weeks in the "Alex," in an eleven-cubic-meter windowless cell, while the authorities decided whether to put her on trial or keep her in protective custody.

In October, it was decided that protective custody without a show trial would suffice to keep her safely out of trouble. She was transferred to the old fortress at Wronke, in Poznan, and detained there for the duration of the war. Punctually, every three months, a new warrant would arrive to guarantee the continuation of her internment.

Wronke was a relatively comfortable prison. Rosa was allowed privacy and exercise walks on the battlements where the sentries stood watch. By some means that she worked out, she carried on a steady stream of correspondence. But even the smuggled articles and letters could not keep her abreast of the latest political developments in Germany and the world at large. She was cut off; her theoretical thinking stagnated; her writing became static, at times stale. With letters she could reach out for her friends, but the responses were never adequate. For the next two years she would be alone with her few books and herself.

XI

Imprisonment was an almost regular occurrence for most revolutionaries. Some, like Trotsky, savored the withdrawal, using the enforced isolation for abstract political writing that might have been impossible amidst the distractions of perpetual meetings and demonstrations. Others, like Karl Liebknecht, devoted their energies to a constant struggle to communicate and keep abreast of political developments. Although the efforts were usually only half successful, no matter how assiduously guards were bribed, an approximation of regular activity was often the only way of staving off the painful loneliness and self-examination that prison can become.

Rosa did a little writing in prison, and sporadically tried to keep informed about the movement. Most of her energies went into creating whole cloth out of the tatters of prison experience. To fill her life with feelings and ideas and things, she turned around the critical telescope that she had used on society so that it made her tiny world seem proportioned and full. In the course of her walks, every animal and flower fell under scrutiny as sharp and intense as she had ever turned on the personalities and ideas of socialism: ". . . I am busily engaged in feeding wrens and magpies. The latter—my sole audience here—I teach the most revolutionary ideas and slogans and then let them fly away again."

With the same fervor she had poured into the *Spartacus Letters,* she resumed the interests that had fascinated her in the university. ". . . The whole world, the party, and my work disappeared and one sole longing possessed me—to wander about in the spring fields, to stuff my arms full of plants and then, after sorting them out at home, enter them in my books. I spent the whole spring as in the throes of a fever. How much I suffered when I sat in front of a new plant and for a long time I could not recognize it or classify it correctly." Her reading settled into a pattern of occasional political or literary items interspersing a heavy quota of natural sciences. Everyone who would read her letters got a stream of exclamations at the new joys she had found in botany and nature. To Sonia Liebknecht: "I feel so much more at home in a garden like this one here and still more in the meadows when the grass is humming with bees than at one of our party congresses. . . . The real deep 'me' belongs more to my butterflies than it does to my comrades." And to Luise Kautsky: "I just must have *somebody* who will believe that it is only by mistake that I am gallivanting about in the whirlpool of history, and that I am in reality born to mind geese."

Yet it was not escapism that turned Rosa to nature. The world of nature was a true miscrocosm, not a laundered one. "In nature I see so much cruelty at every turn that I suffer greatly." Indeed, the world of Wronke was so small, so concentrated, that what might have gone unnoticed in a wartime city or on a battlefield became a mirror of the whole war. She described at least one of these incidents at great length.

Wagons would often pull up to the prison courtyard where Rosa took her walks. One was drawn by a team of buffaloes, who had been so savagely whipped that their tough hides were torn and bleeding.

> While the truck was being unloaded the beasts, utterly exhausted, stood perfectly still. The one that was bleeding had an expression on its black face and in its soft black eyes like that of a weeping child—one who has been severely thrashed and does not know why, nor how to escape from the torment of ill treatment. I stood in front of the team; the beast looked at me; the tears welled from my own eyes. The suffering of a dearly loved brother could hardly have moved me more profoundly than I was moved by my impotence in face of this mute agony. Far distant, lost forever, were the green lush meadows of Rumania. How different there the light of the sun, the breath of the wind; how different there the song of the birds and melodious call of the herdsman. Instead the hideous street, the foetid stable, the rank hay mingled with mouldy straw, the strange and terrible men— blow upon blow, and blood running from gapping wounds. Poor wretch, I am as powerless, as dumb, as yourself; I am at one with you in my pain, my weakness, and my longing.

The publication of these letters after the war did much to eradicate the propagandistic image of "Red Rosa" in all but the most tenaciously reactionary and anti-Semitic circles.

Though she could not follow day-to-day politics, Rosa wrote about the spirit of her politics in language more powerful and direct than in any speech or pamphlet. To one woman who had written of her disappointments in a "weepy-weepy tone," Rosa answered:

> You are "not radical enough" you suggest sadly. "Not enough" is hardly the word! You aren't radical at all, just spineless. *It is not a matter of degree but of kind.* "You" are a totally different zoological species from

137

me and never have I hated your miserable, acidulated, cowardly, and halfhearted existence as much as I do now. . . .

For Rosa, there was no line between politics and life. People were political animals, faced with political value choices as much as with the search for food.

> To be human is the main thing, and that means to be strong and clear and *of good cheer* in spite and because of everything, for tears are the preoccupation of weakness. To be human means throwing one's life "on the scales of destiny" if need be, to be joyful for every fine day and every beautiful cloud—oh, I can't write you any recipes how to be human, I only know how to *be* human and you used to know it when we walked for a few hours in the fields outside Berlin and watched the red sunset over the corn. The world is so beautiful in spite of all the misery and would be even more beautiful if there were no half-wits and cowards in it.

When the poor woman wrote back to defend herself, Rosa praised her bravery, but continued:

> That you want to take me on makes me smile. My dear girl, I sit firmly in the saddle, no one has yet unseated me. I would like to see the one who does it. But I had to smile for another reason; you do not even want to take me on and are closer to me politically than you are prepared to admit. I shall remain your compass because your honest nature tells you that *I* am the one with the unmistaken judgement—since I do not suffer from the destroying minor symptoms: fearfulness, being in a rut, the parliamentary cretinism which affects the judgement of others. . . .

There is more to these letters than self-reassurances. Though she remained physically outside the operational politics of the Spartacists, Rosa was the spirit of the group. Her firm "Either/Or" manifestos, whether in political pamphlets or private letters, sustained a fighting tone and an aggressive dialectic. Without her, they might easily have slid toward a comfortable alliance with the Centrists, leaving Germany without a forceful counterweight to the overwhelming pressure of the state and the SPD.

In her mind, Rosa tried to make the Spartacists into a peer group like the old SDKPiL. But the closeness of the Polish group was based on the members' common background and values, and there was no way in which the disparate individuals of *Spartakus* could experience that commonality. They were of extraordinarily varied backgrounds, even of different nationalities; only opposition to the SPD wartime politics held them together. But Rosa, who saw *Spartakus* as a model for the future socialist society, was reluctant or unable to acknowledge the reality of wartime politics. ". . . No more meetings, no more conventicles. Where great things are in the making, where the wind roars about the ears, that's where I'll be in the thick of it, but not the daily treadmill," she wrote. It was easy to write in prison, where she did not and could not face the daily tribulations of making a revolution.

Although *Spartakus* could not have continued in existence without Rosa's cajoling, it was the behind-the-scenes operators like Jogiches who kept its activities moving. He was content to avoid the limelight while he worked frenetically to get the *Spartacus Letters* printed and distributed to maintain intact the clandestine structure of the group. His unflagging devotion to Rosa was reflected in his efforts to provide her with rice and other foodstuffs to mitigate the harsh prison diet. These acts of love were unacknowledged and unreciprocated; Rosa probably saw them as simple revolutionary readiness.

Rosa was no longer in love with Jogiches. No measure of kindness or gentleness on his part could restore her original feeling. The role of special confidant for Rosa had been filled, after she broke off with Konstantin Zetkin, by Hans Diefenbach, a mild army physician whom in the past she had often rejected. They were probably never lovers (she wrote him as "*Sie,*" the polite, formal address), but during the war her letters to him were far more confessional, more open than her letters to friends like Clara Zetkin and Luise Kautsky. His death, in November 1917, was a terrible blow to Rosa, one of the few events that reduced her to silence. Even days later she was scarcely able to write, except to stammer in prose: "We had a thousand plans for the time after the war, we were going to enjoy life, travel, read good books, marvel at spring, as never before. . . . I cannot comprehend it; is it possible? Like a flower that has been torn off and trampled upon. . . ."

XII

In November 1917, while Rosa was still reeling from the news of Hans Diefenbach's death, Europe learned that there had been yet another revolution in Russia, this time by the Bolsheviks. For revolutionaries of every persuasion, it was a signal event.

The first Russian revolution of 1917, in March, when the Czar's government had toppled, had been less of a shock. The March uprising was an uneasy coalition of proletarians and liberals, a configuration that Europe had witnessed in 1905. November, Rosa recognized immediately, was different. Even before the pact between Lenin and Trotsky—a trade-off of Bolshevik organization for armed insurrection and permanent revolution—she realized that the survival of the Russian revolution depended upon revolutions elsewhere.

139

Although she knew nothing about Lenin's secret train ride across Germany, the Bolshevik seizure of power in November was, for Rosa, a logical historical consequence of the events of March. What mattered, in her view, was the movement of the masses, and on that score she was skeptical about the ability of the West to support the Russians. "Are you happy about the Russians?" she wrote Luise Kautsky.

> Of course they will not be able to maintain themselves in this witches' sabbath—not because statistics show that economic development in Russia is too backward, as your clever husband has figured out, but because the social democracy in the highly developed West consists of pitifully wretched cowards, who, looking quietly on, will let the Russians bleed themselves to death. But such a collapse is better than to "remain alive for the fatherland." It is an historical deed, the traces of which will not disappear in eons of time. I am expecting many other great things during the coming years, only I should prefer to admire the history not merely from behind iron bars.

Although the information she received about Russia was fragmentary, Rosa followed events as closely as she could. Official *Spartakus* policy was to support and salute the Bolsheviks. When, after eight months of watching and thinking, she drew up a balance sheet in a pamphelt entitled "The Russian Revolution," her support of the events in Russia was tempered by qualifications and criticisms.

Rosa's critique of Bolshevik policy is often seen as a manifesto of "Luxemburgism," which some of her "followers" would like to contrast with Leninism. But the comparison is not as easy as the either/or distinctions that could be drawn between Rosa's views and those of the SPD. Rosa's pamphlet on the Russian Revolution, like all her thinking, follows a complex dialectic—from a chapter of praise to chapters of sweeping criticism. What emerges is not a new theory of revolution, but observations of tactics as seen in the light of principles; in short, an inchoate statement of what a revolution *should* be.

Rosa begins with praise:

> The party of Lenin was the only one which grasped the mandate and duty of a truly revolutionary party, and which, by the slogan—"All power in the hands of the proletariat and peasantry"—insured the continued development of the revolution.
>
> Thereby the Bolsheviks solved the famous problem of "winning a majority of the people," which problem has ever weighed on the German Social Democracy like a nightmare. . . .
>
> Whatever a party could offer of courage, revolutionary farsightedness, and consistency in an historic hour, Lenin, Trotsky, and the other comrades have given in good measure. All the revolutionary honor and ca-

140

pacity which western Social Democracy lacked was represented by the Bolsheviks. Their October uprising was not only the actual salvation of the Russian Revolution; it also was the salvation of the honor of international socialism.

Then approbation is qualified by a lengthy bill of particulars. For one, in the matter of Bolshevik land policy, Rosa conceded that the problem could not be solved in a short period. Still, the measure of seizing land and distributing it among the peasants only created a new obstacle of any future socialist land policy. Her second issue was the Bolshevik intention to proclaim national self-determination for every constituent member of the Russian empire. In part her criticism was a recapitulation of her very earliest political arguments, against the old PPS, in which she had argued for the absolute political integrity of greater Russia. But with the Bolsheviks she goes further, pointing out that their slogans strengthened the bourgeois nationalist position in "the coming reckoning of internationalism with the bourgeoisie."

Her next two chapters criticized the Bolsheviks for dissolving the Constituent Assembly and for restricting suffrage. As tactical points, neither was important to Rosa. What mattered was the principle behind these tactics, and in the case of both moves she saw a flagging faith in the masses. Trotsky opposed the continuation of the Constituent Assembly because allegedly it no longer served the role assigned to it. "No," wrote Rosa, "it is precisely the revolution which creates by its glowing heat that delicate, vibrant, sensitive political atmosphere in which the waves of popular feeling, the pulse of popular life, work for the moment on the representative bodies in the most wonderful fashion." As regards limited suffrage: ". . . It is a well-known and indisputable fact that without a free and untrammeled press, without the unlimited right of association and assemblage, the rule of the broad mass of the people is entirely unthinkable."

The list of particulars was really only a warm-up. Her most trenchant criticisms went under the heading "Dictatorship," and here she called into question the very essence of the Bolshevik revolution:

> Freedom only for the supporters of the government, only for the members of one party—however numerous they may be—is no freedom at all. Freedom is always and exclusively freedom for the one who thinks differently. Not because of any fanatical concept of "justice" but because all that is instructive, wholesome, and purifying in political freedom depends on this essential characteristic, and its effectiveness vanishes when "freedom" becomes a special privilege.

Rosa was not writing about bourgeois democracy. What she feared in the Bolshevik revolution was that the Lenin-Trotsky theory of temporary dictatorship would not prove an effective means to true socialist democracy; that instead it would lead to a deformed revolution. In effect, she was still arguing against Lenin's old ideas of party organization, with the difference that this time the ideas were not on paper but a reality. Her conclusion is one of the most quotable critiques of the Soviet government ever written:

> . . . With the repression of political life in the land as a whole . . . without general elections, without unrestricted freedom of the press and assembly, without a free struggle of opinion, life dies out in every public institution, becomes a mere semblance of life, in which only the bureaucracy remains as the active element. Public life gradually falls asleep, a few dozen party leaders of inexhaustible energy and boundless experience direct and rule. Among them, in reality only a dozen outstanding heads do the leading and an elite of the working class is invited from time to time to meetings where they are to applaud the speeches of the leaders, and to approve proposed resolutions unanimously—at bottom, then, a clique affair—a dictatorship, to be sure, not the dictatorship of the proletariat, however, but only the dictatorship of a handful of politicians, that is a dictatorship in the bourgeois sense. . . .

Rosa offers no specific alternatives. Rather, she concedes that much of what has happened was a necessity forced upon the Russians by the circumstances of war and German imperialism. The task of engaging and defeating the latter belonged not to the Russian proletariat but to the German proletariat. The pamphlet ends: "In Russia the problem could only be posed. It could not be solved in Russia. And in *this* sense, the future everywhere belongs to 'Bolshevism.' "

XIII

Spartakus was at a nadir in the summer of 1918. Its following was minuscule, numbering only in the hundreds; its leaders were in prison or internment. There was no one to sustain the flagging spirit of the movement, let alone formulate strategies for the political situation of the fourth year of the world war.

Rosa had been in prison for two years, a year at the fortress at Wronke, then another in the municipal jail at Breslau. At times letter writing, reading, and nature study had sustained her. But the long months took their toll, and by 1918 her correspondence revealed strain close to the breaking point: "Oh God, my nerves, my nerves! I cannot sleep at all."

At one point, Rosa's general health was so low that an attempt was made to obtain her relase on medical grounds. The futility of the protracted court actions only increased her depression. Yet even the worst periods were alleviated by her love for nature and flowers, leaving only the nagging reality of her situation behind:

> . . . The thought occurred to me today while I was arranging the flowers with the greatest care and was occasionally looking into the botanical atlas to determine some little point—the thought suddenly occurred to me that I am consciously misleading myself, rocking in the thought that I am leading a normal life, while round about me there is really an atmosphere of a world going under.

Rosa was in these doldrums, writing sporadically in the *Spartacus Letters* of her disappointment with the German proletariat, when the revolution broke out in Germany.

At the end of September 1918, General Erich von Ludendorff, who for the final years of the war was Germany's *de facto* dictator, informed the Kaiser that the fronts could not be held, and that the Empire would have to sue for peace. After four years of constant promises of imminent victories, the news was a thunderbolt, initiating a steady deterioration of the imperial regime.

A new government was formed under Prince Max of Baden, including for the first time in German history two Social Democrats, one of whom, Phillip Scheidemann, was a member of the SPD executive. For those who could recall the Amsterdam congress of the International, fourteen years earlier— when the SPD delegation resolutely condemned the idea of a French socialist joining the government—it was a moment of supreme irony. But few seemed to remember except the Spartacists and some left-wing members of the USPD. For most Germans, four years of war made anything seem natural, including socialists in an imperial government.

The new government immediately began relaxing the martial law under which Germany had been conducting the war. On October 12 an amnesty was issued for political prisoners. Three days later Karl Liebknecht was freed to a glorious reception by the workers of Berlin. As the amnesty did not apply to detainees, Rosa remained imprisoned, chafing at her fate: "I have stood everything patiently for years, and if necessary I could stand it patiently for years more, but under different circumstances. Now that the general move has started, something has snapped in my psychological stoicism."

Events started on the ships of the high seas fleet in Kiel. In August 1917, the only mutiny of the German war effort had taken place among the sailors, and subsequently the SPD and the USPD had made great efforts to propagandize the navy. At the end of October 1918, the sailors heard rumors that in order to save the honor of the navy the fleet was going to be sent out

143

on the suicide mission of a decisive naval battle in the North Sea. When the order "Action Stations" was given, the stokers raked out the fires, and sailors took over the ships. Portraits of various socialist leaders were hung in place of those of the admirals, and as councils of sailors and workers in the port joined the spontaneous councils on the ships, the revolutionaries began to deliberate the fate of their little revolution.

The record of the deliberations is perhaps the clearest testimony of the political naïveté and immaturity of the German people resulting from almost half a century of life under the Empire. The sailors' thirteen demands were almost entirely apolitical, including the incredible: "No unfavorable entry should be made in their service books." In other words, they were afraid the revolution might be a blemish on their naval records. They did equalize rations of sailors and officers, but the deliberations that resulted in point nine are difficult to imagine: "The address 'Sir' is only to be used at the beginning of an interview—in the course of conversation officers will be addressed as 'you.' " While the ships, guns, and officers of the high seas fleet were in their hands, and the breakup of the German Empire was hinging on their actions, the sailors were debating the form of address to use with officers!

Because of, or perhaps in spite of, the events in Kiel, and the inability of the government to do anything more than send a negotiating commission, the unrest spread throughout Germany. Workers' councils in the factories and cities and soldiers' councils on the front began to assert their right to administer local authority, or at least to exist. The various leaders of the left—Liebknecht for Spartacus, a group from the USPD, and representatives of the Revolutionary Shop Stewards—met to plan an organized uprising, fixing first November 4, then the eleventh as the day. As they jockeyed for different dates, the events of the revolution swept past their abortive efforts.

The SPD had already opened negotiations with the government, threatening that they too would join a rising. They were bypassed by the rush of the revolution. On November 9, a general strike broke out in Berlin, and large groups of armed workers and soldiers thronged the streets. The Empire was finished. As the Kaiser scurried to safety in Holland, Prince Max formally handed over his power to SPD chairman Ebert. Scheidemann, on his own initiative, declared the Democratic Republic, supposedly to prevent the Bolshevization of Germany. Liebknecht, sensing the turn of events, proclaimed the Socialist Republic from the balcony of the Imperial Palace later the same afternoon.

To the SPD leaders, the long awaited revolution had come. The years of discipline and patience had paid off. The revolution was successful, they had seized control of the political power in Germany. But in fact, they had seized nothing. With the wave of strikes, which the SPD neither provoked nor controlled, government in Germany was a runaway wagon. Max of

Baden had readily handed the reins to whoever was willing to take them, and the SPD almost by surprise inherited power and the task of making peace. The provisional government consisted of a coalition between SPD and USPD members.

On November 9, while Liebknecht and Scheidemann were making their proclamations, the revolution reached Breslau. The gates of the city prison were opened, and Rosa Luxemburg was freed. Witnesses recalled seeing the guards weep as she left the prison yard to address the expectant crowds in the center of the town. That afternoon she went to Berlin. Paul Frölich, a witness, described the scene: "She was greeted with joy by all her old friends, but with concealed sadness, for they suddenly realized what the years in prison had done to her. She had aged terribly and her black hair had gone quite white. She was a sick woman."

XIV

Rosa's life work in the socialist movement had been in anticipation of a German revolution. On her arrival in Berlin, she faced the reality, and the difficult task of somehow reconciling her own ideas, the inescapable Bolshevik precedents, and the unique conditions of Germany. Her ideals had never changed; the problem was to refashion a Germany that was ready for real change into the image of her lifelong vision of Marxism.

At first, the revolution seemed to be following the *Spartakus* script. The mass demonstrations and the spontaneous workers' and soldiers' councils were ample proof of the untapped reservoir of energy in the German proletariat, a clear validation of Rosa's faith in the masses. But appearances were deceptive. Behind the initial tumult and exuberance, the red flags and slogans, the shouting and the posters, sentiment was strong for a return to order. For four years most Germans had been living under martial law and the privations of war, trusting in the promises of the General Staff but never knowing when the turmoil would end and conditions return to normalcy. As oppressive as the Empire had been, it did represent stability. Thus when the SPD promised peace, it attracted the attention and support of a wide-ranging spectrum of German society, including much of the middle class that had once been so fearful of the "reds." The steady loyalty of the SPD throughout the war had proved that the party could be entrusted with power, and even if there were many Germans who harbored qualms about a party that called itself Marxist, the only alternative seemed to be the Spartacists—a far worse threat to the security of the concerned and propertied.

Rosa was quick to recognize the danger that the revolution could stop midway, with little more than a transfer of political power to the SPD. As she had written in her pamphlet on the Russian revolution:

Either it must advance rapidly and with determination, breaking down all resistance with an iron hand, and advancing its aims further and further as it proceeds, or it will soon be flung back beyond its own weaker beginnings and succumb to the counterrevolution.

This was the dilemma of the German revolution: *either* a consolidation of the political revolution, as the SPD and the trade unions urged, with an infinite postponement of social changes through the slow process of parliamentary reforms; *or* immediate social revolution, resulting in a socialist state governed by the dictatorship of the proletariat. The latter was the goal of *Spartakus,* expressed at its most eloquent in a long editorial Rosa wrote in the *Rote Fahne (Red Flag)* of December 14, 1918: "What Does the Spartacus League Want?"

The editorial included a list of demands—disarmament of "counterrevolutionaries"; creation of a workers' militia; trial of war criminals by a revolutionary tribunal; abolition of separate political states and establishment of a unified German republic; a complete overhaul of the laws regulating working hours and conditions, health, and food supply; "total socialization" of all business and industry; and immediate establishment of contact with proletarian organizations in other countries in the interest of lasting peace. But the most important section of the editorial was a vision of the society which Rosa hoped the revolution would create:

> The essence of socialist society consists in the fact that the great laboring mass ceases to be a dominated mass, but rather, makes the entire political and economic life its own life and gives that life a conscious, free, and autonomous direction. . . .
>
> From dead machines assigned their place in production by capital, the proletarian masses must learn to transform themselves into the free and independent directors of this process. They have to acquire the feeling of responsibility proper to active members of the collectivity which alone possesses ownership of all social wealth. They have to develop industriousness without the capitalist whip, the highest productivity without slavedrivers, discipline without the yoke, order without authority. The highest idealism in the interest of the collectivity, the strictest self-discipline, the truest public spirit of the masses are the moral foundations of socialist society, just as stupidity, egotism, and corruption are the moral foundations of capitalist society.

Although she closed with Lassalle's famous bloodcurdling exhortation— "In this last class struggle of history for the highest objective of humanity, let the enemy hear this word: thumb upon the eye, and knee upon the chest!"—the overall tone was that of humanistic and humanitarian idealism. Rosa's image of the socialist society was a perfect counterfoil to the situa-

146

tion of degradation and alienation that formed Marx's starting point in his critique and analysis of capitalism. As was Marx in his early writings, she was concerned not with the exercise of political or economic power, but with the proletarian revolution as a liberation from the oppression of alienation.

For all its idealism and humanitarianism, the program of the Spartacists was utopian. The demands they voiced reflected an ignorance of the masses upon whom they depended. The Spartacists deceived themselves into believing that the German people wanted more than the peace and order automatically expected at the end of a war and from the SPD "revolution." Consequently, the efforts of *Spartakus* were quixotic; their determination to carry out their program was suicidal.

When Rosa returned to Berlin, the entire *Spartakus* organization consisted of cadres numbered in the hundreds or perhaps the low thousands. Many of the supporters they had counted on in fact remained loyal to the USPD, and when the chips were down would support the USPD or even the SPD. Still more of their supporters were by no means dedicated revolutionaries, but radical hangers-on—drifters, criminals, and romantic insurrectionists whose ideologies were likely to favor anarchistic gesture or propaganda by deed over considered Marxism. This combined lunatic fringe and *Lumpenproletariat* would frequently resort to looting, indiscriminate street fighting, and other provocative excesses, all in the name of revolution. And because *Spartakus* adhered to Rosa's ideas of decentralized administration, because she refused to admit that *Spartakus* could not function as a peer group writ large, the group's leaders could exercise no authority over these unruly elements. The price they paid for this idealism, for doing in practice what Rosa had urged upon Lenin in words, was increased isolation from much of the German working class. The trade union workers who were anxious to return to normal conditions saw only a threat in the highly publicized Spartacist gestures, and as the blame for these excesses was placed on the movement's leaders, Rosa and Karl Liebknecht became a visible and terrifying threat to much of German society.

Spartakus constantly held the image of the unfinished revolution in the public eye, trying to imitate the success of the soviets in the Bolshevik revolution by demanding "all power to the workers' and soldiers' councils" in Germany. These were to constitute an instant responsive government in a revolutionary epoch, the true and direct representatives of the people as opposed to the hollow and false representation of the people by the National Assembly which the SPD government was proposing.

In fact, the *Spartakus* leaders had read too much from the Bolshevik experience into the German situation. Although the German workers' and soldiers' councils were spontaneous in their origins and perhaps self-consciously or at least subconsciously modeled after the Russian soviets, they were far from radical in their politics or membership. The majority of most was moderate, composed of Social Democrats and Independent Social Democrats, including as well representatives of the middle classes in the towns and factories. Their objectives were practical and immediate: direction of local authority, maintenance of civil order, regulation of food supplies and transportation. In effect, they served as a local government to fill the vacuum left by the precipitate collapse of the Empire. A small minority of the councils did want to emulate the Russian example by calling for a transfer of all political power to the workers' and soldiers' councils, but most considered their function temporary, as they awaited the restitution of more regularized and stable government institutions.

A National Congress of Workers' and Soldiers' Councils met in Berlin from December 16 to 20 to debate whether the future government of Germany should be entrusted to a National Assembly or a permanent council system. By a vote of four hundred to fifty they endorsed the National Assembly, thereby scuttling whatever hopes the Spartacists might have had for the preeminence of councils. This was the first great setback of the revolution for *Spartakus*.

Rosa was bitterly disappointed. In another editorial, she accounted for the decision of the Workers' and Soldiers' Councils by the "general inadequacy of the first stage of the revolution," the "particular difficulties attending this proletarian revolution, and the peculiarities of its historical situation." In previous revolutions, she wrote, the combatants "faced each other with visor up; class against class, program against program, banner against banner." This time, the issues were confused by the fact that the defenders of the old order marched under the flag of Social Democracy. Her disillusionment was scarcely concealed by reiteration of the traditional epilogue of *Spartakus* optimism: "If the cardinal question of the revolution was clearly and openly, capitalism or socialism, the vast masses of the people would not hesitate for one moment." Once again, Rosa had forced the issue into a clear either/or, oblivious to the shades of gray that politics demanded.

XV

New conditions called for new tactics. In the columns of *Rote Fahne*, Rosa and the Spartacists decided now to campaign for the National Assembly they had previously denounced: "Our participation in the elections is necessary, not because we want to make laws in cooperation with the bourgeoisie and its stooges, but in order to chase the bourgeoisie and its stooges from the temple, in order to storm the fortress of the counterrevolution and to hoist upon it the flag of the victorious proletarian revolution." The argument was logical and rigorous, but so subtle and dialectical that it could easily be misread as rank opportunism. What Rosa saw as a necessary course, determined by the will of the masses, others could call revolutionary pandering.

To participate in the elections the Spartacists needed a structure far more formal and effective than their loose organization of cadres. They also needed to define clearly their position vis-à-vis the other parties, particularly the USPD, which in the eyes of much of the rank and file working class was very close to *Spartakus*. By instinct Rosa felt that the time had come to ally with the USPD, to consolidate the mass following of the two groups and to use the collective strength to effect revolutionary changes. But the USPD, loathe to be tainted with *Spartakus* red, rejected the offer for a joint campaign, on December 24, 1918. This led to the final rupture of the always tenuous relations between the Spartacists and the USPD.

On the same day, another left group held a special meeting in Berlin. This was the Left Radicals, also called the "International Communists of Germany," a splinter group with its main strength in North Germany. They were led by Karl Radek, who had gone to Russia with Lenin in 1917 and returned to Germany the following year to bring Bolshevism to the German revolution. The Left Radicals agreed with *Spartakus* on most issues; their only major point of contention had been the affiliation of *Spartakus* with the USPD. When the former broke free, the Left Radicals issued an invitation for a merger, into a German Communist Party.

Rosa was skeptical. Jogiches protested that the formation of a communist party was premature. But Karl Liebknecht and other *Spartakus* leaders were anxious for any affiliation that would increase the organizational strength of the movement, and they soon prevailed. The two groups began meeting in the former premises of the Prussian Diet on December 29.

By January 1, 1919 the German Communist Party (Spartacus League) had been established. The name is usually abbreviated as KPD. As soon as founding formalities were completed, the delegates turned to debate over the question of participation in the forthcoming elections for the National Assembly. Rosa had come out publicly in favor of participation, and had convinced the other Spartacus leaders to support her. But on the floor of the new Communist Party Congress her proposal met fervent opposition. Many of the delegates were so beholden to the Russian model and such revolutionary zealots that they refused to believe that the dictatorship of the workers' and soldiers' councils could not be expected imminently. The recent vote of the councils meant nothing to them.

Rosa urged caution: "Comrades, you make it too easy for yourselves with your radicalism. We must not abandon the necessary seriousness and calm reflection. To cite the Russian example as an argument against participation in the election will not do. . . . The Russian proletariat could look back to a long epoch of revolutionary struggles. We stand at the beginning of revolution. . . ." Her speech was greeted with weak applause.

The delegates voted 62 to 23 against participation in the elections, confirming Jogiches' suspicions about the prematurity of founding the party. Rosa dismissed the vote with a resigned shrug, declaring that a newborn babe always squalled first. Squalling was all right, but the attitude of the delegates also revealed an inclination toward that adventurism which in party lingo was called "Putschism." No tendency was more dangerous for a party that professed to abide by the principles and ideals of Marxism.

In Rosa's situation, Lenin or even Leo Jogiches would have split the party, giving up whatever advantage size offered in favor of tight organization and strict adherence to the proper line. But Rosa would not split a party she had just helped to create; it was not comparable to splitting the SPD after years of loyal opposition. The dilemma meant that Rosa and the other Spartacist leaders lent their support to party policies with which they disagreed. So within the party, the policies of adventurism, rioting, street fighting, looting, and every other excess seemed to carry the endorsement and encouragement of Rosa Luxemburg, Karl Liebknecht, and the other "respectable" figures of the German Left.

The German Communist Party began its efforts to "complete" the German revolution in total political isolation. As its chief agent to effect the revolution, it depended upon the workers' and soldiers' councils, groups which in the majority did not sympathize with the goals or the methods of the communists, and which had indicated in their own national congress that they did not envision any role for themselves beyond short-term administration of local authority. The communists had decided to boycott the elections to the National Assembly, the one institution that most Germans looked to for a resolution of the chaotic conditions at the end of the war. Finally, the communists refused to form political alliances with those groups that were close to them on the political spectrum: The Independent Socialists they branded as no better than the SPD. The Revolutionary Shop Stewards, a radical group in the Berlin trade union movement, found the communists too intractable for a working alliance, although they approved of the idea of small conspiracies advocated by some of the members. Even the defeated *Volksmarinedivision* which had mutinied in Berlin refused to join forces with the communists.

What was off-putting about the communists was the sheer negativism of their programs. The theoretical positions Rosa Luxemburg had taken before and throughout the war were intellectually and dialectically rigorous, but they had been developed as critical stances, focused on the errors of her enemies. At the same time, her faith in the revolutionary consciousness of the masses precluded her deriving or stating a positive program of action or a blueprint for the structure of the post-revolutionary society. The communists, institutionalizing her theory into a political party, made a doctrine

150

solely of the negative criticism. Their goal was to tear down, to remove the abscesses of imperialism and capitalism, without proposing concrete alternatives. As Liebknecht wrote in response to one proposal for mutual action: "The achievement of socialism is only possible if everything is pulled down completely; only after the destruction of the entire capitalist system can reconstruction begin."

The communists advanced this position—more often by deed than by word—during a period when most Germans were searching for nothing more than a way out of disorder and violence, when the promise of peaceful elections for a National Assembly seemed to provide an orderly means of emerging from the horrors of the war. For most Germans the acts and words of the communists seemed like a Bolshevik effort to prolong the woes of Germany. As stories of terror poured out of the East, ordinary Germans grafted them onto the reputation of the communists-Spartacists.

The greatest irony for the communists was that from their position of total isolation they unleashed an unending barrage of calls to the masses to complete the revolution. Rosa did most of the writing, in editorials sharp in revolutionary formulation, provocative in language and tone, and subtle in dialectic logic. She usually tried to achieve a careful balance between the exposition of an appropriate Marxist theoretical position and exhortation to keep up the spirit of the mass movement. The balance was important. To Rosa there was a significant though subtle distinction between laying the groundwork for a revolution and inciting one. As she had written so many times, she did not believe that a revolution could be "made"; all that leaders could do was to clarify the issues in the circumstances. But like so much of her highly refined writing, the distinction was too subtle for most readers of *Rote Fahne*. They skipped over the historical parallels and the careful citations from Marxist texts to absorb only the inflammatory rhetoric:

> The "civil war" which some have anxiously tried to banish from the revolution cannot be dispelled. For civil war is only another name for class struggle, and the notion of implementing socialism without a class struggle, by means of a majority parliamentary decision, is a ridiculous petit-bourgeois illusion.
>
> (November 20, 1918)

> Humanity is faced with this alternative: dissolution and decline into capitalist anarchy or rebirth through social revolution. The hour of decision has come. If you believe in socialism, the time has come to show it with your deeds. If you are socialists, the time has come to act.
>
> (November 25, 1918)

> . . . The strikes which have just broken out . . . are the beginning of a full-scale war between capital and labor in Germany; they herald the onset

151

of the mighty class struggle, the outset of which can be nothing less than the destruction of the capitalist wage system and the creation of the socialist economy.

(November 27, 1918)

The force of the bourgeois counterrevolution must be met with the revolutionary force of the proletariat. The assaults, machinations and intrigues of the bourgeoisie must be met with the unbending determination of purpose, the vigilance and constantly ready activity of the proletarian mass; the threatening dangers of the counterrevolution with the arming of the people and disarming of the ruling classes. . . .

The struggle for socialism is the mightiest civil war that world history has ever seen, and the proletarian revolution must prepare the necessary tools for this civil war, and must learn to use them—to fight and win.

Arise proletarians! To battle! There is a world to conquer and a world to do battle with. In this last class struggle of world history for the highest ends of humanity, the enemy can only think of keeping a tight rein, of holding us down.

(December 14, 1918)

They were stirring proclamations, these calls to action, and if read alone they sounded like a clarion call to the massive civil war that most Germans feared. Few Germans read and fewer still cared about the passages in Rosa's editorials that balanced the rhetoric of these exhortations:

Rivers of blood have flowed in torrents during the four years of imperialist genocide. Now every drop of the precious fluid must be preserved reverently and in crystal vessels. Ruthless revolutionary energy and tender humanity—this alone is the true essence of socialism. One world must now be destroyed, but each tear that might have been avoided is an indictment; and a man who hurrying on to important deeds inadvertently tramples underfoot even a poor worm, is guilty of a crime.

(November 18, 1918)

. . . The dictatorship of the proletariat is democracy in a socialist sense. It is not a matter of bombs, *coups d'état,* riots or "anarchy," as the agents of capitalist profit dishonestly make out; rather it is the use of all the means of political power to realize socialism, to expropriate the capitalist class—in the interests and through the will of the revolutionary majority of the proletariat, that is, in the spirit of social democracy.

(November 20, 1918)

Socialism alone is able to complete the great work of lasting peace, to heal the thousand bleeding wounds of humanity, to transform the plains of

Europe, trampled down by the apocalyptic horsemen of war, into blossom-
ing gardens, to conjure up new forces of production ten times as great as
the old destructive ones, to arouse all man's physical and moral energies,
to replace hatred and dissension with fraternal solidarity, harmony and respect for everything that bears a human countenance.

(November 25, 1918)

In the bourgeois revolutions, blood-letting, terror and political murder were
the indispensable weapons of the rising classes.

The proletarian revolution does not need terror to realize its goals. It
hates and abhors human murder. It does not need this method of struggle
because it does not combat individuals, but institutions, because it is not
entering the arena with naïve illusions which, if disappointed, it would
avenge in blood. It is not a desperate attempt by a minority to forcibly
model the world according to its ideal, but the action of the millions-strong
masses who are qualified to fulfill the historical mission and to transform
historical necessity into reality.

(December 14, 1918)

The humanism and idealism of these passages was totally overlooked by a
government and public that understood little and cared less about the subtleties of Rosa's dialectic. They knew only that radical slogans caused bloodshed, and they were anxious to isolate and silence whoever uttered the
slogans. The fact that *Spartakus* was headed by a man and a woman—
Liebknecht and Luxemburg—added fuel to the fires. The scandal sheets reported "red" orgies, and the public widely believed that Karl and Rosa
were lovers.

By the end of December a right-wing group had put a price on the heads
of Rosa and Karl Liebknecht; bands of hired killers were roaming the streets
in search of the evil revolutionaries. On Christmas Day, 1918, Rosa wrote
to Clara Zetkin that she had received "urgent warning 'from official
sources' that the assassins are looking for Karl and myself, and we shouldn't
sleep at home. . . ." She took to sleeping in a different hotel each night.
There was no time to renew old friendships, or even to write the few friends
she had kept up with from prison. All that would have to await the inevitable ebb that the first Russian revolution had taught her to expect. In the
meantime her only activities were the perpetual meetings of the *Spartakus*
executive and later the KPD *Zentrale*. When she was not in a meeting she
was either writing for *Rote Fahne* or working to make sure the newspaper
got to press.

The only friend with whom she worked closely was Jogiches. From the
beginning of the German revolution he had subordinated his own strong personality to Rosa's preeminence; his preoccupation was supporting and pro-

153

tecting her. As in the days in Warsaw in 1905 and 1906, his presence may have been the impetus to her extraordinary energy. Those who knew her during the weeks of the revolution spoke of her utter disregard for fatigue, constant headaches, and nausea.

XVI

Rosa's and Karl Liebknecht's sloganeering probably had little independent effect on the Berlin masses. The adventurers of the Communist Party were already hell-bent on provocations of the government without any editorial urging by Rosa, and the broad majority of the proletariat was so numb from the years of war and so startled by the ease of the transfer of power in November that they were unlikely to rally from their inertia on the strength of a few wild whirls of rhetoric.

At the same time, the atmosphere of the city was tense, with rival parties jockeying in the streets, on posters, and in the press. Each report of a meeting by any group produced an air of expectancy. The kindling temperature for violence was low enough for the least spark to set off a fraternal bloodbath.

The trouble began with a minor incident. On December 29 the USPD members of the provisional German government resigned to protest the manner in which the mutiny of the *Volksmarinedivision* had been put down. As the dispute between the USPD and the SPD escalated, the USPD and the Revolutionary Shop Stewards decided to call a mass demonstration for January 5 in the center of the city. The plan was communicated to Liebknecht and he agreed to support the call with appeals to the KPD rank and file.

The protest was well attended, and its sponsors recognized the opportunity to exploit popular response with more drastic measures. On the evening after the demonstration, representatives of the KPD, the Revolutionary Shop Stewards, and the USPD held a conference and resolved to overthrow the government by force. By the time they issued a proclamation declaring the Ebert government "deposed," undisciplined and leaderless bands were already rioting in the streets, occupying newspaper offices and skirmishing with the police.

As early as January 6, Rosa and Leo Jogiches realized that the entire undertaking, which they had joined only half-heartedly, was senseless. The revolutionary committee proved incompetent, and the street rioting was uncoordinated and aimless. Within the KPD, Karl Radek, speaking with Lenin's sharp sense of the possible, urged the other leaders to try to call off the demonstrations as soon as possible. But Rosa was of two minds. While she disapproved of the adventure, she was unwilling to abandon the fighting workers to their fate. In any case, she knew well that the KPD had little or no control or influence over the mobs. The party settled for a compromise, printing "defensive" slogans in the *Rote Fahne* in an effort to give the uprising the appearance of a heroic struggle against "counterrevolutionary attacks." The defense was futile.

As early as January 8, the government mobilized every available military unit in the capital. Gustav Noske, a member of the SPD government, led the operation, and on the night of January 10 the troops, many under the command of former imperial officers, began an advance on the center of the city. Three days later the uprising was completely supressed.

In the eyes of the public the blame for the revolt and the consequent bloodshed lay with *Spartakus*. The USPD still retained some aura of respectability from its short-lived participation in the government, and the Revolutionary Shop Stewards, who had never had a knack for propaganda or publicity, remained a rather anonymous group. But *Spartakus* was well-known from Rosa's editorials and from the notorious exploits of Rosa and Karl Liebknecht. Middle-class groups and the leaders of the right-wing, paramilitary *Freikorps* began circulating handbills calling for the elimination of the communist leaders and thus of the threat of future revolts and bloodshed. The military ransacked KPD headquarters in their search for its leaders. While the manhunt was on, *Vorwärts*, the SPD Berlin daily, published a poem accusing Rosa and Karl of cowardice while the innocent workers were being killed:

> Many corpses in a row,
> Proletarians,
> Karl, Rosa, Radek, and Co.,
> Not one of them is there,
> Proletarians.

On January 14 Rosa wrote an editorial on the rising in *Rote Fahne*, "Order Reigns in Berlin." It was a bitter but balanced appraisal, conceding that in the face of "the general immaturity of the German revolution" an overthrow of the government was too much to expect. The editorial ended with a vindication of the masses and a paean of optimism:

> The leadership failed. But the leadership can and must be created anew by the masses and out of the masses. The masses are the crucial factor; they are the rock on which the ultimate victory of the revolution will be built. The masses were up to the task. They fashioned this "defeat" into a part of those historical defeats which constitute the pride and power of the international socialism. And that is why this "defeat" is the seed of future triumph.
>
> "Order reigns in Berlin!" You stupid lackeys! Your "order" is built on

sand. The revolution will "raise itself up again clashing," and to your horror it will proclaim itself to the sound of trumpets:

I was, I am, I shall be.

On January 15, Karl Liebknecht and Rosa Luxemburg were arrested at their hiding place in a block of respectable middle-class flats. They were taken to the Eden Hotel, the temporary headquarters of one of the numerous paramilitary organizations in the center of Berlin. A crowd taunted them when they were brought in, before they were taken to the first floor for formal, though perfunctory, interrogation.

Early in the morning Liebknecht was led out a side door. A soldier had been stationed there with orders to strike the emerging *Spartakus* leaders with the butt of his rifle. The soldier, Runge, performed perfectly. Liebknecht was half-dragged, half-pushed into a waiting car which went off in a direction opposite that of the prison to which he was theoretically to be taken. In the *Tiergarten* he was made to get out of the car and was shot down. The body was delivered to a local mortuary as that of an unknown man found by the roadside. In January there were enough corpses in Berlin for the story to raise no eyebrows.

It was then Rosa's turn. After being jostled and shoved by the crowd in the hotel lobby, she was led out the same door. Runge hit her hard with his rifle butt, and she was lugged half-dead into another waiting car. As it drove away, the officer in charge shot her in the head, and the body was dropped from a bridge into the waters of the Landwehr Canal. The returning soldiers reported that an angry crowd had stopped the automobile and carried her off to an unknown destination.

Since no body was produced, a short-lived myth sprang up that Rosa was in hiding and would soon reappear to direct the revolution. Even *Rote Fahne* did its best to scotch the myth, reporting to its readers that the two leaders had died fighting the counterrevolutionaries. Leo Jogiches sent a short telegram to Lenin on January 17: "Rosa Luxemburg and Karl Liebknecht have carried out their ultimate revolutionary duty."

Jogiches was himself arrested on January 14, but managed to escape by the sixteenth. Loyal to Rosa in death as in life, he immediately set out on a relentless search for the truth about her death, publishing his revelations in *Rote Fahne*. When judicial proceedings were finally held, Lieutenant Vogel, the officer who shot Rosa Luxemburg, was convicted of failure to report a corpse and illegally disposing of it. Runge was convicted of attempted manslaughter.

With Rosa and Karl dead, Jogiches was the effective head of Spartacus. But the group had died with Liebknecht and Luxemburg. In time, the leadership of the Left fell to the *apparatchiks* who were all too eager to take advice directly from Moscow. Jogiches was urged to take leave for safety in the south. "Somebody has to stay," he answered. "At least to write our epitaphs."

On March 10, he was arrested again. This time a notorious ex-Sergeant-Major at the Police headquarters recognized him as one of the leaders of *Spartakus* and shot him dead in cold blood. No official attempt was made to punish the murderer.

On January 25, 1919, thirty-two comrades killed in the January fighting were buried in the Friedrichsfelder Cemetery in northern Berlin. An empty coffin was placed next to that of Karl Liebknecht. On May 31, a body that washed up unexpectedly at one of the canal locks was identified as Rosa Luxemburg's; two weeks later she was buried in the common grave.

Already, she had become a martyr to some elements of the German working class. To avoid any mass demonstration the government took special precautions at her funeral. The myth of Rosa Luxemburg was already bigger than the reality, as followers and enemies used her life and writings for their own purposes. To the German communists she was a heroic leader, fallen in battle. To the middle classes and the secure workers she was the firebrand, the common criminal whose death was, in the words of one paper, the "proper expiation for the bloodbath which she had unleashed. . . ." And to the Bolsheviks, who with the death of Rosa and Karl Liebknecht, were the undisputed leaders of the communist world, she was always the heretic who had dared to criticize Lenin in the tender areas of his doctrines.

Even in the 1970s, the issue of a Rosa Luxemburg commemorative stamp is enough to produce prolonged debate in West Germany. Young leftists use the stamps as a form of protest, while conservatives protest to the postal authorities that "Bonn is now taking orders from the Kremlin."

To this day, Rosa Luxemburg is more paraphrased than read, quoted in defense of "Luxemburgism" but rarely understood, cited in support of positions she would neither have recognized nor condoned. She has become both an idol for the New Left and a "whipping girl" for the Leninist Old Guard, but neither admirers nor critics have paid much attention to exactly what she wrote or believed. Instead, she has been characterized with simplistic positions that do little justice to the subtlety of her views. Her life, too, has been mythologized into heroic or histrionic versions. Neither is true to the humanistic Marxism she believed in and died for. If she was a martyr, it was not for a gesture, but for a vision.

On the fifth anniversary of her burial a memorial was erected to honor her and her comrades. It was razed by the Nazis, then rebuilt after the war by the East German government. Today it is the site of annual pilgrimages by Communist Party members. So important is the abstract heroine in the communist mythology that the epitaph Rosa wanted has been completely overlooked:

> . . . Put on my tombstone two syllables, just "Tsvee-tsvee." That's the call of the tom-tit, and I can imitate it so well that they come fluttering around. It's a clear, fine sound, like a steel needle in the frosty air. But do

you know that for some days now there's been a little warble in it, a faint undertone? And that means the first almost imperceptible sign of approaching spring. Snow still covers the ground, and there's frost in the air, but we know, the tom-tits and I, that spring is on the way. And if I shouldn't experience it for impatience, just remember what to put on my tombstone—nothing else.

A N G E L I C A
BALABANOFF

Whatever the content and promises of its ideology, socialism was a movement. Many of its adherents were more interested in the collective or comradely aspects of the parties than in the fine points of theory and strategies for remaking the world. Artists found in the doctrines of socialism a rationale for their art or for their strange life-styles. Gangsters and thugs used affiliation with revolutionary movements to cloak their activities in respectability, co-opting grand theories and strategies of social revolution to justify mugging, theft, looting, and rioting. Finally, there are the lonely individuals who joined revolutionary movements to give themselves a place in the world. Whether homeless, without family, or in protest against their families' values, they found in the socialist movement a spiritual home and a social milieu that could replace whatever they had lost, rejected, or never had. The party provided ritual, order, authority, responsibility, friendship, enemies—all the emotional supports and needs of the bourgeois or aristocratic societies that had rejected or been rejected by the revolutionaries. Whether in the notoriety of a pariah status or the euphoria of power gained, the revolutionary movements provided an exclusivity that bourgeois and aristocratic society could duplicate only through private clubs and other elitist institutions.

It was this "wanting to belong" that originally drew Angelica Balabanoff to socialism. The story is one she was very willing to tell, so much so that she wrote three versions of her life story: in English, *My Life as a Rebel;* in German, *Erinnerungen und Erlebnisse;* and in Italian, *Ricordi di una socialista.* The emphases of the three differ, to appeal to different audiences. But the details remain the same, and throughout they tell of an extraordinary loyalty, not to a person or an idea, but to a movement. Even as the latter suffered through world war, revolution, schism, and near-annihilation, Angelica remained faithful, ever ready at her post and loyal to the cause that she could somehow pick out of the debates and debacles. Never a great

160

theorist or leader, never a pace-setter in either her ideas or her life, she was the steady bureaucrat, whose life touched on greatness constantly, and who thrived on the greatness of the movement around her.*

I

Angelica was born in 1878, in a twenty-two room house surrounded by a garden and an orchard in Chernigov, a quiet town outside Kiev. Her father was a Jewish landowner and businessman, wealthy enough to have many servants. They were all freed serfs, and stories were told in the household of the "magnanimity" of Alexander II who "freed the peasants and made them happy, whereas before they had belonged to the landlords, just as animals or merchandise." In fact, as Angelica saw it, emancipation meant few changes in the lives of the peasants. When her father returned from a long journey, the peasants on the estate would kiss the hem of his coat. "I cringed with shame," she wrote.

Her father, absorbed in his affairs, remained a distant figure. It was her mother "who ruled my life and for me personified all despotism." Angelica was the youngest of sixteen children, seven of whom had died. All her older sisters were married by the time she was born, and she was forbidden to play with her brothers. She was to be "the crown of the family," with training that would fit her for her destiny—marriage to a wealthy man and a life of ease. School, where she might mix with "ordinary" children, was out of the question. Instead, she was educated at home by a series of governesses, who taught good manners, foreign languages, music, dancing, embroidery, and the like. So taken was her mother with the image of the Russia of *War and Peace* that the Russian language, the language of "ordinary" people, was all but forbidden in the household. Instead, they spoke French or German—the "civilized" languages of refined Russians. To reinforce the good habits that Angelica was supposed to acquire from her governesses, her mother emphasized the regime with trying questions and taunts: "Who will marry you if you do not drink milk or if you do not take your cod-liver oil?" "Where has one seen a girl of good family who does not play the piano?" Or, the most exasperating of all: "What will people think of you?"

Good manners included a measure of noblesse oblige in the form of charity, that constant obligation of Victorian women. With her mother, Angelica

---

* Her perspective and her reactions are so central to her relationship with the socialist movement that I have often used her own versions of events and her own words in this portrait. Where her interpretations stray too far from the facts, I have either indicated so, or have rejected her accounts in favor of others with better documentation.

would visit poorhouses, watching or helping as the old aprons, dresses, and linen were distributed. The overjoyed inmates would kiss little Angelica's hand in gratitude. Once, when a beggar woman came to the door of the estate, Angelica's mother told her to give the poor woman a scarf. She took the wretched beggar to a secluded corner of the estate, gave her the scarf, then knelt in front of the woman and kissed her hand. ". . . I felt that I had established a balance between those who were able to give and those who were compelled to receive." It was her first step on the road to socialism.

Because Angelica was rebellious even at an early age, her mother was harsh with her, especially in front of others. In time, the little girl equated the scoldings with her mother's equally harsh treatment of the servants. "I saw that there were those who commanded and those who obeyed, and . . . I instinctively sided with the latter." Her resentment against her mother grew until, as she put it, "I soon came to understand her temperament, with the result that she ceased to have any influence upon me."

When Angelica was eleven, her mother gave up the battle to keep her out of school. Angelica wanted to attend the local gymnasium. Her mother struck a compromise by sending her to a fashionable girls' school in Kharkov, where a married sister could look after her. The entrance requirement in Russian, her mother had hoped, would keep Angelica out. But in defiance she had secretly been studying Russian all along, and was easily admitted, in fact, to a higher class than anticipated. Before the end of the first year she was promoted for "striking linguistic ability."

With no alternative except the governesses, Angelica stuck it out until she was seventeen. Then, in another obeisance to *comme il faut,* she was persuaded by her mother to come along on a tour of Switzerland. To evade the boredom of hotel life in the Alps, Angelica enrolled in a language school for young ladies. There she was told that she would be an excellent teacher. "It was the first time anyone had suggested to me a career other than idleness, and by the time we returned to Russia the word 'teacher' had become synonymous for me with the word 'escape.' "

The two years after her return from Switzerland were a period of hysterics and stormy battles. For Angelica's mother, it was the last chance for a suitable arranged marriage. For Angelica, it was time to escape, to travel abroad more extensively and to attend a university. Secretly, she taught languages to the daughters of bureaucrats and professional men who were heading to the University of Zurich. One girl, to whom she taught German, told her about the Université Nouvelle in Brussels, a new and innovative university staffed by radicals, with a student atmosphere which replicated the bohemian life of Paris. Although Angelica knew almost nothing of the revolutionary movements in Russia or the West, the tales of her student fired her. Soon she announced to her mother that she was going abroad to the university.

Angelica was nineteen when she broke with the family. Accepting only enough money from her father's estate to enable her to travel third-class and to live "like a working girl," she left without so much as a good-bye or a blessing from her mother. "My last memory connected with her was to be her curse upon me. But I was happier than I had ever been in all my life."

II

The journey from the vast estate in the Ukraine to a student hotel in Brussels was decisive. For the rest of her life, Angelica would live as she lived in Brussels, in "a miserable little room without heat and furnished with only a bed, a table and two rickety chairs." Even when she had achieved positions of prestige and status, she insisted on living "like a working girl," in barely furnished rooms, with a few shelves for her books, a one-burner primus stove to make tea, a cozy for the teapot and a jar of jam to sweeten the tea. For decoration, she kept a few photographs of the men and women she admired. In constant rebellion against the social inequality she had witnessed in her childhood, she rejected wealth or advantage to the point of embarrassing those who offered or enjoyed even a tiny luxury.

The Université Nouvelle proved more than Angelica had expected. It was housed in two shabby old residential buildings, but the staff included such figures as Elisée Réclus, an anarchist and a participant in the Paris Commune who had gone on, like his comrade Prince Peter Kropotkin in London, to become one of the world's foremost geographers.

To Angelica, the professors "were Olympians not to be approached by ordinary mortals." Yet while she faithfully attended lectures as though they were disseminating the Word, the eloquent libertarianism of Réclus and his colleagues did not offer the explanations that she sought. Knowledge, Truth, Justice, Liberty and the other abstractions of the Université lectures stirred her curiosity, but failed to explain the social reality that she had seen as a child. "Why, I asked myself, should mother be able to rise when she pleased, while the servants had to rise at an early hour to carry out her orders?"

In the evenings, at the People's House, a modest establishment where students and workers met for public lectures, and in the endless meetings in the cafés, Angelica heard different sorts of explanations. Many of the students were foreigners—from Russia, Bulgaria, Rumania, Italy—and most had been active in underground revolutionary movements at home. By the hour they discussed the theories of Marx and Bakunin, or told stories of persecution, police terrorism, exile, and the Cause. The Russian students, in particular, had come to the university not to prepare for a profession, but to train themselves for revolutionary work when they returned home. Political discussions were as important as their studies; food and shelter were completely secondary. Many, in fact, took pride in plain or even thoroughly unbecoming appearances—as if it were the mark of true dedication to the movement. Some lived almost communally; those who had more shared it regularly with those who had less.

Angelica looked on with admiration, careful not to reveal her own naïveté and ignorance: ". . . I worshipped them from afar." But as she worshipped, she listened carefully, and from the discussions of these seasoned radicals, from the reports of workers, and from the lectures on economics she had heard from various socialists, she began to piece together insights into economic theory, the mechanics of capitalism, and the history of the revolutionary labor movement.

". . . The most decisive factor in my intellectual life at this time," she recalled, was the work of Georgi Plekhanov. Plekhanov was already well-known by the late 1890s, both for his pioneering attempts to understand Russian economic and revolutionary development in Marxist terms, and for his leadership in exile of the Russian Social Democratic Party. What he had done was demonstrate that the key to social change in Russia was not the terrorist schemes of the Narodniki, or the agrarian utopianism of the Slavophiles, but the urban industrial workers. Even underdeveloped Russia, he showed in his books and his lectures, would follow the Marxist pattern. The industrial proletariat would emerge as the vanguard of the working class, and would lead the revolutionary upheaval that would rescue Russia from autocracy, brutality, and inequality. For those who had despaired of the backwardness of social conditions in Russia, Plekhanov offered an explanation and a "scientifically justified" future.

In 1898, at the very time when Zola's famous letter exploded the Dreyfus Affair in France, Plekhanov came to Brussels to lecture at the People's House. Angelica looked and listened in "bashful veneration." Plekhanov, with his suave appearance and manners, his polished French and brilliant polemic logic, seemed a Russian personification of Zola's challenge in *J'Accuse*. He was the first of many heroes whose portraits were to become icons on the table of the awe-struck Angelica. After the lecture, she remembered not the content, but the impact. "If anyone had told me that a few years later I was to know the speaker of that evening as a friend and comrade, that I was to serve as his aide . . . I would have laughed at such fantasy."

Following a short spell at the British Museum (already a required pilgrimage on the socialist grand tour), she received her doctorate from the Université Nouvelle. Even as she was awarded her degree, she realized how one-sided her education had been. The professors at the Université had been universally critical of orthodox economics and philosophy. To test her new-found Marxism, Angelica decided to spend the next two years studying in the bastion of defenders of the *status quo,* a German university. She chose Leipzig, because it was well-known for socialist activity.

In Germany she discovered the military discipline of the universities, where students clicked their heels and saluted the professors. As a Russian and a woman, her aspiration of studying political economy was looked upon with some suspicion, and she experienced incredible difficulty in adjusting to the formality of German academic life. Once, when a student was ill she ran to a professor to plead that a physician be sent. Carelessly she had omitted one of the physician's titles. "You mean *Geheimrat* Professor Doctor X, do you not?" answered the professor.

In Germany she added to the icons. While in Leipzig she heard that Rosa Luxemburg, already famous for her role in the revisionism controversy, was to speak. Summoning up all courage, Angelica approached her.

"Comrade," she asked, "would you allow me to attend your meeting? I am a Russian student, a believer in socialism, though not yet a member of the Party."

Rosa invited her, of course. Later, a portrait of Rosa Luxemburg was to join the others on Angelica's little tables, along with photographs of August Bebel and Clara Zetkin, whom she also heard and met in Germany.

From Germany, Angelica went to Italy to continue her studies. In Brussels she had felt drawn to the few Italian émigrés by what she called "an almost mystical bond of sympathy." As she explained the fascination of Italy and Italians: "I was a moody, shy young girl and the child-like simplicity, generosity, and warmth of the Italian temperament fascinated me. In the presence of Italians I seemed to emerge from a dark, cold place into the brilliance of Mediterranean sunshine."

The immediate attraction was Antonio Labriola, a Marxist professor in Rome whose reputation was international. Labriola was famous for his broad, philosophical interpretation of Marxist materialism as a world view which negated every kind of philosophical idealism. Angelica was drawn to him, she recalled, because he, like Plekhanov, had a philosophical approach. She was not disappointed in her expectations. Labriola was a broadly educated man who could lead his students carefully through history and philosophy, uncovering facts such that the students would of their own accord come to appropriate conclusions. "A professor using the university to make *propaganda* for socialism," he wrote, ought to be put into a madhouse.

Yet what Angelica recalled in her memoirs of Labriola was not his philosophical approach, but the simple dichotomy of his final lecture: "In the forty lectures I have given you this year I have shown you that society is divided into exploited and exploiters. Those of you who choose to fight with the former against the latter are fulfilling a generous noble task. As your Professor of Morals and Philosophy, I tell you this. I have finished."

165

Angelica applauded more vigorously and more gratefully, she writes, than at any other time in her life. She had found a justification and validation for the life she had chosen. At the end of the year she quit her studies.

When she came to Rome, Angelica met Elena Pensuti, the first woman member of the Italian Socialist Party. ". . . She, like myself, was too shy to approach the party leaders. But even to see these great men, many of whose names were well-known throughout Italy, was to us a great joy." They took their meals in the Piazza Firenze, knowing that the socialists ate there; as they sat in the cafés they would strain to overhear various conversations.

In time Angelica met more new idols: Leonida Bissolati, the founder of the Italian Socialist Party, chief editor of the party paper, *Avanti,* and leader of the party's "gradualist" or reformist wing; and later, Enrico Ferri, a famous criminologist and leader of the party's left wing. With their encouragement, and with her convictions reinforced by Labriola's lectures, she decided to join the party. It was no sudden conversion, only another step on a road she had been traveling. She filled out an application, was interviewed by a small membership committee, and took her place "in the ranks."

Her goal was to begin work as a propagandist. But where? Russian friends discouraged her return to Russia. Her lengthy Western education, they argued, would brand her as "contaminated" by Western liberalism. With no experience of and little taste for underground activity, there was little she could offer the movement in Russia.

What she could offer was a talent for languages. Already fluent in Russian, German, Italian, French, and English, she looked for a place where she could use her skills to interpret the Cause to the multitudes. She settled on St. Gall, the center of an area of German-speaking Switzerland where thousands of émigré Italian workers were employed. Because they knew no German, traditional Swiss xenophobia dealt the Italians the brunt of discrimination in employment, housing, and working conditions. Armed with her party membership, Angelica got a "job" in the Swiss Trade Union Headquarters. "Job" meant an office, a desk, and no pay. It was to become the pattern of her labors in the movement. Although the stipend she received from her father's estate was a pittance, somehow she managed to eke out a living from those few francs and whatever she picked up tutoring languages. Whenever colleagues insisted that she was entitled to a regular salary, she answered with a refrain: ". . . How privileged my life has been, to have an opportunity to work unceasingly for the cause in which I believe."

Within a few weeks she had more work than she could handle, as a translator and as interpreter to the Italian workers. Her activities represented a fulfillment of her ethical vision of socialism. She was ministering to the downtrodden, the suffering, and the poor, alleviating their lot and compensating for the inequalities that through chance and the evils of capitalism had landed her in the wealth of Chernigov and these poor workers in the poverty of an Italian ghetto in German Switzerland.

Finally, she was asked to make a speech to one of the revolutionary clubs. "Speak—why, how can I?" she asked. "I have never spoken before an audience in my life. I wouldn't know how to begin."

She did, of course, and the speech was a rousing success. Intuitively she understood what most propaganda speakers must learn from experience—"in what measure an agitational speech must stem from the emotions and how gradually an audience must be prepared for the absorption of abstract ideas." Within a year she had become one of the more popular propagandists in Switzerland, lecturing often four or five times a day in as many languages.

In St. Gall she met a teacher named Maria, who had fled Italy to escape imprisonment for an article she had written. In Switzerland Maria was having a much-publicized affair, which resulted in "scandalous" pregnancies. She had seven children, but kept her maiden name. Although Angelica did not imitate her new friend's life-style, she did defend the woman's morals, and the two became close friends. Together they decided to establish a propaganda paper for Italian women. Moving to Lugano, where a cooperative printing shop agreed to publish the paper, they launched *Su, Compagne!* (*Arise, Comrades!*).

Both editors were hostile to feminism. "To us the fight for the emancipation of women was only a single aspect of the struggle for the emancipation of humanity. It was because we wanted women, particularly working-women, to understand this, to learn that they had to fight not against *men* but *with* them against the common enemy, capitalist society, that we felt the need of this paper." The editorial line was probably a wise decision, for feminism was not a popular stand among the women of Italy. Unlike England, the United States and Germany, there was almost no feminist movement in Italy in the early twentieth century, and a radical feminist stand would have been the surest way for the paper to brand itself as so outlandish that it would alienate the very audience to which it directed its appeal.

The editorial decision was also wise in terms of Angelica's career. There was little room in the socialist movement for radical feminism. Angelica was one of very few women party members in Italy, and while doctrinal dictates meant that the membership of women would be tolerated and even encouraged, there was little instinct among the party leaders to devote the movement's energies to the cause of women *per se*. Italian politics had only seen women in positions of intrigue. To the extent that the Italian Socialist Party was—like almost all socialist parties everywhere—a microcosm of the national political spectrum, the party allowed small participation for women in leadership or policy-making. If a woman was to rise in the party, she would do so by playing a docile role, as a steady worker carrying out decisions made by the circle of leaders that Angelica had admired from afar.

The paper was a success. Angelica's speeches inspired semiliterate workingwomen to write of the atrocious conditions under which they labored. After judicious editing and polishing, the letters from women in the factories and the rice fields made good copy. The paper exposed the practice by which nuns in the textile areas ran "boardinghouses" for young workers. Their wages were paid directly to the nuns, and after deductions for board, penalties assessed for various "sins," and obligatory religious "donations," the young women received practically nothing. When the exposé articles were compiled in a pamphlet, the government was forced to intervene and regulate the practice.

Priests denounced *Su, Compagne!,* labeling its editor as the "she-devil." At some of Angelica's speeches rioting broke out between her adherents and the followers of the priests. She was mobbed and booed by frenzied crowds who, with the exhortation of the priests, threw dust in her face and spat on her clothes.

The paper's notoriety got Angelica an invitation to address the World Congress of Freethinkers at their meeting in Rome in 1904. The convention of rationalists, scientists, and militant atheists was so heavily publicized that the Pope—then a "prisoner in the Vatican"—had ordered all churches in Italy closed for a week as a counterdemonstration. Although the congress was attended mainly by adamant supporters of capitalism, Angelica agreed to speak because her report on the nuns' work-system would be published extensively in the free-thought journals.

The report was indeed printed worldwide, as promised, and Angelica received numerous invitations to address other meetings. "I had become 'famous,' " she wrote.

III

In 1902, at a meeting in Lausanne to celebrate the anniversary of the Paris Commune, Angelica addressed a large and attentive audience. Throughout the talk, her attention was riveted on a young man in the audience whose unkempt clothes, agitated manner, and general filthiness set him apart from the other workers in the hall. "I had never seen a more wretched-looking human being. In spite of his large jaw, the bitterness and restlessness in his black eyes, he gave the impression of extreme timidity. Even as he listened, his nervous hands clutching at his big black hat, he seemed more concerned with his own inner turmoil than with what I was saying."

During the informal discussion at the end of the meeting Angelica asked about the young man. It turned out that he was a refugee from military service in Italy, that he had appeared at the clubhouse a few evenings before and had been fed at party expense in the cooperative restaurant because he appeared to be starving.

"He sleeps under the bridge except when I can take him in and give him my bed in the daytime while I am at work," Angelica's informant continued. "At home he was supposed to be a school teacher, but it is said that he drank too much, had a terrible disease, and was always getting into scrapes. He claims he is a socialist, but he seems to know very little about socialism. He talks more like an anarchist. But he is in great need."

Another worker, a stonemason, also volunteered a comment: "My wife made him some underclothing from an old sheet. The next time he comes to a meeting, comrade, I will see that he is cleaner. All of us manage to get work, but he says he can't, that he is too sick."

Angelica, always quick to rally to the downtrodden, went over to the man, who was sitting alone in the back of the hall.

"Can I do anything for you?" she asked. "I hear you have no work."

He answered without looking up. "Nothing can be done for me. I am sick, incapable of work or effort." He paused, then began to explain. "I have no luck. A few weeks ago I had a chance to earn fifty francs, but I had to refuse it." (Angelica's memoirs have omitted his vulgar expletives.) "A publisher in Milan offered me fifty francs to translate a pamphlet by Kautsky—'The Coming Revolution.' But I had to refuse. I know only a few common words of German."

"But I know German," said Angelica. "I shall be glad to help you."

"You help me?" he asked. "Why should you help me?"

"Why not? I am a Socialist. I happen to have grown up under privileged conditions with opportunities you were denied. Certainly it is my duty to repay. . . ." It was her whole view of socialism in a few short sentences.

The man was still skeptical. Reluctantly he shook her hand.

"What is your name, comrade?" she asked.

"Benito Mussolini."

Angelica's version of this first meeting is probably overdramatized, but unlike some of her later writings it does not contradict the facts of Mussolini's life.

Mussolini became a major figure in Angelica's life. Never included in the gallery of icons, because his fame came after their friendship had ended, he nonetheless occupies much of her attention in her memoirs and in a book, *Il Traditore: Benito Mussolini and his "Conquest" of Power.* Both the memoirs and the book were written with hindsight, while Mussolini was the dictator of Italy. Both have been "corrected" to show her early "perceptions" of his demagoguery and the shallowness of his ideas. Yet even in her memoirs Angelica is candid enough to admit that she "came to understand these things about him gradually, of course."

Mussolini was raised in the "revolutionary" Romagna, where his father was a well-known militant anarchist. After a short-lived career as a schoolteacher he came to Switzerland. Even with a diploma from a normal school, Mussolini discovered early the misery of being an underpaid white-collar worker. He fled to Switzerland to avoid the draft and what he considered the stifling quality of life in Italy. In Switzerland he was a vagabond, rarely employed more than a few days at a time, cursing the occasional manual labor he could find, and supporting himself on the generosity of those he met. The "terrible disease" Angelica had heard about was syphilis, which Mussolini contracted in his youth. It did not stop his career as a philanderer. As much of his energy that year in Switzerland was devoted to chasing women as to his much talked-about pursuit of work.

Angelica was probably not one of his lovers. She was short and plump, with a round face that gave her the appearance, even as a young woman, of Queen Victoria. She was not Mussolini's type, and she seems not to have been physically attracted to him either. Rather, theirs was a truly platonic relationship of teacher and student. He was lonely, thoroughly outcast, ill-educated in the socialism he was already preaching, and desperately in need of attention.

They were probably drawn together by that mysterious force that attracts opposites. Angelica believed in the essential goodness of people: Only evil social conditions and the oppressiveness of capitalist society corrupted people to produce the bitterness and rancor of a Mussolini. When social conditions were rectified by socialism, she believed, then the basic goodness of all human nature would emerge. By contrast, Mussolini was a skeptic. Seeing himself in others, he was distrustful of human nature. As a young man he had spent much time discussing Machiavelli's *Prince* with his father. One passage in particular impressed him:

> . . . What is quite manifest from even a superficial reading of *The Prince* is the acute pessimism of Machiavelli in regard to human nature. . . . In chapter XVIII of *The Prince* Machiavelli thus expresses himself: "This may be said generally of men: that they are ungrateful, voluble, deceitful, shirkers of dangers, greedy of gain." . . . Much time has passed since then, but if I were allowed to judge my fellows and my compatriots, I could not attenuate in the least Machiavelli's verdict.

The work of the translation did not last long, and by the time they were finished Angelica could see how much intellectual labor stimulated Mussolini's spirits and ambitions. She urged him to read, lending him books and pamphlets.

"It is not enough to be a rebel," she told him. "You cannot abolish injustice by merely raging against it. You cannot lead the workers intelligently unless you know something of the labor movement. You must understand its history—its failures as well as its successes and the reasons for both.''

Her self-effacing manner, as a teacher and as a collaborator, increased his bravado and self-confidence. Soon he was calling himself an intellectual and a writer, citing with offhand ease dozens of authors and philosophies that only a day or two before he had heard of for the first time. Yet the bombast was never turned on her. Mussolini felt comfortable with Angelica in a way that he could never have felt with a man, from whom he would have hidden his weakness, or one of his lovers, to whom he was forever proving himself. He also respected her class background with snobbish pride. Angelica was convinced that she was the only human being with whom Mussolini was completely himself, to whom he told all without bluffing.

As they got to know one another, he bared himself, revealing the raw energy encapsulated in the once wretched and lonely figure. He told of passing a park when he was almost insane with hunger, and seeing two Englishwomen on a parkbench with their lunch—''bread, cheese, eggs!'' (Mussolini had a phenomenal memory for food.) ''I could not restrain myself. I threw myself upon one of the old witches and grabbed the food from her hands. If they had made the slightest resistance I would have strangled them—strangled them, mind you—'' (In retelling the story Angelica, always a prude, omits Mussolini's interjected obscenities.) He paused in the telling, then laughed. ''Don't you think it would have been better if I had killed those parasites? Why does not the hour of revenge arrive?''

Angelica protested that assassinations were not the key to the problem of human hunger. Yet, while repulsed by his story, she recognized the vast difference between his personal sense of inequality and wrongdoing and her intellectual commitment to the cause. For Mussolini the conditions of the world had meant real hunger, anger and jealousy—which roused him to a fervor and passion that Angelica could never match. ''He used to envy my will power,'' she wrote, ''my not losing my temper, etc., and this too aroused in me constantly the comparison between the luxurious house and immense garden, and the abundance which surrounded me in my childhood and the filthy environments and the deprivations he was again and again referring to when dealing with his past, present and future.''

He was never a Marxist, and never would be. His reading of philosophy and social criticism was always sporadic, geared to a search for passages that struck his fancy. He was especially drawn to writers who stressed the power of the individual act—Nietzsche, Schopenhauer, Stirner, Blanqui. What he liked in Stirner and Blanqui—their sense of ego and admiration of a planned coup d'état—was exactly what Marx had rejected. Yet what Mussolini lacked in intellectual rigor he made up for with sheer hatred and will. And even as she despised his stories, Angelica came to believe more and more in Mussolini: ''I felt assured that if he once achieved a more normal life in Switzerland, earned enough to assure his bodily needs, regular meals, a place to live; if he no longer had to suffer the humiliation of being dependent upon the charity of his fellow radicals, he would become less agitated in mind and spirit.''

After a while, he gained some respect in the émigré socialist circles of Switzerland, despite his habit of arguing with anyone at any time, and shouting down opponents over the smallest points. He was finally invited to present the anticlerical position at a talk given by a priest. Mussolini did not yet have the poise and exquisite control of the audience that was to mark his famous balcony speeches. Instead, he substituted histrionics. At this first lecture he asked one of his listeners to lend him a watch. He then struck a dramatic pose and said: ''I will give God just five minutes to strike me dead. If he does not punish me in that time, he does not exist.''

Angelica despaired of these gestures. But in fact, with the semiliterate audiences they were very effective. Mussolini was soon a popular speaker on anticlericalism and antimilitarism, so much so that by 1905, the violence of his utterances had earned him an expulsion from Switzerland.

In the two years since Angelica had known him, Mussolini had changed considerably. He had gained self-confidence and enough learning to pose as a self-taught expert on socialism. When she met him he had mouthed the socialism and anarchism of his native Romagna; now he could cite Marx and Engels well enough to drown out most arguments. He had become a popular speaker, had published a pamphlet entitled ''God Does Not Exist'' at the expense of his radical friends, and had traveled through most of Switzerland without having to hold down any regular job.

Yet underneath the surface there was the same Mussolini. On the evening he left, Angelica walked him down to the boat on Lake Lugano. As they waited for its departure, he waved his arm toward the fancy restaurants and hotels along the pier. ''Look! People eating, drinking and enjoying themselves. And I will travel third-class, eat miserable, cheap food. *Porca Madonna,* how I hate the rich! Why must I suffer this injustice? How long must we wait?''

IV

From 1902 to 1905, the period of her early friendship with Mussolini, Angelica lived in Lugano, just across the border from Italy. Besides editing the weekly newspaper for women, she spent most of her time in propaganda and speaking tours of Italian towns and cities. She was not officially a leader of the Italian Socialist Party, but with her international connections and her linguistic abilities, she formed one of the important links between the socialist movement in Italy and the movement in other countries. Almost alone of those active in the Italian movement, she followed events elsewhere and interpreted their significance to Italian workers and socialist intellectuals.

Italy was immature politically. Unification of the country was less than fifty years old, and national parties had been late to form. Indeed, they were so divided internally that political coalitions were normally formed between splinters of the various parties, so that at any given moment, a party might be both in power and outside the ruling coalition. The socialist party was relatively unified, since neither the left nor the right wing was ever invited into any government. Yet it suffered from the same immaturity that plagued the other parties, coupled with the usual pressures that a developing capitalist society would apply against the threat of socialism.

At the same time, the latter half of the nineteenth century had seen a proliferation of secular and socialistic ideas in Italy. Unions, schools, libraries, cooperatives, and other institutions sponsored or supported by the socialists (and in some cases, the anarchists) began to share the extraordinary role once exercised by the church. Among large segments of the working classes, clergy were called on less frequently to officiate at weddings, births, and deaths. Children were less likely to receive the names of saints and more likely to be named Égalità, Libertà, or Unità, or perhaps, like Mussolini, to be named after some revolutionary hero.

As the socialist campaigns progressed, slogans and songs were popularized among both the workers in the cities and the peasants and small landholders in the countryside. The close proximity of farm country and cities in Italy facilitated the spread of ideas among the rural population, where cooperatives caught on early. Slogans such as "You are small because you kneel; rise and you will be big!" were as likely to adorn peasant dwellings as the walls of the tenement squares.

Finally, two other elements molded the character of the socialist movement in Italy. One was the vast number of émigré workers who had been employed in Swiss, German, or French factories. They had witnessed the scope and discipline of the foreign socialist parties, and developed an appreciation of the potential power of a well-organized and structured movement such as Italy lacked. In addition, the émigré workers, many of whom had been brought in as scabs, had seen at first hand the effect of the struggle of worker against worker. They had gone innocently to Germany or Switzerland in pursuit of promised high wages. When they arrived they often took the jobs of workers who were on strike, and by doing so they had lowered the wages the employer had to pay. It did not take long for the workers to understand the game the employers were playing; when they returned to Italy they were worldly wise in the game of strikes and strikebreaking. In the parlance of the socialist movement, they had developed the class consciousness of the proletariat. During the periodic waves of strikes

173

that beset the infant Italian industries, the former émigrés were often spontaneous leaders of the workers.

The other unique element in Italy was the large number of respected intellectuals who were Marxists. A referendum conducted by a radical magazine showed that a substantial number of the best known writers, artists, and scientists were avowed socialists. Lombroso, the criminologist; Chiaroggi, the embryologist; Catelli, the physicist; Sanarelli, the discoverer of the yellow fever bacterium; De Amicis, the most widely read novelist; Grel, Gueriai, Pascoli, the poets—all were socialists. Many of the party leaders were also respected intellectuals. Turati was a criminologist and social critic; Ferri was a rival of Lombroso as a criminologist. Outside the university, as well, were many individuals who had turned from a life of comfort in the bourgeoisie or the aristocracy to join with and take a position of leadership in the socialist movement. There was little xenophobia in Italian socialism. The few outsiders, like Angelica, were readily welcomed for whatever talents or energies they might bring, and rarely distrusted as Rosa Luxemburg and Leo Jogiches were in Germany.

The experience abroad of so many Italian workers, and the party's relative lack of xenophobia made the Italian workers more eager for foreign news than were the socialists of most countries. Angelica's descriptions of working conditions in Switzerland or party structure in Germany met a receptive audience. By far the most popular topic of her talks, though, was the 1905 revolution in Russia. News of the revolution was as much a surprise in Italy as in the rest of Western Europe. But in Italy the parallel of Italian with Russian conditions made it directly relevant. Both Italy and Russia were backward and underdeveloped, with industry in only a few areas. The industries in each country were on a large scale, though, which meant that in certain cities there were great agglomerations of workers. In both countries, the movement had been built up by disillusioned aristocrats and bourgeoisie. Also, while Italy did not have an underground socialist movement as in Russia, the movement was still relatively small, unstructured, and undisciplined.

Thus for the Italian workers and peasants, the fact of strikes and an uprising in Russia offered hope that Italy could also produce a revolution. Theory had always claimed that revolutionary change would come first in the countries with the most highly developed industry and the most disciplined working class organization. The Russian revolution demonstrated that there was an alternative, giving a sense of expectation to the working classes of Italy and other countries that saw their situations as roughly parallel to the economic and social situation in Russia.

Angelica's speeches about the Russian revolution, and particularly her angry attacks on Czarism and the drastic measures the Czarist government was taking to suppress the uprising, were also popular among the Italian bourgeoisie. Among the constitutional monarchies and parliamentary regimes of Western Europe, Czarism was generally viewed as the most barbaric extreme of "oriental despotism." The middle classes of Italy, France, England, and Belgium took pride in the gulf separating their own "democracies" from the autocracy of Russia. Denunciations of Czarism, even from a socialist agitator, were popular lecture topics, and when the lecturer was herself a Russian, attendance at the lecture proved a remarkably self-satisfying experience for the middle classes. How liberal and democratic Italy seemed when compared with the brutality the Russian government had introduced in the wake of the revolutionary upheaval! In her speaking tours of Italy, Angelica raised three times as much money for the support of the Russian revolutionaries as Maxim Gorky had raised on his much-publicized fund-raising tour in the United States.

V

Although Angelica's sympathies lay with the Italian socialist movement, as a Russian living in Switzerland she could not escape the Russian Marxist movement. So many leaders of the various Russian factions lived in Swiss exile that Geneva was in fact the capital of the Russian movement. Plekhanov had left Switzerland because of his health, and settled in Nervi, on the Italian Riviera, a short train ride away from the unending theoretical discussions of Geneva. Martov, Axelrod, Lenin, Zinoviev were all living in Switzerland; Trotsky was next door in Vienna. The universities of Zurich and Lausanne were filled with Russian students, and the students were themselves affiliated in their own organization.

None were to join the icon collection, but in 1906 and 1907 Angelica met all these leaders in the course of Russian party meetings. In 1906 she spoke on the same platform with Trotsky. She immediately recognized the brilliance and effectiveness of his oratory, and was as immediately put off by "certain of his mannerisms and his general self-consciousness." Strikingly, she does not remember exactly when she met Lenin, although he was someday to play a more important role in her life than any other figure in the revolutionary circles.

"Lenin had no exterior characteristics that would lead one to single him out among the revolutionary figures of his day," she wrote. "In fact, of all the Russian revolutionary leaders, he seemed, externally, the most colorless." It is an unusual observation. Most people were struck even on a first meeting by Lenin's appearance. His tiny, steely eyes, the Tartar features and the extraordinary concentration of his look are mentioned by almost everyone who met him. Even his speeches were unimpressive to Angelica. She somehow failed to notice the intense single-mindedness that others saw:

"Do you mean to say that all these splits and quarrels and scandals are the work of one man?'' asked one observer of the Russian party. ''But how can one man be so effective and so dangerous?''

''Because,'' answered Paul Axelrod, ''there is not another man who for twenty-four hours of the day is taken up with the revolution, who has no other thoughts but thoughts of revolution, and who, even in his sleep dreams of nothing but revolution. Just try and handle such a fellow.''

This was the Lenin that most people met and remembered.

To Angelica the Russians were an enigma. Night and day they argued theory, strategy, and tactics with an earnestness and pedantry she had never before seen. Every aspect of the development of industry, society, and the consciousness of the working class was debated over and over, as advocates of each possible position (and a number of positions that almost everyone could agree were not possible) presented data and logic to buttress his or her stand. In exile, with almost no functioning party structure at home, the Russians were impotent to effect any kind of revolutionary change. But that did not stop them from discussing in minute detail the various theories as to correct organization of the revolutionary party, tactics for the seizure of power, and strategies for the gradual preparation of the working class.

Although they were all clearly revolutionaries, to Angelica their discussions were academic claptrap. ''It never occured to the Russians that these lengthy theoretical discussions might be subordinated—as they frequently were among other revolutionists—to practical and tactical matters, or that their prolonged polemics represented a waste of time.'' What she only dimly realized was that the theoretical discussions were not only a substitute for the action that was impossible for the Russian exiles, but were also a means of ironing out conflicts of personality and in-house power struggles.

It was in London, at the 1907 Russian party congress, that Angelica began to sense the nature of Russian party politics. The titans were there: Plekhanov, Lenin, Trotsky, Axelrod, Martov, Zinoviev. Rosa Luxemburg and Leo Jogiches made their appearance together, though few of the other delegates knew the emotional pain that appearance, so soon after they had severed their close relationship, cost them.

Angelica was invited as a fraternal delegate of the organization of Russian university students. She traveled to London via Berlin, where she picked up a substantial check provided by the German party to finance the cost of the Russian party meeting. When she was first admitted to the congress, the salutation of the delegates was: ''To which faction do you belong?''

It took a week to elect a chairman. Everyone knew who the candidates would be: Lenin for the Bolsheviks and Plekhanov for the Mensheviks. But since the chairman would have strategic control of the agenda, even the nominating speeches became a full-scale debate ranging over the whole

176

gamut of ideology that separated the factions. Lenin was determined to impose his ideas of a tight, centralized party structure; the Mensheviks were determined to maintain a broad-based party. In between was a gallery who took intermediate positions, or who put their energy into cheering and booing. Some heckled both sides.

To Lenin or Rosa Luxemburg, these debates were deadly serious. Just because the Russian socialists were far from power, the "correct" theory became important. After all, 1905 had shown how close power could be, and the failure of 1905 had shown how important preparation could be. Yet to Angelica these debates were nonsense. Her idea of socialism had always been practical and direct. Philosophy and theory, for her, meant a kind of egalitarian ethic, a quasi-religious socialism which exalted the poor and downtrodden and demanded they be granted full human stature. Of what use to the poor could these debates be? How could complex and abstruse arguments about the proper role of the revolutionary vanguard do anything about the concrete situation of the workers and peasants of Russia and the world?

Her role at the congress was in finance. When the debates over organization and chairmanship exhausted the money provided by the SPD, a committee was formed to raise more funds. A Bolshevik and a Menshevik, joined by two neutrals (Gorki and Angelica) set to the task, and concluded that the best possibility was to borrow from the rich liberals who were literary and journalistic "fellow travelers" of the Russian party. They finally got enough money to continue the congress by borrowing from a wealthy industrialist and patron of the arts, Mr. Fels of Fels-Naptha soap fame. He was a vociferous sympathizer with the victims of the Russian revolution, and loaned the sum with no security beyond the signatures of the more famous revolutionaries. There was even a dinner in their honor at his home and a tour of his collection of paintings. In front of one masterpiece Gorki exclaimed, in Russian, "How terrible!" Mr. Fels turned to Plekhanov for a translation, and Angelica felt a panic about the future of the loan. But Plekhanov was a true Menshevik, willing to compromise a little to save the day. "Comrade Gorki has merely exclaimed, 'How remarkable!' " he assured the host.

What Angelica could not understand in Russian socialism was the absolute dedication bred by underground activity, arrests, Siberia, and exile. Lenin, Trotsky, Zinoviev, even Plekhanov and Martov, were men who knew what it was like to flee the police and who were well acquainted with the terrors and the exaltation of revolution. The tough business of revolutionary politics was not an act of noblesse oblige for them, but a commitment totally lacking in charity or ethics. If they had once undergone a moral crisis in the formation of that commitment, they were by the time Angelica met them total revolutionaries. No acts were beyond them, and no sense of duty to the downtrodden could get in the way of their earnestness for the difficult and sometimes uncharitable aspects of revolution.

Angelica was not alone in her contempt for the Russians' factional squabbling. Throughout Western Europe, the socialists watched with amazement and disbelief as the Russians seemed forever bent on destroying whatever party organization they could build. Great effort was put into preventing the split of the Bolsheviks and Mensheviks, and into recementing the party after the split in 1903. The Germans had been willing to finance the London congress in the hope that a unified party would emerge. Their money was used instead to finance a week of bitter debate.

What grated most of all was that the Russians had met on the eve of what was to be the greatest display of socialist unity ever held, the sixth congress of the Second International in Stuttgart. To show off their own might, the SPD had gone all out in its preparations. Over one thousand delegates were invited, and the opening rally was attended by a crowd estimated at fifty thousand. With pride of membership, Angelica's memoirs compare this spectacular assemblage, which required Stuttgart's largest auditorium, to the last meeting of the First International, in a small café in The Hague in 1872. It is a remarkable contrast. The Hague was a squalid little "family" affair, the final "settlement" of Marx's dispute with Bakunin. Stuttgart, by contrast, was a magnificent display of unity and might, with slogans on the walls and a mass singing of socialist anthems by delegates from every European country, from Japan, India, the United States, and Latin America.

Angelica had come as an observer, but the linguistic difficulties of the debates soon had her involved as a translator in the various commissions and subcommittees. In the main debate over the proper attitude and action of socialist parties to the threat of war she remained only an observer, watching with joy as a series of compromises produced a resolution which satisfied the demands of all parties. For the French it provided an acknowledgment of the imminence of war, for the Germans it carefully avoided committing any party to specific actions, and for Lenin and Rosa Luxemburg it provided a closing paragraph that called the parties and the workers to "strive with all their power . . . to rouse the people, and thereby to hasten the abolition of capitalist class war." This kind of successful hodgepodge compromise was, to Angelica, the spirit of internationalism: people from different situations working together to solve problems, not to intensify them by doctrinal pedantry and divisive loyalties.

In Stuttgart she met the greats of international socialism—figures who were to be added to the collection of icons. Jean Jaurès spoke often in the debates, and Angelica joined the many who had been overwhelmed by the eloquence and power of his rhetoric. Up to and long after his assassination in 1914, Angelica kept a small picture of him on a table in her room. It served to remind her of what she admired in him: "The attitude of Jaurès was not abstract, and therefore his speeches . . . seemed like prophecies as well as exhortations."

In Stuttgart she also met Karl Liebknecht, then already an outsider in the SPD. Angelica, who did not know the SPD well, thought he was "the most popular of the younger German Socialists and a leader of the party's left wing." It may have been her memory playing tricks with her, or simply that she was very taken with the fact that she was chosen to serve on the Youth International that Liebknecht had proposed.

Bebel was there, of course, and Angelica was again impressed by the power and stature of this shadow emperor. With affection and admiration she remembered the time that he discovered that she was riding on the same train as he. Although he was entitled as a Reichstag deputy to travel free first-class, he insisted on joining Angelica in second-class. She was equally impressed by Victor Adler, the leader of the Austrian social democrats, who had given up a comfortable bourgeois life to work in the socialist movement. Though not a professorial and donnish figure like Kautsky, Adler was a man of extraordinarily broad learning and culture. He often slipped out of what he considered unimportant meetings to attend a Beethoven or Mahler concert, and on the wall of his living room he had hung a portrait of Eleanora Duse. To Angelica he was proof of the compatibility of socialism and culture.

With leaders like Bebel and Jaurès, Adler and Luxemburg, and with the ability to compromise and act that Stuttgart had proved, Angelica trusted completely in the International. More even than the Italian Socialist Party, the International was the world in which she belonged, surrounded by those who shared her ideals and respected the goals for which she worked. Over the next years she attended more of the congresses, and in 1912, when the International met in Basel to discuss the threat of war that had arisen in Tripoli and the Balkans, she was one of the Italian delegates. The only item on the agenda was the war threat, and the congress was intended more as a demonstration of socialist readiness than a session for deliberation.

The various speakers all declared their implacable opposition to war. After Angelica's translations into French, German, Italian, and English, the entire audience, "including the press representatives and the visitors, arose from their chairs and cheered," recalled Angelica. "It was not until Bebel stepped forward and embraced me that I realized that the applause was for me."

"Comrade Balabanoff," he said, "in hearing you I felt that I was listening to and seeing a living incarnation of the International."

It was an important moment in Angelica's life. Like everyone else at the congress, she was so elated at the spirit of defiance, so convinced by the demonstration of socialist might, that she truly believed slogans and speeches and resolutions could keep Europe out of a world war.

VI

Although she continued to live in Switzerland, after 1905 Angelica's activities had become directed more and more to Italian affairs. She spoke more often in Italy than in Switzerland, and became closely involved in the affairs of the Italian party. It was only a matter of time before her path crossed again with the ascending star of Italian socialism, Benito Mussolini.

After expulsion from Switzerland, Mussolini had taken advantage of an amnesty declared on the birth of a royal heir to join the army. He served for a year, then returned to his previous career of teaching and debauchery. After attending a course in French at Bologna he obtained a teaching post that paid well enough to enable him to devote himself to writing for various papers and journals. What his articles lacked in intellectual rigor they made up in venomous anticlerical and antimonarchical rhetoric. Though more often than not pseudonymous or anonymous, these articles soon brought Mussolini into conflict with local authorities. The resultant notoriety earned him an appointment as a full-time publicist for the socialist organization of the Italian population in the Austrian Trentino. In Trent he became the editor of a four-page weekly, *L'Avvenire del Lavoratore*. With his own paper there was no limit to his rhetoric. He called the Vatican a gang of robbers, branded priests as rabid dogs, and only occasionally introduced propaganda for international socialism into his tirades. In six months his journalism and speeches earned him several short terms in jail, sufficient fines to exhaust the treasury of the local socialist group, and a deportation back to Italy. He left behind two mistresses, each with a child.

By the time he left Trent, Mussolini was infamous. The socialists in Forlì, in the heart of that revolutionary area of the Romagna where Mussolini had grown up, invited him to become their secretary. He founded a new weekly journal, *La Lotta di Classe,* which he used to continue his attacks on the Church and the monarchy, and to denounce the members of the reformist wing of the socialist party as cowards. Mussolini had already begun to identify himself with the party's extreme left wing, which, in Romagna, hovered between Marxist socialism and the anarchism so endemic to the area. His motto was "Provided we fight." When there was no possibility of fighting the state, Mussolini thought it useful for the socialists to fight one another, since to do so was to "strengthen our muscles and prepare our minds." He introduced resolutions calling for the expulsion of all party members who practiced religion, and devoted columns of his journal to praise for various arsonists, assassins, and bomb-throwers.

In 1911, when the Italian government declared war on Turkey and launched its colonial expedition to Libya, Mussolini took a leading part in the antiwar campaign. It is one facet of his life that he does not mention in his autobiography, but at Forlì he made a fiery speech urging the crowd to declare a general strike, erect barricades, destroy the rail lines to prevent the transport of war materiel, and to organize active resistance to the government. Riots followed the speech, and the authorities, having taken notice of his eloquence, arrested Mussolini, tried him on eight different charges, and sentenced him to twelve months' imprisonment. On appeal the sentence was later reduced to five months.

His war protest was of little more than local significance, but the publicity of his trial and the appeal proceedings in Bologna brought him recognition in the Italian Socialist Party. At the party congress in 1912, Mussolini was fresh out of prison and a hero to the congress, which elected him to the party's executive committee.

Another new member of the executive committee was Angelica Balabanoff. While Mussolini claimed the credit for splitting the party and reducing the right wing to powerlessness, to Angelica fell the task of explaining the schism to the public, lest the bourgeois press impugn the party moves as a reflection of personal motives. Her speech was a masterpiece of party loyalty:

> Only a party like ours, which is rooted in a mass movement, whose future is intimately linked to the fate of the masses, can expel from its midst men like these whom we are going to part with today and who may be followed by others—men whom other parties would be honored to have in their ranks. But such is the fate of those who join a movement like ours. When the masses disapprove of us we have to go. Maybe such will be the fate of those of us who expel you today, or perhaps life will be merciful enough to spare us.

The speech was received as soothing rhetoric. Few realized how prophetic it would be.

One of the first acts of the new executive committee was to appoint a new editor for *Avanti,* the party's weekly newspaper. The secretary of the party, Lazzari, nominated Mussolini, dismissing his youth (he was twenty-seven) with the explanation that the executive was responsible for the paper, and it was not too important who actually functioned as the editor in Milan. Mussolini accepted, with one condition: Angelica was to be coeditor.

The newspaper was a formidable responsibility. *Avanti* was one of the largest socialist newspapers in Europe, comparable to *Vorwärts* in Berlin or *l'Humanité* in Paris. Although published in Milan, it was read by workers throughout the industrial towns in Italy, where it assumed the function that the party organization filled in countries with more structured socialist parties. In editorials and reportage it brought the wider world of socialism to the Italian working class, and at the same time provided an antidote to the clerical and monarchical bent of the Church-dominated education that most workers had received.

When Mussolini and Angelica moved to Milan, they lived a few houses apart on the same street. Mussolini had by this time "married" Rachele Guidi, without benefit of ceremony or license. On the few occasions that he introduced her, she was simply "Comrade Rachele." Her role was to bear with his infidelities and his incredible moodiness, a role which she silently filled to the end. It fell to others, especially Angelica, to be Mussolini's companions and confidants.

In *Avanti* Mussolini was all bravado, stretching the paper's editorial policy to fit his charged demands for revolutionary preparations among the working classes. It is difficult to determine the authorship of editorials, since the party executive often intervened to tone down the language of Mussolini's exhortations. At the same time, it is probably true that, as Angelica reports, Mussolini left the unpleasant chores to her. The unpopular stands, the speeches to hostile crowds, the responses to angry readership—these were tasks that Mussolini felt suitable for his coeditor. Even the dismissal of employees was her responsibility. She never refused him, because, as she put it, "the interests of the Party required it."

Their relationship was quick to return to its old terms. Angelica was the person to whom Mussolini would confide his fears and weaknesses; the escape valve allowed him to maintain a public image as the implacable revolutionary. In public he often contradicted himself, and even in *Avanti* his articles lacked both logic and facts. But with a large crowd he was at his best. As long as he had the distance of the newspaper or the stadium between him and his audience, Mussolini was a convincing propagandist—a man who seemed to know his mind and who demonstrated the kind of energy that could overthrow a government.

Angelica still believed in Mussolini. He was lacking in common sense, and even more lacking in a political education, but Angelica saw in him a devotion to the cause, a fanatic industry, and a fiery temperament that could be the making of a real revolutionary. Although much of the credit for his editorship belongs to her, she was willing at the time to remain on the sidelines, compensating for his excesses and supplying the material that he called his own. It was enough for her to be a part of the movement; she seems to have visualized no role for herself beyond the support of a man who seemed destined for power.

For three years they worked together. Mussolini would write the editorials and reserve himself for an endless series of speaking tours; Angelica was left with the editing of the paper and those distasteful duties which Mussolini rejected. When friends of his asked him to identify a corpse, he deferred to her because the task was odious to him. When political opponents came to the offices of *Avanti* to protest editorials, he would slip out, leaving her to confront them.

The period, especially 1913 and 1914, was marked by incessant civil strife in Italy. The development of Italian industry had been accelerated since the turn of the century, but manufacturers were still up against the stiff competition of English, German, French, and American goods. To meet the competition they held down wages, refusing to sacrifice profits to improved working conditions. At the same time, the growth of industry brought together large numbers of workers and an expanding working-class organization. The result was pitched battle between bosses and workers in a series of strikes and lockouts. Troops or police were often called in, and bloodshed was common.

Mussolini enthusiastically supported every uprising, urging the workers to convert the strikes into revolution. What his exhortations lacked in theory they made up in fiery enthusiasm; and in the opinion of many Italian socialists he was the spirit of the party.

The peak of his rise to socialist power came in the week of June 7, 1914. A nationwide demonstration had been called on behalf of a soldier, Masetti, who to the cry "Long live Anarchy" had shot and wounded his colonel during the Tripolitan War. Before the rally, the various labor groups had agreed that if there were any acts of repression on the part of the police, a general strike would be called.

The protests were calm in Milan, but in Ancona three demonstrators were killed by the police. Mussolini immediately devoted a whole issue of *Avanti* to the "proletarian massacres" and "premeditated assassination." In response, a general strike was launched, with substantial success, throughout Italy. There were riotous demonstrations in Rome, replete with barricades. In some communities local leaders declared republics, the red flag was hoisted, taxes were "abolished," prices were reduced by decree, churches were attacked, railways and telegraph lines were sabotaged, villas were looted, troops disarmed, even a general captured. Mussolini was in his element, surveying the scene "with something of the legitimate joy with which the craftsman contemplates his creation."

Red Week, as it came to be known, ended after seven days, when the Confederation of Labor called off the general strike. To Angelica the week of almost revolutionary fervor had proved the vitality and readiness of the masses, and the ability of the leadership to call off the strike had proved the effectiveness of the relationship between the leadership and the masses. Mussolini drew different conclusions. The revolution had not come, he noted, and the reason was "the act of treason" of the leaders. Only he was without blame, for his support had been steadfast. It was the beginning of a subtle campaign by Mussolini to separate himself from the other leaders of the Italian left. No one, not even Angelica, noticed.

Through the summer of 1914, Italy continued to await revolution. The climate of expectation, coupled with steamy weather, compounded the widespread tension. It was not until Austria and Serbia were shelling one another that the Italians emerged from their introspection to realize that the world war might include them.

Ostensibly, the Triple Alliance bound Italy to the side of Austria and Germany, although neither the Italians nor their Germanic allies expected Italy to honor the alliance. In the short life of the Italian nation, the finesse of treaty obligations had become a steady habit. Still, while the diplomats worked on interpreting and reinterpreting the clauses of the Triple Alliance (and other diplomats went to London and Paris to hear the counterproposals), Italians added the worry of war to their woes.

VII

Even the socialists took time off from the thoughts of revolution to ponder the problem of war. A grand congress to celebrate the twenty-fifth anniversary of the Second International was scheduled for August 1914 in Vienna. When war threatened to interrupt the congress, the various leaders of the International called an emergency meeting in Brussels, the seat of the bureau of the International.

Twenty socialist leaders gathered there on July 28, five days after Austria's ultimatum to Serbia. The climate outside was gloomy and rainy. Inside it was worse.

Victor Adler, representing Austria, said that the party could do nothing to stop the war. It was not the news the others wanted to hear, but he spoke with such logic and poise that no one dared challenge him. The Germans and the French made hopeful speeches, but no one seemed to know exactly what to do. When war had been "prepared for" in previous congresses, its possibility had always been remote. The socialists had remained smug behind their glorious resolutions and the massive solidarity of their meetings. Now there were but twenty of them to represent the millions of workers of Europe. Suddenly the glorious resolutions and the massive solidarity meant nothing.

Angelica took the floor to remind the meeting that earlier international gatherings had considered the general strike a primary means of averting war. With the experience of Red Week, it was an obvious suggestion. Adler and Jules Guesde of the French party looked at her as if she were crazy. It would be utopian and dangerous, said Adler. Guesde took the position that a wartime strike would imperil the socialist movement. "The slogan of the general strike would be effective only in countries where socialism is strongest, and thus the military victory of the backward nations over the progressive ones would be facilitated." Already, nationalism was rearing its ugly head among the socialists.

The other delegates present paid no attention at all to Angelica's reminder. As a recommendation for specific action the group decided to intensify antiwar demonstrations. Their only other act was to advance the date of the twenty-fifth anniversary congress and change its site to Paris.

That evening Jaurès spoke in the Cirque Royal. With the hall and the streets all around completely packed with workers, he delivered another of his passionate pleas against war. "Jaurès himself was quivering, so intense was his emotion, his apprehension, his eagerness to avert somehow the coming conflict," wrote Angelica. When the speech ended, the entire city seemed to shake with the applause and the reverberating cries of "Down with war; long live peace!" and "Long live International Socialism!"

But the speeches, the shouts, and the fervor were too late. When Angelica left Antwerp the following day, it was on the last regular train leaving Belgium. In the morning, while she ate breakfast in Basel, she heard that the German socialists were depositing their money in Switzerland for safekeeping, an admission that they expected war. The next day she heard that Jaurès had been assassinated in Paris by a deranged nationalist. The last clear voice against the war was silenced.

While the executive committee of the International was meeting in Brussels, the Italian Socialist Party had issued a manifesto against the war: "You, proletarians of Italy, who in the painful period of crises and unemployment have given proof of your class consciousness, of your spirit of sacrifice, must now be ready to prevent Italy from being dragged down into the abyss of this terrible adventure." Mussolini had been one of the signatories.

As soon as Angelica returned to Italy, a meeting was called in Milan, with representatives of all Italian working-class organizations summoned to reaffirm the resolute antiwar stand of the Italian left. Even groups who had been mutual enemies in the domestic in-fighting responded to the call. A resolution introduced by Angelica, declaring that war on either side was "incompatible" with the goals of the working classes, was passed unanimously. Mussolini had privately told Angelica that he was in favor of the stand of absolute neutrality, but he left the meeting early, in the midst of the discussion, and failed to vote.

On the question of neutrality, the Italian left was, for a change, not alone. All but a tiny minority of Italians were opposed to entry into the war. That tiny minority was the nationalists, who for years had preached the glories of

185

combat; they were convinced that Germany would win the war, and saw the Triple Alliance as a bulwark of monarchy against the republicanism of France. For most of Italy, the war in Libya, fought at great cost and for little gain, had been enough.

Yet a terrible fact stared in the face of the Italian left. On August 4 the German Social Democrats had voted to finance the war. On August 5 the Austrian socialists announced that if their parliament had been in session they too would have supported the war. The Austrian declaration had been printed in the socialist press under the banner headline, "The German People's Historic Day." With the most powerful socialist parties backing the war, it became very difficult for the Italian socialists to repeat the old slogans about the international solidarity of the workers. No information at all about the antiwar stands of Rosa Luxemburg, Karl Liebknecht, or Friedrich Adler reached Italy, and to the Italian working class it looked as though the Germans and the Austrians had decided to postpone the struggle against capitalism in favor of a struggle for nationalism.

Bissolati, a former leader of the reformist wing of the Italian socialists who had been expelled from the party, wrote in a democratic paper that the Socialist International, being based upon reciprocity, no longer existed. Since the German social democracy had collapsed, he argued, international socialism had collapsed, and it was the duty of all true socialists to carry on the struggle for socialism, which meant to support the war on the side of the allies.

Bissolati was not alone in his stand. Angelica received a letter from Plekhanov, early in the war, asking her to visit Geneva. When she arrived, he asked, "What is your and your party's attitude toward the war?"

The question amazed her. Surely Plekhanov, the great theoretician, would know that the answer was implicit in the very theory of Marxism.

"We will do our utmost to prevent Italy from entering the war and to end the war as soon as possible," she answered. "As far as I am concerned, I shall naturally do all in my power to assist the Party."

Plekhanov was visibly angered by her reply. "So you would prevent Italy from entering the war. How about Belgium? Where is your love for Russia?"

"What do you mean—my love for Russia? Must my attitude toward war change because Russia is involved? Would other imperialist governments not act as Germany had done in Belgium if it were necessary to gain their ends? Wasn't it you who taught me the real causes of war? Didn't you warn us that this slaughter was being prepared and that we must oppose it?"

"So far as I am concerned," Plekhanov answered, "if I were not old and sick I would join the army. To bayonet your German comrades would give me great pleasure."

"*My* German comrades! Are they not yours as well? Who, if not you, taught us to understand and appreciate German philosophy, German so-cialism—Hegel, Marx, Engels?''

Angelica left Geneva that night. When she got back to Milan, she re-moved one of the icons from her little table.

In Italy too the interventionists gradually picked up supporters. Republi-cans, freemasons, and democrats urged alliance with France, the country of the Rights of Man. Volunteers, raising the slogans of the days of Garibaldi and Mazzini, rushed off to enlist in France. The interventionists discovered powerful arguments that could be made against neutrality. To remain out of the war put Italy in a no-win situation. If Germany and Austria won, Italy would be subjugated as the errant and unfaithful ally. If the Entente won, Italy would never get a chance at the eventual distribution of prizes in the Adriatic and the Mediterranean. France and England, with their shared spoils, would surround Italy and cut off her future access to Africa. Finally, there were the Italian feelings of inferiority as a new nation. They were a great power *manqué,* and many felt that only by being on the victorious side in the world war could Italy ever take her place among the nations.

The socialists led the defense against the interventionists, with Mussolini, as usual, in the vanguard. Throughout July he had preached in his editorials that if the government declared war, he would declare revolution: ''We can assure you that if Italy mobilizes her army and commands it to march to the direct or indirect support of the Germans against the French, that very day there will be no need of any effort on our part to make the Italian people revolt. The insurrection would be unanimous and terrible.'' His readers could remember Red Week, and that alone made his threats vivid. Whoever supported the war or failed to accept the party slogans was a ''traitor'' or a ''renegade.''

Conservative papers attacked the socialists, though with little effect. Then, in the early fall, a conservative paper in Bologna, *Il Resto del Car-lino,* published a statement implying that a member of the socialist party ex-ecutive had said: ''Don't be afraid of the socialists; you can be certain that when the government decides to support the Allies, the socialists will as-sent.''

Mussolini denied that he was the member alluded to, and most of the ex-ecutive believed him. A special meeting was called to discuss the issue. Mussolini and Angelica traveled in the same train compartment, and throughout the journey Mussolini spoke of the attacks that had been made on Angelica.

''Don't concern yourself about them,'' he said. ''Our adversaries are capable of anything.''

Just then another member of the executive entered the compartment. Ig-noring Mussolini, he said to Angelica:

''Have you read this morning's *Avanti?''*

187

"Not yet."

"And Mussolini has not spoken about his article?"

Angelica took the paper and read for herself. In an editorial Mussolini advocated the change "from absolute to active neutrality," attributing the change in attitude to the party. It was an open declaration of sympathy for the Entente.

Angelica finished the article and said to Mussolini: "The man who wrote this has no place in the Socialist Party. He belongs at the front or in a madhouse."

"The whole executive will approve and follow my lead," he answered.

Mussolini sat in silence through the meeting of the executive session.

The outcome was a foregone conclusion. Mussolini was deprived of the editorship of *Avanti* and his seat on the executive committee.

"Comrades," Angelica said, "before we part I should like to have a temporary allowance made for Mussolini. Until he finds something else to do, we should provide for his family." After ten years Angelica still remembered him as the desolate and dissolute vagabond.

Mussolini finally spoke. "I don't want your allowance. I'll find work as a stonemason. Five francs a day are enough for me. Of one thing you may be sure. I shall never speak or write a word against the Party. I would rather break my pen and cut out my own tongue. Whatever action you take, I shall remain true to socialism. You may deprive me of my membership card but you will never be able to tear socialism out of my heart—it is too deeply rooted."

In Milan, Mussolini was summoned before the socialist branch to which he belonged. There he maintained that the executive committee had never given him a fair hearing: "Even a bourgeois tribunal gives the accused a chance to defend himself." "You persecute me because you love me," he shouted.

The audience was so noisy that the chairman had to call the meeting to order repeatedly. Mussolini tried one of his rhetorical ploys:

"If you proclaim that I am unworthy—" he began.

The crowd shouted "Yes!" from all sides. He left the hall in a rage.

On November 15 Mussolini launched his own newspaper, *Il Popolo d'Italia*. Under the masthead were two slogans, from Blanqui and Napoleon: "He who has steel has bread" and "The Revolution is an idea that has found bayonets."

On November 24, he was formally expelled from the Socialist Party. A subsequent issue of his newspaper carried a cartoon of a man trampling on a red banner, the beginning of his campaign against the socialists, who now received his customary vilifying labels of "coward" and "traitor." From "Revolution if War," his slogan became "Revolution if No War."

Mussolini's conversion, or as the socialists would have it, his betrayal, was a surprise to most Italians. In July he had been the most fervent advocate of neutrality; in November he was the most vociferous sword-rattler. Charges and countercharges of his being "bought" by the Allies circulated freely, and in the 1920s a number of accounts of his receiving French funds were published. These probably were decisive for Mussolini, not for any personal use, but because they enabled him to run his own newspaper, free from any restraints of an executive committee. Mussolini was happiest as a fighter. Once neutralism had been accepted as government policy it was respectable. There was little joy in preaching it, and no path to power in advocating it.

With Mussolini now as fervent in support of intervention as he had once been against it, the face of Italian politics changed. His following as the editor of *Avanti* had been in many respects a personal following; many of his former readers now shifted to *Il Popolo d'Italia,* and their opinions from neutralism to intervention. By the end of 1914 the government too was flirting with intervention. Sidney Sonnino, who became Foreign Minister in November, was holding an open auction between the Entente and the Austrians, promising Italian loyalties and arms to the highest bidder. The pressure of Mussolini and his following for war on the side of the Entente prejudiced the acceptance of bids to the point where the continued negotiations with Austria were only a means for extorting the highest possible offers of postwar spoils from the English and the French.

Italy's slide toward war left the socialists once again a beleagured minority, fighting a rear-guard action in what, by the spring of 1915, had become a hopeless cause. They had lost much of their mass support, suffered the loss of their propaganda leader, were vilified in the press (especially by Mussolini), and found themselves with no dynamic leadership. As Italy drew closer to a declaration of war against Austria and Germany, the socialists found that their newspaper appeals and their rallies were censored; they were viewed by many as potential traitors and saboteurs.

No one was more disillusioned by the spring of 1915 than Angelica Balabanoff. The great figures in whom she had put her trust had all either betrayed her or were dead. Plekhanov, whose writings had introduced her to Marxism, was supporting the war. The German and Austrian social democrats, who had formed the shock troops of international socialism, were doing likewise. Mussolini, upon whom she had placed so much hope, whom she had nurtured as a potential leader of socialism, had betrayed her and the party to support the war. Jaurès, the one voice which had spoken to the end against the war, was dead, as was Bebel, the great leader of the masses. The others—Victor Adler, Rosa Luxemburg, Karl Kautsky, Eduard Bernstein, Paul Singer—were silent.

No one, it seemed, saw the question in the simple we/they terms of her socialism. It was no longer socialists vs. capitalists and "Down with Imperi-

189

alist Wars!,'' no longer international socialism vs. nationalist states, no longer workers against oppressive bosses, the downtrodden against the privileged. The war had turned the world topsy-turvy. Comrades had become enemies, enemies were supposed to be allies, and the one organization in which she had placed her faith—the International—was no more.

Angelica was determined to remained loyal—but to whom, to what?

VIII

Shortly after hostilities broke out, in September 1914, the Swiss and Italian Socialist Parties sent representatives to a meeting in Lugano. They were a powerless group, but since two countries were represented, it was at least an international effort. Angelica helped to draft their pitiful resolution, condemning the war as "the result of the imperialist policy of the Great Powers," and calling upon socialists everywhere "to uphold the old principles of the International of the proletariat," and to put pressures on their governments "with a view toward a speedy close of this mass murder of the European people." It was a frail gesture, but for Angelica and the other socialists who still believed in the International, it was a first step.

The Italians and the Swiss also attempted to organize an international conference, but the obstacles introduced by various socialist parties now competing to see who could be more loyal to their respective war efforts proved more than the efforts of the neutral states could overcome.

Since the men seemed determined on war, in December 1914 the women of the socialist movement took the situation in their own hands. As early as November, Krupskaya, Lenin's wife, had broached the idea of a conference of women. In December, Clara Zetkin took up the idea, issuing an appeal to socialist women to meet and inaugurate a struggle for peace. Despite her reservations about women's movements, Angelica joined the effort, and helped to convene an International Socialist Women's Conference at Bern in March 1915. Delegates came from Germany, France, England, Holland, Switzerland, Italy, Russia, Poland, and Hungary—the first time that socialists from opposing belligerent nations met at the same congress. They had two tasks: to publicize the fact that in spite of the vetoes of governments and the opposition of "loyal" labor leaders, representatives of the old International had met together; and to formulate slogans and propaganda for a women's struggle against the war. Their leaflet began:

> Where are your husbands, your brothers, your sons? Why must they destroy one another and all that they have created? Who benefits by this bloody nightmare? Only a minority of war profiteers. . . . Since the men cannot speak, you must. Workingwomen of the warring countries, unite!

190

The leaflet had small distribution and less effect, but the conference itself was a moral victory, and paved the way for future meetings. A month later an International Conference of Socialist Youth assembled at Bern, again at the urging of the Italian and Swiss parties, and with Angelica as coordinator.

To Angelica, the importance of both conferences lay in the impression of international unity that they conveyed to the world. "The absence of one signature on our manifesto—an absence which would be exploited by the nationalist press—would be sufficient to convince the general public that 'the Internationalists cannot agree among themselves.' " Yet even in the face of the situation, at both conferences Angelica discovered that the Bolshevik delegates insisted upon the introduction of resolutions which were "irrelevant to the specific purpose of our meeting and which the majority could not sign." To secure the Bolshevik signatures, Angelica had to negotiate complex compromises, delaying the proceedings and revealing that the unity which the congresses were supposed to demonstrate was at best a rather elusive quantity.

Lenin was living in Switzerland at the time, where Bolshevik delegates to the conferences could confer with him frequently on the tactics of introducing and pressing their resolutions. During the youth conference, Angelica met him in a restaurant.

"Vladimir Ilyitch," she asked, "did you come here for tea or for the resolution?"

He answered with an annoyed glance, incredulous that she could joke about what he considered a deadly serious matter. Resolutions and tactics were a matter of utmost concern to Lenin. Even for a clandestine conference of thirteen delegates, he could put hours into the wording of a single sentence, or nights into the forging of a delicate compromise. When he realized that he could not convert other delegates to his position, he would spend days polemicizing his viewpoints. His arguments might not carry, but with history as a witness, it was important to Lenin that the correct theoretical stands be articulated, explained, and defended.

His attitude and behavior was incomprehensible to Angelica. "I was particularly surprised to find him behaving in such a fashion during the war, when the general tragedy was so overwhelming and our movement so weakened that the purely theoretical decisions of an insignificant minority of intellectuals seemed of so little importance." It was inconceivable to her that a vote or resolution could matter when the very International was at stake. How could anyone let petty bickerings get in the way of resolutions against the single and overwhelming enemy? Before the war a certain leeway for disputes was possible; now, the lines were so clear, the positions of right and wrong so obvious, that any deviation from the lines of battle was a blow against socialism.

What Lenin understood, and what Angelica failed to grasp, was that the Second International was moribund. Even at the height of its power and prestige, at the Basel Congress of 1912, the International was constitutionally and institutionally incapable of exercising authority. It was a loose international federation, and like the League of Nations and the United Nations later, it suffered from the fact that its constituent members could not or would not surrender their sovereignty to a central or collective body. Even as the various parties formulated resolutions proclaiming their faith in internationalism and their comradely solidarity, each was careful to guard its own interests by maintaining complete autonomy. Parties were frequently condemned or praised for various actions, but the only sanctions of their activities were weak resolutions. The occasional instances of voluntary compliance with these resolutions produced the aura of internationalism that the International stressed in its propaganda. The many instances when the stronger parties refused to obey the resolutions were rationalized by the argument that the strength of a party could not be risked in a foolhardy gesture. Most of the resolutions were calls for revolution or promises of action in the circumstance of imperialist exploits or war, but with no executive authority to enforce these resolutions they carried no more weight than the paper and ink of the thousands of copies that were printed.

The only "executive" in the International was the International Bureau, in Brussels. It was no more than an administrative clearing house, great at shuffling papers, but lacking the power even to call a meeting. The parties, especially the stronger parties, insisted upon this arrangement.

Thus the only real weapon of the International was its ability to coordinate international demonstrations and protests, which, if powerful enough, carried the hidden and persuasive threat of revolution. This was the weapon that the International had hoped to use at the start of the war, but the demonstrations of the summer of 1914 were dwarfed by the waves of jingoism and chauvinism that accompanied the mobilizations and declarations of war. When larger crowds would take to the streets to clamor for war, the socialists everywhere found that there was nothing to bind them to the International any longer. Their members were in the pro-war demonstrations. Could they risk losing their membership by proclaiming loyalty to the International? To do so was to be branded as traitors at home, and nowhere was treason a popular cause in the summer of 1914.

Although he was shocked by the German Social Democrats' support of the war, Lenin concluded early that the Second International had collapsed. The workers had been betrayed by the opportunism of their leaders. It was the duty of true Social Democrats to expose the opportunism of the sham "socialists," to build a new international free from the debilitating weaknesses of the old, and to turn the weapons of war that were being spent by worker against worker into a revolutionary struggle of worker against the bourgeoisie. What he wanted, and what he elaborated in his *Theses on the War*, was only what the old International had already agreed to—the final clauses that he and Rosa Luxemburg had worked into the 1907 resolution on war: "Should war break out in spite of all this, it is their [the parties'] duty to intercede for its speedy end, and to strive with all their power to make use of the violent economic and political crises brought about by the war to rouse the people, and thereby to hasten the abolition of capitalist class rule."

In November 1914, Lenin intoned the death of the Second International in the first number of the revived journal of the Russian social democrats: "Overwhelmed by opportunism, the Second International has died. . . . Long live the Third International. The task of the Third International is that of organizing the forces of the proletariat for a revolutionary onslaught on the capitalist governments, for civil war against the bourgeoisie of all countries, for political power, for the victory of socialism." At the conferences of women and youth, he had pressed for resolutions calling for an immediate organizational break with the majority parties of the old International and the formation of a new International.

His resolutions were rejected because many former internationalists thought his obituary premature. The Bureau of the International had moved from Brussels to The Hague, appointing a number of Dutchmen to the staff to preserve its neutrality in the war. As long as the Bureau existed, representatives of many of the parties waited for it to spring into action, hoping somehow to avoid a split in ranks of socialism that could be exploited by the nationalist press. They waited in vain.

By the summer of 1915, it became obvious that the International would not act. "So long as German soldiers are in Belgium, no talk of peace is possible," said Émile Vandervelde, a leader of Belgian socialism and the chairman of the International.

To fill the vacuum of internationalism, the Italian Socialist Party decided, on its own initiative, to take steps to revive the International. In the spring of 1915, before Italy entered the war, the party sent secret invitations to socialist factions in every country where there had been any indication of support for internationalism and opposition to the war. Angelica was dispatched to Switzerland to supervise the preparations, and to obtain whatever material was available from the neutral center. She read extensively in the legal and underground press, and translated significant articles by Trotsky, Rosa Luxemburg, and others for *Avanti*.

Working with Robert Grimm, a Swiss journalist and socialist leader, she sent out invitations for a secret preliminary conference to determine who should be invited to a full-scale socialist conference. With careful preparation, she hoped, a split in the socialist movement could be avoided.

193

In fact, by this time, the socialist parties in almost every European country had already split, often into three distinct factions. The *majority* or right factions supported the war efforts of their respective homelands, using various rationalizations to explain the about-face to chauvinistic nationalism that they had taken. The Germans were defending the Fatherland against the threat of "Oriental despotism," the French and Belgians were defending themselves from the *Boche,* and so on. For some of the leaders, the position of support represented a sincere conviction. For many others, it was a response to the workers' jingoistic nationalism at the outbreak of the war. It was more important to maintain support of the workers than to follow the proper theory, they argued, despite the fact that the argument put them in the position of urging a bloodbath of workers fighting workers with little possibility of profit for the socialists no matter what the outcome. The majority socialists boycotted and campaigned against all international socialist conferences. To sit at a table with Germans, while German troops were on French soil, was "treason" in the minds of the French socialists. Their governments facilitated the boycott of conferences by refusing to issue visas and by censoring all publicity about antiwar or socialist-unity conferences.

As the quick victories promised by the governments failed to materialize, segments of mass support began to defect from the majority position. Most gravitated to the centrists, personified by Kautsky in Germany and later by Jean Longuet, Marx's grandson, in France. The centrists opposed the war, hoping that a quick end to hostilities would permit the socialists to get back to the essential business of preparing for revolution and exercising pressure for concrete reforms. Their position was pacifist, rather than revolutionary, and their demands were for a peace without annexations or reparations. The centrist slogans were versions of "peace at any price."

Finally, in a few countries, a revolutionary left emerged. Lenin in Russia and Rosa Luxemburg and Karl Liebknecht in Germany were the most prominent leaders. They hoped to convert the war into a revolution, using the arms, energy, and organization of the war effort against the ruling classes instead of for them. The viewpoint was a difficult one to impress upon the masses, partly because anyone advocating such a stand was generally either in prison or exile, and even more because workers and soldiers already exhausted and benumbed by war were scarcely a willing audience for the specter of suffering and exertion that revolution promised. By the sheer force of their ideas and the brilliance of their articulation these few leaders were able to gain some attention and publicity for their position. Lenin and Rosa Luxemburg had seen in Russia in 1905 how easily war could be transformed into a revolution; to them the world war offered the great opportunity for world revolution that Marxism promised. Of all the factions, the left was most anxious for internationalist conferences, both as a forum to denounce the majority and the Centrists, and as a means of publicizing their revolutionary ideas.

The first full-scale wartime conference of international socialism opened in September 1915, in the tiny Swiss town of Zimmerwald. Delegates from Germany, France, Italy, Russia, Poland, Hungary, Holland, Switzerland, Sweden, Norway, Rumania, and Bulgaria were present. But as Trotsky observed in his wry if grim jest, "half a century after the founding of the First International it was still possible to seat all the internationalists in four coaches." The great figures of the Second International—Adler, Kautsky, Bernstein, Vandervelde, Guesde, Plekhanov, Longuet, among others—were absent, either because as majority socialists they had opposed the gathering, or because, as in the case of the English delegates, they were unable to obtain passports. Those who attended all represented the Centrist and left positions of the socialist movement. Even without spokesmen for the majority position, there were enough disagreements to make the conference a constantly fiery debate. For Angelica and Robert Grimm, it was a full-time task to maintain a semblance of peace at this antiwar conference.

The declarations and resolutions were memorable. The French and German delegates issued a joint statement to the effect that "this war is not our war." The Germans further suggested that the immediate evacuation of German troops from Belgium be one of the demands. An almost unanimous statement condemned the war as imperialist on both sides, repudiated the voting of war credits, and called for a struggle against war and for socialism. The unanimity was rent by Lenin, who wanted a repudiation of the Second International, organization of a Third International, and a resolution calling for "civil war" within the warring nations. He had tried to pack the conference with delegates who shared his views, and he spent his time twisting arms, including an eight hour discussion with a French delegate. In the end he had to settle for a compromise.

The final manifesto, passed unanimously, was stirring: "The war makers lie when they assert that the war would liberate oppressed nations and serve democracy. In reality, they are burying the liberty of their own nations as well as the independence of other peoples. . . . To you, men and women of labor, to all those who suffer by and for war, we say: 'Above the frontiers, above the battlefields and devastated countries, Proletarians of the World, unite!' "

Despite the efforts of a newly appointed International Socialist Committee, consisting of Angelica, Robert Grimm, and representatives of the Italian and Swiss parties, the manifesto was only slowly publicized. It was published in Italy, Britain, and the neutral countries, but could be distributed only by clandestine channels in Germany, France, and Russia. The only full report on the conference was in *Avanti,* which took advantage of Italy's still lax wartime censorship to print Angelica's dispatches in full. Everywhere else governments were unwilling to permit publicity for revolutionary pacifists. The socialist press, controlled by the majority parties, dismissed the conference with contempt or silence.

The Zimmerwald conference polarized the socialist movement as much as the first votes for war credits had done. It did not precipitate an open break, but with representatives of the Centrists and left meeting and discussing the "treasons" of the majority socialist parties, and the majority parties at home in turn denouncing the "treason" of Frenchmen who would meet with Germans while German troops were on French soil, the bonds of international socialism had loosened considerably.

The underground news of Zimmerwald gradually helped to catalyze antiwar opposition in many of the belligerent countries, strengthening the campaigns of Rosa Luxemburg and Karl Liebknecht in Germany or Friedrich Adler in Austria. When a few parliamentary deputies began, in early 1916, to speak out against the war effort and the cost of the prolonged war, the International Socialist Committee lobbied among the various parliamentary delegations to try to get a uniform protest declaration introduced in several countries. Initially, only the parliamentary delegates of the Italian socialist party went along with the idea, introducing a version of the Zimmerwald manifesto in parliament and in municipal councils. To strengthen the movement among other parliaments, it was finally decided to call another international conference.

This time the anticipated opposition of various governments was so strong that Robert Grimm leaked fake information about a conference in The Hague, hoping to throw off the immigration authorities who might use news of the real conference to deny visas. The actual conference took place in the village of Kienthal, high in the Swiss Alps, in April 1916. Forty-three delegates came, including three from the French Chamber of Deputies. Again the conference was divided between the center and the left, with Angelica's problems of translating and interpreting complicated by the fact that the French deputies, while honored as the "pilgrims of Kienthal," were not Marxists and were not accustomed to the language and antics of an international conference. The serious Marxists were bored by the rather commonplace speeches of the deputies, and the deputies in turn were mystified by the erudition and jargon of the Marxists.

Her task was made even more difficult by the new attack that Lenin leveled against the old majority socialists, whom he now labeled "social chauvinists." Again, Lenin failed to persuade a plurality of the delegates to support his demand for a declaration in favor of a revolutionary civil war in the midst of world war. In the seven months that had elapsed since the Zimmerwald conference, many who had once believed in the Second International had grown progressively disillusioned. The old International had still done nothing, and Lenin's motion of censure of the old International because it had "completely failed" in its duty and had "become an accomplice in the policy of betraying principles, political truce, and so-called defense of the Fatherland," received strong endorsement. Even his initial draft resolution on civil war and the founding of a new international received twelve of the forty-three votes.

The split within the group was now so aggravated that wording a manifesto for the conference proved almost impossible. Angelica was up for over forty-eight hours drafting and redrafting the statement, incorporating mention of concrete measures to stop the slaughter demanded by the Leninist delegates, and deleting enough references to civil war and revolution to placate the more moderate delegates. After each introduction of a new draft, another debate would take place, and before a vote could be taken the various delegations would call for a recess to caucus. Even within these caucuses the arguments went on for hours. The final plenary session to vote on the manifesto was not held until three o'clock in the morning on May 1, 1916. Then, recalled Angelica, "something occurred which had probably never happened before at meetings of the Socialist parties. During the vote most of the delegates rose to speak so as to explain that it was only with certain reservations that they were able to accept the resolution."

A manifesto was finally passed, calling for immediate peace without annexations, and stressing that "Lasting peace can result only from victorious Socialism!" When the vote was completed, Angelica, though near exhaustion, suggested that the delegates await the sunrise of International Labor Day—the symbol of working-class unity. The gesture of waiting together, and the significance of the day, were more binding and more important to her than the acrimony of the debates and votes.

IX

Every Russian revolutionary in exile dreamed of the inevitable impossibility—a revolution in Russia. The dream was so real and so persistent that the reality, in March 1917, came as no surprise. News of the Tsar's abdication produced few celebrations among the exiles, and almost none of the outward displays of excitement and emotion of radicals of the West.

For Angelica, recovering from a severe case of influenza in Zurich, the March revolution presented more questions than answers: "What is to be done now? How can I take my place in the ranks of the revolution?" The other exiles in Switzerland were absorbed by the same thought: How could they get back into Russia and the revolution? Although Angelica had given only passing attention to Russian affairs in her twenty years of exile, a real revolution so overshadowed socialist activities in the West that there could be no choice of loyalties, no comparisons of importance.

The endless theoretical debates in coffee houses turned from the question of setting off the revolution to the question of sustaining it. Most sympathetic observers in the West, and many of the Russians, took the position that the only salvation for the Russian revolution was in simultaneous revolutions in the West. Rosa Luxemburg was of this view, and almost immediately after she received the news of the Russian revolution she began her efforts—from prison—to bring revolution to Germany. Revolutions on both sides of the trenches would mean peace, and peace would mean that revolutionaries everywhere could turn their energies from war to the vast task of social change.

But at least one voice in Switzerland took a different view. Angelica regularly attended the meetings of the various exile groups in Switzerland after the news of the revolution, and one evening she heard Lenin speak to a gathering of the Bolsheviks. One line of his talk stuck in her head: "Unless the Russian Revolution develops into a second and successful Paris Commune, reaction and war will suffocate it." He was arguing a position that almost no one else would have advocated: Russia could not wait for the West. To preserve its revolution, Russia would have to advance it—among soldiers, peasants, and workers. According to textbook Marxism, Russia was not ready for socialism, but Lenin was arguing that given the conditions of world war and with the indomitable energy and experience of the Russian people, the revolution could move to socialism even before the level of industrial development had reached the Marxist "take-off" point. Like so many of Lenin's views, it was prescient and brilliant, but so strange and unbelievable that few in his audience could subscribe. In March 1917, such an opinion remained the personal viewpoint of an infamous but relatively powerless intellectual in Zurich.

While the intellectuals argued the revolution, they diligently concocted plans for returning to Russia. The Zimmerwald group negotiated a scheme whereby the Russian government would exchange German prisoners of war in return for the exiles being permitted to cross German territory on their way to Russia. The Germans were willing, of course, since they had been assured that the return of the exiles would mean the end of the Russian war effort. Within four weeks of the Russian revolution, a train carrying Lenin and other Bolsheviks made its way across Germany to the Finland Station in Petrograd.

The journey had been arranged in what were to be "extraterritorial" trains. The restrictions on the journey—that no one leave the trains on German soil and no one speak with Germans when the train stopped en route—gave rise to the legend of sealed trains. Vast crowds gathered to see off the émigrés, including many of Angelica's colleagues in the Italian, Swiss, and Zimmerwald movements. She was going to Russia as the official representative of the Zimmerwald committee. Robert Grimm, who had departed for Stockholm ahead of the group to establish there a new base for Zimmerwald propaganda, planned to join them for a triumphant entrance into Russia.

Throughout the journey, the émigrés discussed the revolution. The entourage included Bolsheviks, Mensheviks, Social Revolutionaries, anarchists, and adherents of various splinter sects. Families, including children born in exile, were packed together on the third-class benches. Shortly before they crossed the border, a Georgian jumped off the train at a Finnish station to pick up a stick. Angelica attached a red scarf to the stick, and embroidered on it: "Long live Zimmerwald; Long live the Russian Revolution." That afternoon, carrying the homemade banner, Angelica entered "the revolutionary Holy Land."

To Angelica's amazement, the crowd at the station included one of her brothers. She had maintained almost no contact with her family since leaving Russia, except occasional visits with her eldest sister, who traveled to expensive resorts in Switzerland and Germany. Since the war, Angelica's modest stipend had been cut off, and to avoid embarrassing her family she refrained even from writing them during the war, as the receipt of letters from a Zimmerwald member could bring accusations of treason. She had not informed any member of her family of her return to Petrograd; they apparently picked up the information from the newspapers.

The brother had come to bring Angelica to their sister's home. Angelica was reluctant, concerned that it was simply not right for a revolutionary to accept gifts or hospitality from the wealthy—even relatives—when the hardships of the workers and soldiers were so evident everywhere. She finally agreed to spend a few days with her sister, before seeking housing of her own.

They had scarcely embraced when Angelica noticed her sister's agitation. Although they could not understand one another politically, Angelica had been close to her oldest sister; the difference in age had made Anna a surrogate mother, whose love had often filled the vacuum left by Angelica's break with her real mother. Suddenly, Anna showed her news clippings that labeled Angelica a Bolshevik.

"Are you really a Bolshevik?" she asked. "That means a fight against the new government as well as the old—more bloodshed, more persecutions. Even if you were a Menshevik or belonged to one of the other groups, it would not be so bad. But a Bolshevik—where will you go, how will you find shelter?"

Angelica was not a Bolshevik. Strictly speaking, she was not formally a member of any faction, although she generally concurred with the Bolshevik positions on the war and the revolution. She also sensed that the emotion in her sister's voice was motivated by fear as much as concern. "Bolshevik" had already become a synonym for "bandit," "murderer," and "German agent."

Knowing their break had to be decisive, Angelica answered, "Yes, I am a Bolshevik." The next day she moved in with her brother at his flat in the city.

Petrograd was in a state of chaos. Although Kerensky was trying to carry on the war, the army was collapsing from within, and the streets were filled with soldiers and peasants from the countryside who had come to the city to seek shelter and food. The railways were near breakdown. The large-scale expropriation of the apartments belonging to the wealthy which would provide housing after October had not yet begun, so lodgings were almost impossible to find for many of the returned exiles, including Angelica.

This was the period of the revolution that Trotsky has described as the era of "dual power." Officially the Provisional Government was trying to consolidate itself, hoping to placate the middle classes by checking revolutionary enthusiasm and slowing the pace of "experimentation." With little success, it tried to sustain the war effort. At the same time, the soviets were exercising authority in the cities, and shop committees had taken over in many of the factories. The soviets picked up Lenin's slogan of "Peace and Bread" and on their own issued the famous manifestos on "Peace Terms of the Russian People" and an "Appeal to the Socialists of All Countries." The Russian revolutionary movement had split completely, with the Mensheviks and a segment of the Social Revolutionaries supporting the Kerensky government, while the Bolsheviks and the left-wing of the Social Revolutionaries supported the soviets (except when the soviets defied the proffered leadership of the Bolsheviks). The smaller parties and groups divided, or if they could not position themselves, faced annihilation by alliance or inaction.

The precarious balance, with both the Provisional Government and the soviets exercising power, provided a perfect situation for Bolshevik propaganda and tactical activity, allowing them to plan and regroup forces, to prepare shock troops, and to campaign broadly against the war and in favor of the revolution. The Provisional Government, though anxious to stem the Bolshevik propaganda efforts, was relatively powerless, as it faced a full-time job in maintaining the war effort and a semblance of order.

Angelica's task was to coordinate the Zimmerwald propaganda with the Bolshevik efforts, using the Zimmerwald pipelines to funnel news about the Russian revolution to the West. Her chores were greatly complicated by the fact that the Bolsheviks were no more popular in the West, especially among the majority socialists, than the Zimmerwald movement had been. The governments of the Western European states did all they could to limit the dissemination of propaganda, and to discredit the Zimmerwald movement, the Bolsheviks, and the Russian revolutionaries in general.

Zimmerwald, and especially Angelica, also served the reverse function. Lenin and the Bolsheviks were of course anxious for reports of revolutionary activity in the West, and Zimmerwald, with its network of contacts, was a source of valuable information. The war made almost every means of communication unreliable, and only the clandestine messages exchanged with the Zimmerwald adherents gave Lenin and the Bolsheviks any news of the Spartacus movement in Germany or the other sporadic revolutionary movements.

What did receive considerable publicity in 1917 was the forthcoming peace conference in Stockholm that the Dutch and Scandinavian socialist parties were organizing. By this time, a number of majority socialist parties had begun to show interest in a peace conference, and several had received feelers from their governments indicating that the interest was shared in official circles. Particularly in countries where the war effort had begun to flag, such as Austria, the peace conference idea caught on as a forum for informal consultation on the possible terms of an armistice.

The Stockholm conference posed a dilemma for the Zimmerwald movement. On the one hand, it promised to be the largest international gathering since the beginning of the war, with representatives of the majority parties, Centrist groups, and the Left invited. For Zimmerwald to refuse such an invitation was, in effect, to turn its back on the internationalism it advocated, and to miss a splendid opportunity for propaganda and publicity.

On the other hand, Lenin denounced the Stockholm plans as a convention of "social chauvinists," urging that the left immediately break with those centrist elements planning to go to Stockholm. The time was ripe for a new Third International, he argued. "We ought to remain in Zimmerwald only to gather information." In Germany, the Spartacus group had joined Lenin's boycott of the Stockholm conference.

Thus if the Zimmerwald adherents attended the Stockholm conference they would lose the support of the Russians—the only party which had successfully participated in the wartime revolutions that Zimmerwald policy encouraged. If they remained allied with the Russians, they would have to forego the greatest propaganda and publicity opportunity the war had yet allowed, and they would surely lose their identification as the only representatives of true internationalism. The dilemma was one of the first signs of that trauma that the Russian revolution would mean for international socialism.

The Stockholm conference question was a special crisis for Angelica: She was being asked to choose between her loyalty to Russia and the revolution, and her loyalty to the international movement to which she had pledged herself. Her inclination was to uphold the boycott and maintain the doctrinal and moral integrity of Zimmerwald, but she argued that the small group of Zimmerwald representatives in Russia had no right to make the decision for the rest of the movement. The final compromise, which she supported, called for a special Zimmerwald conference in Stockholm, prior to the Dutch-Scandinavian conference. The main item of the Zimmerwald agenda would be whether to participate in the subsequent conference.

Long before plans for either conference were settled, rumors began to circulate in Russia that Robert Grimm was a German agent. Why else, it was asked, would the Germans have allowed him to cross their territory and travel to Russia? The same rumor had been floated about the returning exiles, but it was complicated in Grimm's case by the discovery of a telegram of his to the Swiss Foreign Minister, requesting a clarification of the German position on peace negotiations. At a meeting of the All-Russian Workers', Peasants', and Soldiers' Soviet, called to decide on the summer offensive, Kerensky was able to build support by shouting: "I call to your attention the fact that agents of the German government have been agitating in our midst for a separate peace—a separate peace!" As the campaign against Grimm gained momentum, other Zimmerwald members were also named as foreign agents. Angelica, the rumors claimed, was an Italian agent, sent to Russia to negotiate a separate peace between the Italian Socialist Party and representatives of the German government, who according to the gossip, were everywhere in Russia.

The Italian Socialist Party promptly denied the charges against Angelica, clearing her of the various allegations. Those against Grimm could not be so easily brushed aside. He had indeed sent the telegram, although it was an innocent effort to prepare for the various Stockholm conferences, and with that kind of concrete evidence being discussed in the press the Zimmerwald movement had to make a strenuous effort to clear its name. Finally, a special Zimmerwald investigating commission determined that the charges of his being a German agent were untrue, but conceded that he had acted without proper consultation and approval of the Zimmerwald members. His action had given the enemies of Zimmerwald an opportunity to label the whole movement an instrument of German imperialism. The commission concluded by disavowing his action and declaring that his usefulness to the movement was at an end.

The upshot was that Angelica had to take over the direction of the entire Zimmerwald movement. After only five weeks in the new socialist Promised Land, she had to leave for Stockholm, where the Zimmerwald Commission had been relocated. She and the other Zimmerwald representatives were already being pilloried by the press, as a new military offensive recaptured the minds of Russians wearied by war and revolution. In June she had come to Russia expecting a revolution in full swing. In July she left on a train on which the only conversations were of the offensive and the hopes for victory. "We must fight to the bitter end" was the slogan of the day that she heard on the train. "All the Germans, all the Internationalists, must be exterminated." "Have you heard the story about the German spy, Grimm, and the whole Zimmerwald crowd?" "What a shame! They should have been shot!"

X

Angelica had no sooner settled the Zimmerwald Commission in Stockholm when she was besieged from all sides by pressure groups. Representatives of the German center and the Russian soviets urged her to declare openly that Zimmerwald would support and attend the Stockholm conference. Karl Radek, Lenin's official representative, demanded she confirm that Zimmerwald would boycott the conference. She tried to stick by the earlier decision, that a preliminary Zimmerwald conference would decide on the question, but with constant postponements of both the big socialist conference and the Zimmerwald conference, the lobbyists had months for their unrelenting pressure tactics.

At the same time, the propaganda duties of the Zimmerwald Commission were made incredibly difficult by the fact that they had identified themselves with the Russian revolution and internationalism. Coupled with their appeals for an immediate peace were additional pleas designed to mobilize working-class opinion in support of the Russian revolution. Because they were not a harmless peace movement, but an international control center for revolutionary movements, the Zimmerwald members found that their task of distributing propaganda was constantly complicated by government spies and *agents provocateurs*. In every country they were either declared illegal or pressured against in the press; their manifestos were invariably censored, then denounced by every newspaper from the far right to the social-democratic left.

When the Zimmerwald conference finally met, at the beginning of September, it was a meeting of delegates who had trekked to Stockholm illegally. Their governments had denied them passports, and most had followed the underground railways into neutral Sweden. Since Stockholm was already a gathering place for spies, journalists, and pacifist tourists who had come for the social democratic congress scheduled later in the month, the Zimmerwald conference had to meet in the strictest secrecy—a situation which the Bolsheviks cherished. Five days of "rigidly conspiratorial" meetings were exactly what Lenin felt he needed to bring Zimmerwald around.

In fact, it was unnecessary. With marvelous timing, the Allies turned out to be Lenin's partners in sabotaging the big social democratic congress. When the Zimmerwald group met, the Allied governments had already refused passports to the delegates of the social democratic congress. Although representatives of the Central Powers and the Scandinavian nations would meet, the much publicized social democratic conference was effectively dead, giving the Zimmerwald Commission a marvelous opportunity for publicity against the "fruits of collaboration with capitalist governments."

Without delay, Radek shifted the focus of the conference to Russian affairs, particularly the question of whether the Zimmerwald conference would coordinate a broad program of support for the Bolsheviks. For five days, the conference witnessed another episode in the famous controversy between the Mensheviks and the Bolsheviks. The former argued that the revolution in Russia had not developed sufficiently to justify seizure of power; the latter retorted with the Zimmerwald slogan: "Either the revolution will end the war, or the war will end the revolution." Many of the important Bolshevik leaders were absent, and this lent authority to Radek's arguments concerning the seriousness of the situation in Russia. Even Angelica abandoned her position of "neutrality" at the head of the Zimmerwald Commission to support the Bolshevik position.

More than anything else, the third Zimmerwald conference demonstrated that the leadership of international socialism had shifted from the Germans to the Russians. Before the war socialism had been dominated by the Germans, to whom every other party (including the Russians) looked in awe. Now, the only functioning forum of internationalism was devoting its entire conference to a debate on what should be done about the Russian situation. Even the German Spartacists, theoretically the staunchest allies of the Bolsheviks, were but poor cousins in the Zimmerwald movement. Nothing is as revolutionary as a revolution, and with the March revolution in Russia verifying much that Lenin had argued throughout the war, the prestige of the Russian party gave it a leverage that no other party could outweigh. Although the conference was still unwilling to seal the demise of the Second International by declaring itself a new Third International, its tone and content proved that the socialist movement was too mangled ever to heal its wounds on the model provided by the old organization. Lenin and the Bolsheviks had achieved a commanding position in the movement from which they would not easily be dislodged.

The conference's final resolution called for a general strike in all of the warring countries. The general strike was the most discussed and most fearsome weapon of socialism, but one which had never been used in wartime. The plan was that a general strike would take place everywhere, demanding immediate peace and solidarity with the Russian revolution. It would have to be simultaneous everywhere, both for maximum impact and to avoid the charges of treason that would be brought on strikers of one side of the lines if they acted when there was no corresponding strike on the other side. The plans for the move were to be kept in complete secrecy, lest their discovery initiate the kind of negative publicity that the Grimm Affair had occasioned.

The conference was scarcely over when Radek, in the name of the Bolsheviks, demanded that the resolution be printed. A call for a general strike in support of the Russian workers would greatly increase the prestige of the Bolsheviks at home, and since the Bolsheviks had already decided upon the seizure of power, they were anxious to assure the Russian workers that Bolshevism had strong international support. Radek and his few allies did not care at all whether the publication of the resolution was followed by a strike. He refused to await the reports from various deputies on the possibilities of holding a general strike. The pledges of secrecy, the mutual resolution, and Angelica's responsibility to the movement also meant nothing. All that mattered was the Bolshevik cause: "Will the Revolution kill the war, or will the war kill the Revolution?"

Angelica was again torn. Loyalty to Russia and to the Bolsheviks with whom she sympathized demanded that every possible step be taken to support the revolution. On the other hand, she was barraged by pleas from precarious groups, like the Germans, who warned that a premature publication of the general strike appeal could mean annihilation of their antiwar efforts. Despite her ambivalence, she wrote, she "felt that there was only one course to pursue—to keep [her] pledge and obey the unanimous mandate of the Zimmerwald Convention."

Days after she informed Radek of her final decision on the matter, the manifesto was published in a Finnish paper controlled by the Bolsheviks. It was not the first and certainly not the last time that the Bolsheviks had defied international agreements.

XI

A successful revolution can be a profound shock to the revolutionaries. For the schemers and conspirators, the success marks the end of the excitement of adversity: The close camaraderie of the cadres is replaced by the bureaucracy of power, clandestine meetings give way to official councils, secret messages become memoranda in multiple copies. For the propagandist, success means the end of the pleasures of opposition criticism. The self-righteousness and morality of opposition must give way to the trials of defense: Criticism must be parried, "necessary" if distasteful revolutionary acts must be explained, and the vagaries of the revolution must be molded into patterns that will reflect the promises. Compared to the joys of pointing out the foibles, weaknesses, and malfeasance of the government in power, the obligations of defending the exercise of power are a drain. In an ideologically based revolution, where every act must be explained in the context of the theory of revolution or social change, the task is even more formidable—especially since in the course of the explanation many of the explainers only for the first time recognize the true consequences of what they have so long advocated.

A small group of Zimmerwald members and Russian exiles in Stockholm watched events in Russia with increasing excitement during the first week of November 1917. The news from Petrograd and Moscow filtered through slowly, so that every phone call or telegram only heightened the general anxiety.

Word of the Bolshevik seizure of power came in the early hours of the morning, after a long evening of patient waiting. Later that day Angelica took the Zimmerwald appeal, in twelve languages, to the printer. The duties of the Zimmerwald executive were already clear: "We must rally the workers of the world to the support of the new revolutionary regime and an immediate peace which would permit it to consolidate its power. The warweary and suffering masses of Europe must be made to realize that their own salvation was bound up with the fate of the Social Revolution in Russia, and the Russian workers must be assured that they were not alone in their fight." Within weeks the manifesto had been disseminated throughout Europe, in thousands of clandestine leaflets.

Peace was the first priority for the Bolsheviks. In Lenin's words, they needed a "breathing space" in order to begin fulfilling the promises of bread to the hungry, freedom to the oppressed, and land to the landless.

But it takes two to make peace, and the Bolsheviks had to propagandize for peace among the Central Powers especially, but also among the other warring nations. The way to peace everywhere, the Bolsheviks assumed, was the way that had brought them to a position of seeking peace—revolution. "We are in a beleaguered fortress," wrote Lenin. ". . . We are counting upon the inevitability of the international revolution." They circulated manifestos and appeals: "To All the People of the Whole World," and later, "To the Toiling, Oppressed and Exhausted Peoples of Europe." "The workers and soldiers must arrest the business of war and peace from the criminal hands of the bourgeoisie and take it into their own hands," wrote Trotsky. "We have the right to demand this from you, because this is what we have done in our own country." Propaganda newspapers were printed— huge editions in dozens of languages, for clandestine distribution across the lines on the battlefields.

Zimmerwald, as the chief link between the Bolsheviks and the West, had the responsibility for feeding this material to underground and legal newspapers, a task made no simpler by the fact that the "treasonous" reputation of the Zimmerwald internationalists was now coupled with the "criminal" reputation of the Bolsheviks. Neither bourgeois nor labor journals were willing to publicize the Bolshevik Revolution or its peace demands, with the exception of the Bolshevik-controlled *Politiken* in Sweden and *Avanti* in Italy. Therefore, propagandizing was confined to the underground of leaflets passed around in the cities and the trenches.

The November revolution completed the transformation of the Zimmerwald movement. From a control center and administrative base for internationally minded socialists, it had finally become what Lenin wanted of it all along—the Western propaganda arm of the Bolshevik party. The message was clear: Bolshevism was international socialism, and whoever would call themselves internationalists had to deal with the reality of the Bolshevik revolution and the administrative prestige it gave the Russians. Since the all but defunct Second International could not offer any alternative to the Bolshevik-Zimmerwald model of international socialism, the possibility of a movement of international social democracy along the lines of the prewar federalized structure became nearly unthinkable. Lenin had long recognized what he considered the chief weakness of the Second International: its structural flabbiness, with decisions made too far from the center of power, and decision-making power spread too thin. Through the Zimmerwald leaflets he made it clear that the future would not repeat the mistakes of the past.

Because they believed so strongly in the essentiality of a revolution in Central Europe, Lenin and Trotsky tended to overestimate revolutionary activities in Austria and Germany. The massive strikes in Austria in January 1918 actually came nowhere near approximating the revolution the Bolsheviks thought they needed to save their own, but in their evaluations they exaggerated the disturbances into the prologue of a revolution. Later, with hindsight, Trotsky would admit "we mistook the second month of pregnancy for the ninth," but in the early months of 1918, the Bolsheviks expected palpable results from their propaganda efforts in the West. To Angelica, Lenin wrote:

> Dear Comrade: The work you are doing is of the utmost importance and I implore you to go on with it. We look to you for our most effective support. Do not consider the cost. Spend millions, tens of millions, if necessary. There is plenty of money at our disposal.

Angelica's reply was naïve. She did not need so much money, she answered. Although well aware of the monies available to the Bolsheviks, since they had taken care not to repeat the mistakes Marx criticized in the Paris Commune, and had expropriated the banks and private fortunes of money and jewelry, Angelica could not appreciate what need this money would serve in her efforts. "I could not see that our campaign of propaganda, in behalf either of Russia or the World Revolution, required such huge sums. I had always believed, as I still do, that the methods by which the workers emancipate themselves cannot be imposed from above. They must flow from the experience of the workers themselves, as an exploited class, and from their understanding of the goal which they seek to achieve."

Angelica's faith was similar to Rosa Luxemburg's belief in the masses

207

and in the process of consciousness-raising that Marxism promised. Although Angelica was never a theoretician of Marxism, she had grasped and believed the essential process by which a class recognized its own interests and its own identity. But in 1918, when the Russian revolution stood alone, the view and the faith were indeed simplistic. To most of the world, the word "Bolshevik" was a synonym for bandit or criminal; mention of the Bolshevik revolution conjured up visions of Mongol hordes sweeping across the steppes of Russia to loot, plunder, and level. To counter this negative image, which the Central Powers and the Allies alike promulgated in their reports of the revolution in Russia, the Bolsheviks required more effective means than the slow if inexorable processes of growing class consciousness could provide.

More than the naïveté which she acknowledges in her autobiographies, Angelica's reply revealed the political differences between Lenin and herself. He was the consummate politician, always operating on the edge of the possible, relentless in the pressure he placed on adversaries, and most important of all, convinced that the end justified any means. Without that conviction he could neither have fought the long battles that led to November 1917, nor sustained the revolution that the war had ushered in. Angelica, though she would subscribe to the goals of the revolution, and believed as much as anyone in the justice and righteousness of its fruits, could neither accept nor understand the politics and methods that practical success demanded.

Through 1918, Angelica requested permission to return to Russia. Each time, she was given reasons why she was more important in Stockholm. Observing that the vast sums for propaganda purposes were being routed through other channels, she suggested she could perform more valuable work in Russia. But the Bolsheviks were not about to give up their link to the only wartime international socialist organization.

She was also a fill-in for V. V. Vorovsky, the *de facto* Soviet ambassador to Sweden. His main responsibility was to negotiate the purchase of machinery and other goods in Sweden; when he was away for his frequent trips to the Soviet Union, she was called upon to represent Russian interests in these negotiations. Public relations and industrial purchasing were hardly the ambitions Angelica had dreamed of in the years when she studied, wrote, and spoke on behalf of a socialist revolution.

In August 1918 came the news of an attempt on Lenin's life by a Social Revolutionary named Dora Kaplan, followed by the institution of the "Red Terror." Reports circulating in the West were sensational, but to Angelica, unbelievable. That excesses of violence and repression could be committed by revolutionaries, by the same revolutionaries who had struggled against repression and war, was scarcely conceivable to her. Unable to believe the rumors of mass executions, deportations and internments, she determined to return to Russia no matter what and see for herself.

Her first attempt was unsuccessful. The train was stopped at the Finnish border, and on account of the fighting between the Reds and Whites, she was refused permission to enter Russia.

In October 1918 she finally did get through. The Civil War was in full swing, with Trotsky's Red Army fighting Koltchak's Whites and the Czechs in Siberia, the English at Archangelsk, and the Japanese at Vladivostok. The breadbasket of the Ukraine was under German and Austrian occupation, and vast sectors of Russian industry were only slowly recovering from the war. Although only semiofficial, an Allied blockade effectively cut Russia off from the rest of the world, exacerbating the food and coal shortages occasioned by the German occupation.

The morning after Angelica's arrival, she began to inquire about Lenin's health from a group of his Kremlin colleagues. His physical condition preoccupied her, as it did most followers of the revolution. But another question nagged almost as much: What would happen to the assailant? The foreign press had reported that she would be executed, or that a secret execution had already taken place. "Is it possible," Angelica asked herself, "that a revolutionary government executes someone who has acted with the intention of serving the people's cause? Did we not protest when the Czar and his police-spies did it? Is this the respect for human life for which we have fought so much and which we have claimed as one of the basic rights of the socialistic regime?" The reality of revolutionary necessity distressed her.

A personal note brought by a messenger summoned Angelica to an "audience" with Lenin. When she reached the house, Lenin embraced her and let loose with a barrage of questions. How strong was the communist influence in various labor movements? How close were the Germans and the Austrians to revolution? Would the revolution in Germany galvanize and consolidate the international movement? How great was the working-class sympathy for the Bolsheviks? Did Zimmerwald command a larger following than the majority socialist parties of the West?

Lenin insisted she stay for dinner. She brought up the question of Dora Kaplan, the would-be assassin. "The Central Committee will have to decide," he said. The subject clearly bothered him.

The modesty of the dinner impressed Angelica. "Look," said Lenin. "This bread has been sent to me from Jaroslaw, this sugar from comrades in the Ukraine. Also the meat. They want me to eat meat during my convalescence." He tried to refuse the cheese and chocolate she had brought from Sweden. "Give it to the children in Moscow," he said. To Angelica, this asceticism in the face of widespread scarcity was the mark of the true revolutionary—more important than the mastery or application of any theory. The heart, more than the head, made a revolutionary.

No one knew Lenin well, and Angelica was no exception. He was "close" to her only because he felt that her knowledge of and connection with the socialist movement in the West could be useful. Throughout many of the great socialist battles of the war, Angelica had been on Lenin's side. She did not support his positions without reservation at the Zimmerwald conferences, but neither had she been an antagonist or rival. And she had been a steadfast opponent of the majority socialist parties and the International Socialist Bureau of the Second International. "The enemy of my enemies is my friend" was a concept that explained many of Lenin's friendships and alliances.

At the end of her long evening with Lenin, Angelica told him that she planned a trip to Switzerland and Italy. She was anxious to reestablish her contacts with the socialist movements there, and to survey at close hand the state of the various European socialist movements as the war drew toward its close. Lenin urged her not to go. "Think it over," he said. "I am sure you will run into difficulties. You are secretary of Zimmerwald; you are known all over the world. There will be trouble." When he realized she could not be dissuaded, he let the matter drop.

There was one detail to be taken care of before Angelica could leave on her tour. From Stockholm she had applied for membership in the Communist Party, sending Alexandra Kollontai to file her papers. In Moscow, she was summoned before a committee of old-guard Bolsheviks, asked a few perfunctory questions, and made to sign a paper to the effect that she had never been a member of the party. She was cheered by the audience at her formal hearing, and given party membership with twenty-five years seniority. Her service in Zimmerwald had been so "loyal" that she became one of the old guard in a party to which she had never belonged. When she left for Switzerland, she was a Bolshevik.

XII

Angelica's trip to the West was an eye-opener, revealing the extent of Bolshevik overestimation of the "revolutionary" situation in Europe and gross underestimation of how feared and despised the Bolsheviks were in Western Europe. She traveled with Red Cross papers, which enabled her to stay clear of the Soviet embassies, but her name was too well known for journalists not to make the connection.

On the train to Switzerland she read a small notice in one of the newspapers: "Angelica Balabanoff, the well-known revolutionist, is on her way to Switzerland from Russia with many millions for the purpose of provoking a revolution here and in Italy." Her immediate reaction was amusement, since the Bolsheviks were hardly foolish enough to send money by well-publicized courier. But at the train station in Zurich her Italian comrades greeted her with jokes about her "many millions."

The next day a stranger approached her on the street.

"Would you do me the honor, signora, to have dinner with me?"

"Why should I?" she answered. "I don't know you."

The stranger kept walking alongside. "I have heard how generous you are, signora. And I am in great need. If you could loan me a small sum, you will never regret it. Just sixty thousand francs, a mere trifle to you now."

He was the first of many. Insurrectionists seeking money for dynamite, people selling their houses or furniture, spies and provocateurs posing as journalists—all trooped to her hotel or wrote her with their proposals for her millions.

The Swiss press added fuel to the fire. She was a celebrity at the commemoration of the first anniversary of the November revolution in Bern—a fact which, to the press, proved the intentions of her visit. A coalition of Swiss unions was threatening a general strike, which the press attributed to Angelica's agitation and money.

When the general strike began, troops filled the streets, and Angelica ended up under siege in the Russian embassy. Without being informed of their destination, the Bolsheviks were escorted to heavily guarded automobiles and driven to the German border for an unceremonious expulsion. They arrived in Germany on the day of the armistice.

Four days later they were expelled from Germany. "As we left Germany," wrote Angelica, "I experienced again the depression with which I had left Berlin a few weeks before. The old oppressive military bureaucracy had been destroyed and to this extent the suffering of Germany had not been in vain. But this destruction had brought with it no sense of liberation, none of the enthusiasm needed to build something new in its place. The German workers and their leaders felt themselves defeated in the defeat of their own oppressors."

It was an accurate summary, not only of Germany, but of Europe as a whole. The end of the war had not brought the world revolution that the Bolsheviks expected. Except for short-lived revolutionary outbursts in Hungary and Bavaria, the disappearance of the empires and the change of governments had constituted more an act of resignation and exhaustion than an outburst of revolutionary fervor. The Bolsheviks were everywhere unwelcome. Even the Scandinavian countries had broken off diplomatic relations with Russia—as if diplomatic quarantine could somehow keep out the infectious revolutionary bacillus.

There was no hope of reviving Zimmerwald in Western Europe. The movement, indeed, returned to Russia with Angelica when she was expelled from Germany. Yet Moscow was by no means a workable center for propagandizing in the West. The Allied blockade meant no regular mail, no newspapers and no books from abroad. The only information to get through was via a few couriers. Nor was there any way to reach the working classes of the West. In effect, Zimmerwald was dead.

There was little Angelica could do, except continue her regular round of propaganda speeches. She briefly considered writing a book about the influence of the Russian revolution "on the thought of the masses and their attitude toward religion," but dropped the idea when she was warned not to offend the high dignitaries of the Church. On her request, Angelica was assigned by the Commissar of Justice to work in the Cult department, dealing with church matters. As was every other task she dealt with in revolutionary Russia, the position was an eye-opener.

During the war, the bells had been removed from churches all over Russia to prevent the Germans from seizing them and melting them down for armaments. When the war ended, delegations from remote villages came to the capital to retrieve their bells. Angelica would greet these delegations, and ask why they wanted a church bell now that the revolution had come. All had ready answers:

"You see, the bell is necessary in case of fire or some other disaster to warn the population." Or, "Sure, if all were like me, we would not need bells, but the old folks. . . ." Not a single man admitted he was in any way concerned with the church or religion.

"In their shrewd and humble way they were adapting themselves to the new regime. They spoke now as though they had always been Bolsheviks, were perfectly at home in the new regime, and already understood all the new laws—and how to evade them." These episodes marked Angelica's earliest awareness of how difficult and complex it was to make a successful revolution. To seize power, to pass new laws and to enforce the new order was one thing; it was another matter to change the minds and hearts of people who had lived through years of czarism and Church authority, and whose heritage was symbolized in the church bells they came to seek in Moscow.

Because it was so important to change the hearts and minds of the people, correct deportment on the part of the revolution's leaders was as significant to Angelica as correct tactics. She had been impressed by Lenin's abstemiousness, even in his illness, and she was determined that in her own life she too would be the true revolutionary.

Her attitude was typical of socialists who have rebelled against privilege. Angelica's Marxism was heavily tainted with an attitude of noblesse oblige, of moral righteousness demanding a certain code of behavior and style of life as the outward signs of doctrinal and political purity. She perhaps never understood the gap between her own abstemiousness and Lenin's utter disregard for comfort or material goods. If he declined extra food or an increase in his monthly wages, it was because he simply could not be bothered with either. He had never known material pleasures, and his duties to the revolution allowed him no time to begin indulging. No revolutionary self-righteousness was involved in what he did; only politics. When he saw that the situation required that he live in an isolated country dacha, he would do

212

so. But for Angelica, socialism was the rich helping the poor. She insisted her life-style be a model of self-denial.

She paid a price for this adamancy. Her health so deteriorated during a speaking tour that her temperature was consistently below normal. Only a case of near-exhaustion finally got her to rest in bed. A physician ordered a diet including white bread. Angelica, knowing that even the ordinary bread of bean meal and straw was rationed, refused the prescription.

Even Lenin urged her to take care of her health, sending her to an oculist when he found her using a borrowed pince-nez in order to be able to read. She had to be forced to accept one of the fur coats that had been expropriated from emigrating families. Only under extenuating circumstances would she use the automobile provided for her, and her embarrassment at staying in either the National Hotel or one of the aristocratic residences caused real difficulties in finding quarters for her.

In time Angelica found another of her little student's rooms, where she could set up her collection of icons on the table and get down to the endless work of propagandizing the revolution and its blessings.

XIII

Throughout the revolution and the armistice, Lenin had never given up his hope of founding a new International free from the opportunism of the Second International, and with a coherence and disciplined structure that could function to instigate revolution, on the Bolshevik model, throughout the world.

These plans were still unrealized at the end of 1918, when news arrived in Moscow that the English Labor Party had issued a call for an international Socialist and Labor Congress—in other words, for the revival of the Second International. At any expense, it was important to Lenin that the "traitors" of the Second International not be allowed to recapture the leadership of international socialism. At a time when the Bolsheviks had not been able to establish firmly their own influence and leadership, a reassertion of leadership by the moderates of the Second International could be disastrous, especially if the international gathering scheduled for Bern could use the open transportation and communication of the West to woo away the allegiance of leftist socialist elements from the Bolsheviks. And while the moderate elements of the labor movement were still disorganized and factionalized by the war, they were unified enough to agree on a resolution condemning the "dictatorship" in Russia.

To counter the Bern conference, Lenin determined to call a conference of his own, despite the fact that the blockade had made any kind of written communication with the West impossible. The Soviet Foreign Ministry used radio to issue the call for a conference on January 24, 1919—a few days before the scheduled opening of the Bern conference, which the Russians carefully denounced as a "gathering of enemies of the working class." The invitation was filled with optimism about the "gigantic pace of the world revolution" and "the internationalization of the entire revolutionary movement," but when the date for the congress rolled around, in mid-February, only a single group in the West—the Spartacists—had duly elected a delegate.

When the congress opened finally, in March, there was as the English journalist Arthur Ransome later remarked, "a make believe side to the whole affair." Most of the thirty-five delegates had been carefully handpicked by the Russians. The sealed borders meant that few foreign representatives arrived, and substitutes were arranged from "qualified" individuals resident in Russia. The official record lists thirty-nine different parties, but careful examination reveals that many of the "parties" were from new "nations" that had suddenly appeared with the dismemberment of the Russian Empire. Poland, Finland, Estonia, Latvia, Lithuania, White Russia, the Ukraine all now had new "parties" loyal to the Bolsheviks. Many other countries were represented by former prisoners of war or foreign radicals long out of touch with their homelands. The Swiss delegate was Fritz Platten, who had arranged Lenin's trip from Switzerland to Russia, accompanied him, and been in Russia ever since. Holland, the Socialist Propaganda League of America (an organization of Slavic immigrants), and the Japanese communists were all represented by a Dutch-American engineer named Rutgers who had once spent a few months in Japan. England was represented by a Russian émigré named Feinberg who served on Chicherin's staff at the Russian foreign ministry. In fact, the only duly elected delegate was Hugo Eberlein, the Spartacus representative.

Eberlein was the guest of honor. His status as the representative of the only true communist party in Western Europe, and the faith that the Bolsheviks placed in the German revolution (almost two months after the defeat of the January rising and the murder of Liebknecht and Luxemburg!), entitled him to the place of honor next to Lenin on the presidium. German was adopted as the official language of the congress, and the Spartacus party was listed ahead of the Russians on the program and in the minutes.

He was not a very cooperative guest. The sign over the dais said, "Long Live the Third International!" Eberlein wasted no time in reminding his hosts that the congress was not a meeting of a new International, but only a preliminary gathering to offset the impact of the Bern conference of the moderate socialists. His mandate from the Spartacists, he repeated over and over, did not support the declaration of a Third International or the forced splitting of the labor movement. For two days he fought off the imprecations

214

of the other delegates, and while Lenin could command an overwhelming majority, he was loathe to declare a new International without the support of the only legitimate Western communist party.

On the third day a new delegate arrived, an Austrian named Steinhart. He had traveled seventeen days, crossing the lines of both the Whites and the Reds at great peril. In an emotional speech he described his adventurous journey. Everywhere he had been, he reported, capitalism was disintegrating and the masses were on the verge of revolt. In Germany and Austria, the proletariat was on the point of establishing a dictatorship. The revolution was imminent, and everyone was looking to Moscow for guidance.

He undoubtedly believed all that he said, as did the congress delegates. In the mood of glee, they persuaded Eberlein to abstain on the voting. The Third International was founded, and a few basic principles of the platform were set down, including soviet dictatorship and the duty of severing all ties with patriotic or pacifist socialists in every country. The Russians were in full charge.

The next step was to vote on a resolution submitted by Lenin, Trotsky, Racovsky, Zinoviev, and Platten—all members of the Zimmerwald left— which denounced the centrist (pacifist) members of Zimmerwald and declared: "The Zimmerwald Union has outlived its purpose. All that was really revolutionary in it goes over to the Communist International."

Angelica protested. She conceded that Zimmerwald had been created for a specific wartime purpose, and with the war ended the purpose no longer existed. But, she pointed out, most of the members of the Zimmerwald conference, although invited to Russia, had not been able to come and to consider the question. She could not act in their name.

The Bolsheviks, outraged by her legal squeamishness, passed a resolution to the effect that "the First Congress of the Communist International resolves that the Zimmerwald agreement be liquidated." The transformation that Lenin had worked on since the first women's conference of 1914 was now complete.

Angelica was anxious to be done with the conference, and from her encounters with Lenin, she had reason to think that the Third International was anxious to be done with her as well. As she was leaving the Kremlin, getting ready to return to the Ukraine to continue her propaganda speeches, she said good-bye to Trotsky. He was surprised.

"What, you are going to leave?" he asked. "You know you have been nominated Secretary of the International?"

"I? Not in the least! Let me do my work among the masses. . . ."

"But you are the only one capable of holding that office. Come with me to Comrade Lenin, he is around here. He will tell you what the Central Committee has decided."

Angelica knew exactly why they wanted her as Secretary: She represented a kind of quasi-neutral respectability. She was not a Bolshevik old-timer, and her long experience in Italy and Switzerland would make the International seem less of an all-Russian show. She confronted Lenin:

"Comrade Trotsky tells me you want me to take the post of Secretary of the International, but I ask you to be excused. As long as the work was very difficult and taxing, especially in wartime, I have never refused. Now the Secretariat is in a socialist country, the procedures are normal again; you can find a replacement for me."

Lenin took on what she called "one of his characteristic looks," shutting one eye: "Party discipline exists for you too, dear comrade," he said. "The Central Committee has decided."

It was like a father saying, "Your mother and I have decided." There was no appeal. As Angelica put it, "I knew it would be useless to argue."

The appointment was confirmed formally when she returned to her hotel room. That evening, the inauguration of the International was celebrated in one of the largest halls in Moscow. Angelica was feted and praised: ". . . for a few moments I felt profoundly happy. . . . It was one of the few moments in my life when it seemed to me that I had not lived in vain. Here was the result of the tenacity of the Zimmerwald movement—the ties of international brotherhood had been renewed. I was almost grateful to Lenin and Trotsky for having induced me to accept the nomination and for having given me the opportunity thus to serve the international working class again."

XIV

Angelica was actually only a front, nominated for the sake of her international prestige. The man she fronted for, the Chairman of the International, was Gregory Zinoviev. Aside from Mussolini, Angelica considered Zinoviev "the most despicable individual I have ever met."

He was a brilliant speaker and debater with a remarkable gift for dealing with people in a way that thoroughly concealed his duplicity. It was intrigue that most appealed to him, and his virtuosity ultimately exhausted the patience of even the most sympathetic comrades. He had made his career by slavish devotion to Lenin, and by parroting Lenin with a polemical and literary flourish that Lenin's own writings often lacked. Yet at crucial moments he had refused to follow Lenin; in November 1917 he twice publicly denied any responsibility for the Bolshevik seizure of power. His trespasses disqualified him from any high office in the party or the Soviet state. The consolation prize, in consideration of his talents and his general loyalty, was the chairmanship of the International.

Almost immediately, Zinoviev and Angelica clashed. She continued to assume that the whole thrust and purpose of the International was propaganda and comradely aid to left-wing forces throughout the world. "I knew that their respect could only be won by the quality of our program and the superiority of our leadership." As she soon discovered, Zinoviev entertained a very different notion of the organization's purpose. In his view, the size and international character of the International would give it sufficient leverage to dislodge or destroy rival parties, and to nurture or even establish parties sympathetic to the Soviet cause and program. It was his practices and policies that made the name Comintern (for Communist International) synonymous with intrigue, double-dealing, pressure politics, and purchased support.

The real decisions of the International were made in secret Party committee meetings. There, even Zinoviev was a front, selected because his skills were useful. Angelica was not a member of the committee, and until many years later did not even realize its existence.

Its most important function was to coordinate the efforts of the Comintern and the parallel efforts of the Commissariat for Foreign Affairs. Prior to the founding conference of the International, the Commissariat of Foreign Affairs had set up what were called "foreign sections of the Communist Party." * The program was widely heralded, but, as Angelica later discovered, it was a first-class fake. The members of the sections were almost all war prisoners in Russia, new recruits to the party with little or no knowledge of the revolutionary or labor movements in their home countries. They were groomed to return to their native countries where they were to "work for the Soviet Union." Their tasks were to coerce and control the left-wing socialist parties in their home states, or, if that were impossible, to create rival parties. Most of the representatives at the first congress came from the ranks of these trainees.

At one point Angelica met two Italians from Trieste who were about to return to Italy with special credentials from Lenin and a large sum of money. After speaking with them in Italian for a few minutes, she concluded that they knew almost nothing of the Italian labor movement or even the basic terminology of socialism. She protested to Lenin, describing the situation.

"Vladimir Ilyitch, I advise you to get back your money and credentials. These men are merely profiteers of the Revolution. They will damage us seriously in Italy."

"For the destruction of Turati's party," he answered, "they are quite good enough."

Angelica was shocked, but as the months wore on the whole procedure became commonplace. Adventurers, former criminals, even former Red-

---

* Angelica attributed the move to Karl Radek, who in fact was in prison in Berlin in 1919, and did not return to Russia until January 1920.

baiters were trained, outfitted, and supplied with funds. They departed on various secret missions, and with the prestige of the Russian revolution behind them, they created an enormous stir in many of the revolutionary labor parties of the world. New parties were created, old ones split, and everywhere factions with undivided loyalty to the Comintern and the Soviet Union were organized and funded. The International itself functioned as Lenin had always believed a revolutionary organization should function: with a tight, centralized organization in Moscow, and with rigorous discipline extending from the executive committee to the lowest ranks. Parties in the farthest corners of Europe, even of the world, could be depended upon to react swiftly to decisions reached in Moscow.

XV

It was soon clear to Angelica that Zinoviev was eager to be rid of her. Her name would appear on documents and appeals that she had never seen. When she complained, Zinoviev, with Lenin's backing, would insist that the Executive had made the decision informally, and that naturally they had intended consulting her. If she pressed the point, Zinoviev would fall back on his favorite argument: "Party discipline. . . ."

Then at one meeting, after a glowing report of expansion of Comintern activities, Zinoviev announced that a new office of the International would be established in the Ukraine, with Comrade Balabanoff in charge. When Angelica questioned the decision, she was assured that it was her talents that had prompted the decision. "The Ukraine is the most important issue in our fight just now," said Lenin. "Why should we keep all our best speakers in Moscow?"

She went, and during the worst months of the civil war in the Ukraine she gave an average of five speeches per day, urging support of the Red Army and adherence to the strict rationing the war had imposed. Although she was in the Ukraine only a few months, she gained a reputation for being "soft-hearted," mainly because of her efforts to get the prisons opened and to distribute foodstuffs to all who applied for help.

But there was one exception to her generosity. At a public meeting in Odessa she was informed that someone wished to speak with her. Angelica went to the waiting room and there saw the woman—old, trembling, dressed like a beggar, with a shawl over her head. It was her sister Anna, who came to tell the tale of the deprivations the family had suffered through the revolution and the civil war. After losing everything, they lived in a single room with no light. They could not afford candles. In the mornings, Anna (who was over sixty) would wash linen in cold water and attempt to dry it by the

218

sunlight of a single window. There was no heat in the winter and little food. Her son had to give up his scientific studies and writing because there was not enough light for reading. He who had one of the finest and most expensive scientific libraries, who had never stayed in a second-class hotel or worn ready-made clothes, now faced the horror of being conscripted into the Red Army.

It was a tale Angelica had heard often: the trials of the wealthy middle class in the wake of the revolution. This time it was her sister telling the tale and begging Angelica to save her son—Angelica's nephew—from the Red Army that he so feared and loathed. Day after day Anna came, repeating the same monologue in her low, broken voice. She seemed to know that Angelica would refuse to extend any privilege to her family. A year later, when Angelica returned to the Ukraine, she heard that the family had escaped to Turkey. Several years after that she heard that her sister and brother-in-law had died of starvation in Istanbul.

Early in 1920, reverses in the civil war necessitated the evacuation of Kiev. Angelica returned to Moscow, eager for a further assignment. To her amazement, the only order she received from the Central Committee was to leave Moscow for a sanatorium. It was well-warranted: her speech-making had left her in a state of physical exhaustion, seriously underweight, and again with a temperature that constantly registered below normal. She refused, arguing that she was neither sick nor old enough to retire. Her reaction was not prompted by fear; the Soviet sanatoriums had not yet acquired their reputation as asylums for incurable political deviants. For Angelica, the refusal was simply based on her firm belief that any hint of privilege, even a well-earned rest at state expense, smacked of antisocialist decadence.

The official response to Angelica's "disobedience" was unexpected. N. Krestinski, the General Secretary of the Party, seemed prepared for her refusal. "Look here, Comrade Balabanoff, we have a piece of work which will certainly satisfy you and which is extremely important to us. We would like you to take charge of a propaganda train which we are preparing to send to Turkestan."

Turkestan, in Central Asia, where a typhus epidemic was raging, was an odd assignment for someone whose health allegedly warranted a spell in a sanatorium. Even the ultramodern propaganda trains, with their special cars for printing and movies, were no protection against the epidemic, as the very nature of the journeys necessitated stops in every little town and a crisscrossing of the area where the epidemic was at its worst.

"Why Turkestan?" was Angelica's response. "Is that a joke? I know neither the country nor the psychology of the people, who, no doubt, are very primitive; my propaganda work would be wasted there. Besides, very few understand Russian."

"But we need a famous name, like yours."

219

Although assured she would have plenty of time to decide whether or not she would go, she discovered that arrangements for her departure had already been made. Friends warned that it was all a maneuver of Zinoviev to get rid of her. Resolutely she ignored the warnings, despite her feelings about Zinoviev.

It was not long after the "invitation" to Turkestan had been extended that Angelica learned that the arrival in Moscow of a delegation from England was scheduled immediately after her proposed departure. She became suspicious. "My hesitation regarding the Turkestan trip became a decision when, soon after this, came another announcement that the visit of the English commission would be followed by one from Italy. . . ." A telephoned protest to Zinoviev got no response, and at the next meeting of the International Executive she brought up the matter.

"I should like Comrade Zinoviev to tell me why I have to leave Moscow at the very time that the delegations from Western Europe are arriving. I was elected Secretary, presumably, because of my contacts with the labor movement abroad—especially Italy. Then why must I be separated from my Italian comrades on their arrival in Russia? And what can I do in Turkestan that any other Party propagandist can't do?"

The answer was silence. Several members spoke of the urgency of the Turkestan trip, using arguments that sounded weaker with each repetition. When Angelica held her ground, Zinoviev said—in the shrill and petulant voice that marked his anger—"Well, if you don't wish to obey the Party Central Committee, we shall take up the matter tomorrow. We have urgent problems to deal with now."

The timing of the next meeting was carefully arranged to coincide with a speaking engagement Angelica had in Kronstadt. She returned to Petrograd in time to confront Zinoviev as he left the meeting.

"The Executive has decided that you must obey the Central Committee's request that you go to Turkestan," he said.

"I will not go," she replied.

"And the Party discipline . . . ?"

"I am second to none in the observance of discipline," she said, "but this is no longer discipline, this is absurdity, idiocy! You will regret your actions. You want me out of the way exactly when my presence might be useful, when the comrades from abroad finally arrive. And you want me to miss the encounter with the Italian socialists. I will not stand for that!" *

Angelica's defiance was a first for the Bolsheviks: Never before had an official as highly placed and as well-known challenged the party leadership. Yet in Angelica's mind the decision to no longer collaborate with Zinoviev

* At the congress of the Russian Communist Party someone coined a wry expression around the fact that Turkestan was a peach-growing area. Angelica, the saying went, had been sent off to "eat peaches." When the same tactics were applied to other obstreperous officials, the wags would say, "They wanted him to eat peaches as they had tried with Comrade Angelica."

and the Comintern was only, as she put it, "half-formed." She realized fully that she could not fight him on his own level, with his weapons of intrigue and subterfuge, but was she ready to break with the one victorious revolutionary party and all that it meant for socialism and for her life?

It was not until she spoke with John Reed that she began to see the reality of her position.

"They want to get rid of you," he told her, "before the foreign delegations arrive. You know too much."

"But surely they don't doubt my loyalty."

"Of course not, but neither do they doubt your honesty. It is that they are afraid of."

From John Reed, whose own honesty was prompting certain doubts on the part of the Bolshevik leadership, the warning was portentous.

For two weeks nothing happened. Then one day Reed came to Angelica's room.

"Are you, Angelica, still the Secretary of the Communist International?"

"Of course I am, at least nominally."

"And why, then, are you not at the meeting?"

"Which meeting?"

"The meeting of the Executive Council which is taking place in Litvinov's office."

She phoned. An employee muttered a feeble excuse: He had forgotten to invite her. Forgotten to invite the Secretary of the International!

When she walked into the meeting, even the imperturbable Zinoviev was embarrassed by the nakedness of his latest subterfuge.

"Well," Angelica asked, "what have you decided about the train to Turkestan?"

"What? Has Trotsky not told you? Strange, we have asked him to do so." Zinoviev often called in a Gray Eminence to break the news of his schemes.

"But what has Trotsky to do with it? I ask you."

"The Central Committee has decided that you may not go to Turkestan, but at the same time you are relieved of the office of Secretary of the International. Trotsky will explain to you."

This time Angelica was speechless. After what she had considered a career of unwavering loyalty and devotion, she had been dismissed with less ceremony than her mother would have used in firing a housemaid. If there was any relief in knowing that an end had been put to the intolerable situation, there were also the humiliation and doubt about a career that suddenly seemed to amount to zero. On top of a state of health that the party had once thought merited a visit to a sanatorium, the news precipitated a physical and nervous breakdown. For weeks, Angelica was bedridden, unable to deliver speeches or to function in any productive activity.

Zinoviev called on her to announce that she had been reinstated. She demurred. Then Trotsky came to urge her to resume the post. Like Zinoviev, he had heard reports from Western Europe that the removal of Angelica would cause dissatisfaction and apprehension among the parties where she had ties.

"Dear Comrade Angelica," Trotsky said, "as you know we have annulled the absurd decision of the other day. I have always been against your removal, and I voted against Zinoviev's proposal. Now. . . ."

"Listen, Lev Davidovich, it is not a matter of revocation or of how you voted on that occasion, but rather of the whole system of lies and intrigues which you should not tolerate."

"What do you want me to do, dear comrade? I know you are right. . . . But you must come back to the International."

She refused. Trotsky tried another tack. "You do not want the office of Secretary? Accept another one then: Comintern correspondent for Italy, as Marx was for Germany."

"Thank you very much, but it is no use insisting. . . ."

Hell hath no fury like the wrath of a woman spurned. The movement and the party had been more than a belief or life-style for her, it had been a love affair—the love of her life. For that love she had put up with the inane squabbling, the deceit, and the unfaithfulness of the party. What had been a minor tactic for Zinoviev and Trotsky, like the harmlessly intended ploys of sparring lovers, had been enough to kill the affair. And once spurned, Angelica could not be wooed back. It was over.

XVI

Angelica fell out with the Bolsheviks in the spring of 1920. Within weeks of her suspension as Secretary of the International a delegation of the Italian labor movement arrived in Moscow. There had been other foreign delegations, including the English, but for Angelica the visit of the Italians was a special event, because of her long association with the Italian socialists.

As early as 1917, the Italian party had been more sympathetic to the Bolshevik revolution than had almost any other party, with the exception of those factions in Germany and other states that identified wholly with the Bolsheviks. In Italy it was not a splinter but the whole party that supported the revolution, and favorable editorials appeared not in a tiny underground paper, but in *Avanti,* a national journal.

After the war, Italy was the country of the West which most closely approximated conditions in Russia. Ostensibly a victor in the war, Italy had in fact emerged a defeated nation. Industry was in shambles, the government unable to cope with the problems of rebuilding the nation, and the rent in

Italian society that divided the rich from the poor was seemingly irreparable. The situation was another example of what made Lenin and Rosa Luxemburg, and before them Engels, realize that war would so weaken some nations that either victory or defeat could produce a revolutionary situation.

In the elections of November 1919, the socialists had emerged the largest party. At the opening of Parliament, the socialist delegation refused to hail the king, and instead shouted, "Long Live Socialism." For Italy, it was an unprecedented display of socialist disloyalty. Through 1919, shops were looted, peasants rose in many areas to redistribute land, and waves of strikes repeatedly swept from one industrial city to another. In 1920, a large-scale passive-resistance strike was retaliated with a lockout. The workers then occupied the factories—the first time this strategy was used in a strike. Within a few weeks mutual fears on both sides had heightened tensions to the point where the socialist party had to choose between social revolution or defeat. "The bankers, the industrialists, and big landowners were awaiting the social revolution like sheep awaiting the slaughter," wrote Gaetano Salvemini. "If Communist revolution were something which could be caused by the bewilderment and cowardice of the ruling classes, the Italian people could have had as many Communist revolutions as it liked in September 1920."

Yet revolution was not so easy. If Italy resembled Russia in many ways—with peasants who were not conservative, with an intelligentsia that was largely socialist, and with whole regions that were disaffected with the governing of the country—it remained a country of the West. The labor movement had been educated and influenced by the examples of the West; German militant "preparation" and French theory were more influential than the Russian example. Revolution was still viewed as a fairly distant possibility, not a present reality. Sober minds in the party were quick to point up the effects that the inevitable Anglo-French-US blockade would have on a revolution. The Russians would offer aid, perhaps, but it would have to come through the Dardanelles, which were controlled by the Allies. When the moment came for the crucial decision, the trade unions threw the balance against revolution, and to the relief of most Italians the strike ended peacefully.

The events in Italy were incomprehensible to the Russians. By 1920, the Comintern was so absorbed by a millennarian belief in the imminence of social revolution in Western Europe that the behavior of a party which had so obviously turned away from a possible opportunity for revolution could be explained only by treason. The resultant Russian attitude and behavior toward the Italian socialists is one of many examples of the results which obtained when the perceptions and methods of the Comintern crossed with the traditions and policies of Western European parties.

The fever of agitation in Italy had not risen to the great strike yet when the labor delegation arrived in Moscow in May 1920. But the visit itself was enough to create a stir in Italian politics. Mussolini, his fascist movement still only embryonic, denounced the trip as a delegation to a country of "vermin" and pauperism. Serrati, the head of the socialists, answered that they were going to The Holy Land.

Whatever their public statements, the Italian delegates were prepared for a country of hardship and poverty. They brought with them as gifts to the Russian people over one hundred large cases of canned foods, oil, sugar, medicines, soap, and other needed supplies—a gesture which immediately endeared them to the Russian masses. Wherever the Italians went in Russia, large crowds would follow, singing revolutionary songs and cheering at every opportunity.

The reception by the Bolshevik officials was not so friendly. On the surface all was fraternal camaraderie, but even as the initial receptions were in progress, Zinoviev approached Angelica to ask if she would bring "the most radical" members of the Italian delegation to him. Although she did not recognize it at the time, the inquiry was the first step in a Comintern plan to divide the Italian socialist party.

In this, as in so many cases, Comintern policy was utterly paradoxical. The very month of the Italian visit, Lenin had published *Left-Wing Communism, an Infantile Disease*. The book is a handbook of revolutionary tactics, fully worthy of its frequent comparison with Machiavelli's *The Prince* for its force of argument, realism, logic, and compelling directness. In genesis the book was an attack on the antiparliamentarianism and antiunionism of the English communists, but the overall tone and thrust are apparent on every page. "We in Russia . . ." are the first words, and Lenin's basic assumption is that "some elements," as he puts it, of the Russian revolutionary experience are of international value. In fact, the book became a scriptural justification for imposing the Russian revolutionary model on all parties and under all circumstances. That the enforced application of Russian experiences might cripple or destroy fledgling communist parties in the West was a possibility that Zinoviev and his colleagues chose not to consider.

The Italians were perhaps the first party to feel the brunt of this approach. They were on tour in Russia, with Angelica as a sometime guide and interpreter, when the Comintern summoned a second world congress of affiliated parties.

There had been not a single instance of sustained successful revolution in the West since the Russian revolution. The Hungarian Soviet Republic had lasted three months, the Bavarian three weeks. Undaunted, Zinoviev opened the conference on a note of defiant optimism, based mainly on reports of Russian successes in the war with Poland, and the entire agenda was carefully orchestrated on the theme of Lenin's latest polemic. The unmistakable thesis was that the class struggle was "now passing into civil war." Collapse of revolutionary struggles in most of the Western countries was seen by the Russians not as a sign that their optimism was misplaced, but as a sure proof of the unsuitability of Western leadership which had left the masses in the lurch. The congress was a means of driving a wedge between that leadership and the masses—in short, splintering the western labor movement.

For over three weeks, Angelica translated these speeches and answers, watching as Zinoviev's hammering tactics threatened to shatter the delicate structure of the Comintern. For many parties, especially for the Italians, who were the largest Western affiliate of the Comintern, affiliation had been possible only with the assignment of a measure of national independence to each party. The Italians had given their allegiance to the Zimmerwald movement throughout the war, and at the founding of the Third International they had dutifully and in good faith transferred their allegiance to the new International.

The second congress, under Zinoviev, put an end to this trust once and for all. He presented to the congress the infamous Twenty-One Points. Any party which wanted to maintain its affiliation with the Comintern had to agree to accept the points and institute whatever policy changes the points demanded as a precondition for continued affiliation. The Twenty-One Points were nothing more than an elaboration of the Bolshevik line that had served Zimmerwald and the Russian revolution with such success. All the key words and phrases were there: rigid control of the party press by a central committee, removal of "centrists" and "reformists" from the party, organization of underground machinery, continued propaganda against the army, work among the peasants, campaign against the pacifists and patriots to achieve a total break with "opportunist" elements, aid to revolutionary movements in the colonies, work within the trade unions, strict subordination of parliamentary delegations to the central committee of the party, accentuated centralization of party organization with "iron discipline," periodic purges, support for every Soviet republic, all future party programs subject to the approval of the Comintern executive committee, recognition of the authority of the Comintern to overrule even Party Executive Committee decisions, renaming of all adherents as Communist Parties, mandatory publication of all documents of the Moscow Executive. All points were to be accepted or rejected within four months.

Many parties objected, maintaining that adoption of the Twenty-One Points would mean the split or possibly the destruction of their organizations. The Twenty-One Points were in places contradictory. For example, to purge rightist elements and then to insist upon working with the trade unions—who generally represented the right wings of parties—was utter absurdity. To demand rigid central control of the party newspapers in a country with regions as disparate as Italy would mean the destruction of the press.

The Russians were oblivious to the protests. When the congress adjourned, the Italians were given the same four months as every other party to decide if they fully accepted the Twenty-One Points. If they did not, they would no longer be members of the International.

Serrati returned to an Italy on the verge of revolution, as the demonstrations and looting of the immediate postwar year escalated to the strikes that would culminate in the great lockout and factory occupation. He was accused of absenting himself at the crucial moment because of cowardice, and the charges were repeated as he and Lenin waged a duel in the journals on the correct position and posture for the Italian party. "Making a revolution," wrote Serrati, "is less a matter of egging people on to violent behavior . . . and more a matter of preparing the conditions in which we, as a party, have a chance of exploiting the inevitable eruption when it comes." The real prerequisite of a successful revolution, he continued, is to preserve "the unity of our party with all its offensive and defensive weapons and with its vanguard and rear guard intact."

To Lenin, Serrati's views, especially his insistence upon "relative autonomy" of action, smacked of heresy: "Serrati has failed to grasp the peculiar qualities of the moment of transition which Italy is now passing through—a period in which we are approaching the decisive struggle between the workers and the bourgeoisie for the possession of state power. The vital thing," continued Lenin, *"the absolutely vital thing* for the victory of the revolution now is to ensure that there is a real Communist party to act as a vanguard for the revolutionary workers of Italy, a party which is incapable of being swayed. . . ." His definition of a real communist party, of course, was spelled out in the Twenty-One Points. The collapse in Italy of the mass strike movement, when the labor leaders called off their potential revolution, was just the proof that Lenin needed of the absolute validity of his position.

To reinforce the case Lenin was building in his *Pravda* articles, Zinoviev whipped up a smear campaign against Serrati, built around a loan Serrati had once contracted. Lenin even approached Angelica for help in the campaign, hoping perhaps that she would be flattered by the invitation: "And you, Comrade Balabanoff, would you be willing to write a pamphlet against Serrati?"

"I, against Serrati? But I fully agree with him. You should write that pamphlet. But you know only too well that Serrati is a man of integrity and one of the best socialists, and deep inside you, you admire him for the courage with which he attacks your doctrines, your methods, and yourself, but you want to compromise him in the eyes of others." That the Bolsheviks would sink to asking her to turn against Serrati only showed that their amorality was ignorant as well as intemperate.

The convention to decide the Italian reaction to the Twenty-One Points was held in Livorno in January 1921. It was a showpiece, complete with a dove of peace and two delegates handpicked by Lenin and Zinoviev, Mathias Rakosi and Christian Kabakchiev, both experienced in Bolshevik methods in Hungary and Bulgaria respectively. The message sent with Kabakchiev read the ultimatum in categorical terms: "Before knowing what will be the majority opinion at your congress, [we declare that] those who refuse to accept the separation from the reformists violate an essential order of the Communist International and, by that alone, place themselves outside of it."

The question, quite simply, was whether the party was willing to purge itself of its entire right wing. Exclusion of the right wing would so alienate the trade unions, with their vast following, that in effect the move would have emasculated the party. Serrati made desperate efforts at compromise, but the fate of the Italians had already been sealed in Moscow. The closing words of the message from Moscow which Kabakchiev read were: "The Italian Communist Party must, one way or the other, be created. . . ." One way was for the entire party to accept the Twenty-One Points, and that was impossible. The other was for the party to split.

When the vote was taken, one-third of the delegates left the conference to march across the road and declare themselves the Partito Communista. They remained loyal to the Comintern, but the rest of the Italian socialist party was irrevocably lost. The tactics of Zinoviev and Lenin had succeeded in creating, one way or the other, an Italian Communist Party, but in the process they had lost the support of the one large country in which the labor movement, as a whole, had been sympathetic. And by dividing the party, Moscow had destroyed it. In the next Italian election, the Socialists elected only 122 delegates to the 275 of the Liberals and Democrats. The Communists elected 16. The only Communist victory was in the city government of Bologna, where Communists still hold office and still administrate with impeccable efficiency. The way was open for Mussolini to fill the gap left by the split and demoralization of the labor movement.

Years later, when it was too late, the Bolsheviks made overtures to Serrati in the hope that a united front could defeat Mussolini. He rallied then, in 1924, not because he believed in the Bolsheviks, but to prove his willingness to make any sacrifice for the cause. Yet while he became a "rank and file member" of the Communist Party in name, he could never really identify with or support the methods of their struggle. A follower without faith, he died prematurely and suddenly on his way to a clandestine meeting. Angelica diagnosed a broken heart: "Serrati could not survive the break with what he had loved and believed in so fervently: the Italian Socialist Party."

XVII

Neither could Angelica survive the break with what she had loved and believed in so fervently: "I felt that something more terrible than anything that had gone before now divided me from the Bolsheviks." She was determined to leave Russia with the Italian delegation after the Comintern congress.

When she told Lenin of her decision, he gave her a handwritten "letter of introduction": "The President of the People's Commissars of the Socialist Soviet Republic asks all institutions and individuals to give Comrade Angelica Balabanoff *every assistance* required. [Lenin's emphasis.] Comrade Angelica Balabanoff has been for many years a member of the Party. She is one of the most prominent militants of the Communist International."

Personal tributes were rare from Lenin. Angelica was so moved that she hesitated.

"How difficult it is to satisfy you," he said. "We once offered to make you ambassador to Italy and you refused. If we prevented you from leaving Russia, you would still be unhappy. Now you are free to go and you still seem unhappy. What do you object to in my note?"

"Object? Why should I object? Any other Communist would have given ten years of his life to have such a certificate from you—but to me—"

"Well," he asked, "what can I do to satisfy you, to make you happy?"

"What I would like most you cannot give me, Vladimir Ilyitch—the political and moral possibility of remaining in Russia the rest of my life."

"Then, why don't you?" he asked. "Why must you leave?"

"You know very well, Vladimir Ilyitch. Russia does not seem to need such people as I."

"She needs them," he said, "but she does not have them."

Angelica found that even with the letter from Lenin, she could not obtain a visa to Italy, probably (as she suspected) because Zinoviev had taken steps to make her exit difficult. She said good-bye to the Italians in Estonia, then returned to Moscow.

It was September 1920. For more than a year Angelica had to wait in Moscow, watching from afar as Italy was torn by the wave of strikes, lockouts and factory occupations, and as the Italian socialist movement was split into the Communist and Socialist parties. Although still a party member, she held no official position, and could do nothing to affect affairs in either Russia or Italy. She could speak as a general propagandist, but to do so was to appear an accomplice of the Bolsheviks. There was no way she could express her disagreements in either the press or public meetings. So she waited, her disillusionment compounding, as experience after experience confirmed her suspicions and fears.

Clara Zetkin came to Moscow for consultations in the fall of 1920. As the leader of the Marxist women's movement, and as one of the epigoni who tried to pick up the pieces of German communism after Rosa Luxemburg's death, she was feted by the Bolsheviks. Angelica had long admired Clara Zetkin as one of the dynamic women in the socialist movement, and after the death of Rosa Luxemburg, Clara had reciprocated by pronouncing Angelica her closest friend. When Angelica recounted her disenchantment and her decision to no longer work with the Comintern, Clara begged her to stay, perhaps as the secretary of the International Women's Movement. "You must stay, Angelica. You are one of the few honest people left in the movement."

Angelica declined, referring to this as the second time in her life she had turned down the appeal of someone she admired. (The first was Plekhanov, at the outbreak of the war.) "Had I yielded to pressure in either case," Angelica mused in one of her autobiographies, "my life would be quite different from what it is, but I would have missed the greatest satisfaction of my life—the knowledge that I have been strong enough to swim against the stream."

Lenin and Zinoviev also entreated Angelica to return to the fold and avoid the embarrassment that an open break would signal. For the third congress of the Comintern she was invited to serve as official translator. She declined. To give her boycott an official character—lest Zinoviev announce that she was "indisposed" or use another of his clever cover-ups—she appeared at the opening session of the congress. At the door she met Lenin.

"I am glad to see you in good health. I had heard that you would not participate and I thought. . . . All the better. . . . You will be of great use to us."

"No," she said. "I have not been ill. I have come here to show that I am well and that I do not intend to collaborate with the Comintern. The way you deal with the Italian Socialists is contemptible and abject. Even if I did not agree with the Italian Socialist Party—which happens not to be the case—I would side with the Italian comrades against you."

The break was open. Angelica had decided to leave at all costs. Hearing that the new social democratic government in Sweden might grant her a visa for reasons of health, she quickly obtained a certificate from a physician to the effect that her physical state required her to leave Russia. The visa was granted. But again, weeks went by with no response from the Central Committee on her request for permission to leave Russia.

After bureaucratic delays, during which other party leaders tried to persuade her to stay, Angelica finally received a sealed envelope marked

229

"Quite Confidential." Inside was a statement: "Comrade Balabanoff is authorized to leave Russia on her own responsibility. She is prohibited to express her opinion, verbally or in writing, on the Italian question."

Angelica left at the end of 1921, four and one half years after she had returned to Russia to work for the revolution.

XVIII

Love comes easily to some. For them, the end of an affair may be unpleasant, but it is a temporary misery that can be lost in a new liaison. The catharsis of pain and suffering can even be a welcome punctuation between loves.

For others, love does not come so easily. They are those who can have but one love. When it comes to an end, they have lost a piece of themselves. They are the widows and widowers who never recover from their mourning, the spurned lovers who never love again, no matter how hard and how often they might try.

So it was with Angelica. Socialism, by which she meant the great movement with its people and ideas tied up into one all-consuming experience, was the love of her life. When her pride and her lover's intransigence ended the affair, she found she could never love again. There were groups, and people, and little movements with whom she associated herself. But they would never fulfill her as the great movement had. One by one she would drop them, until finally age let her forget the differences and she could dream and pretend that love was the same as it had once been.

Even her health never quite recovered after she left Russia. In the passion of the revolution and the years of her break with Bolshevism, she had paid little attention to food and living conditions. Work and undernourishment had left her so weakened that, leaving Russia, she "felt like an old woman at forty-three." In fact, she was close to a nervous breakdown, as the precarious health of her body was exacerbated by the emotional strain of her intense feelings. Later years would find her robust and seemingly healthy, but she could no longer continually push herself as she had done in the heady years of the revolution.

Loneliness often makes us turn not to companionship, but inward, to soul-searching for the secrets that a busy life can keep locked within. When Angelica was about to board the boat for Stockholm, she was so apprehensive about the rough winter sea that she went to a drug store to seek an antidote for the anticipated seasickness.

"I can't give you anything that will be of any use to you," said the girl behind the counter, "except some advice—that is, to sing. Try to sing on the boat."

It was not the prescription Angelica sought, but on the boat, as the storm began, she remembered the advice. Sing? She had never sung in her life. Then as she watched the movement of the waves, the meaning of the words dawned. She began to recite poems she had learned in childhood, and as she recited she would translate them into the different languages she knew so well. The songs and the translations came easily. Later she found that unconsciously she would jot down translations of the Lermontov verses she had learned as a child.

Like so many Russians, Angelica was in awe of the power of music and poetry. Tolstoy had warned that poets and musicians could intoxicate with their work; Angelica called music and poetry "the highest form of human expression." The thought of herself as a poet was incredible. In all the years of her public speaking, when she would coax the crowd to sing revolutionary songs, she would remain silent, sure that she had no voice or ear.

When she arrived in Stockholm, the encouragement of a friend who saw some verses she had translated, together with the experience on the boat, set her off on a binge of writing poetry. She wrote in five languages—English, French, Italian, German, Russian—with little attention to the traditions of verse in any of them. Her poems were made up of the phrases of her speeches, a rhetoric that had been effective with ill-educated crowds, but came out as clichés in her poems. And while much of the motivation for this poetry was undoubtedly her break with all that she had loved, the poems were impersonal and abstract: Her own life was still not important enough to be a mirror for the world around her and the tragedy of socialism she had been through.

> Each man says he loves
> And yet, he does not love
> And yet, he does not lie.

> What he calls love
> Is an illusion;
> What he can prove
> Is a deception;
> What he promises
> Is a failure,
> What he takes
> Is a life,
> What he gives
> Is a lie,
> And yet, he does not die.

> Each man kills the thing he loves
> And yet, he thinks he does not,

And yet, he does not lie,
And yet, he does not die!

Year after year Angelica poured out these lines, always the same themes, usually the same images and words—mothers, tears, martyrs, slaves. The same rhythms and words are used in all five languages. Many of the poems read as subconscious translations of other poems, altered only to make the rhythms scan.

As poetry, these are not much. Yet as therapy they served their purpose. The simple phrases were an effective vehicle to express Angelica's straight-forward ideas of socialism:

Don't ask me wherefrom
  I come
I have no home.
I am where
A man stretches out his hand in despair.
  I am where
  There
Is suffering and fear
Where brethren hide the face
  In shame and disgrace
    Where hunger
    Is stronger
    Than pride.

In part, the verses were a kind of autobiography. Through these first liter-ary exercises Angelica found the confidence to begin pouring out her autobio-graphical writings. When she finally published some of her poetry, in 1943, the introduction to the volume was a statement of her socialist credo:

> I am one with these men and women, one with the victims of injustice, the underprivileged of the world. The tears about which I have written are their tears, the sorrow is the sorrow that I shared with them during the long years I have been fighting for human freedom, for human brotherhood, for solidarity in a new Socialist Society. There is no contradiction between this deep sense of human tragedy and my lifelong struggle for Socialism. I became a Socialist *because* I protest with all my heart and with my whole mind against the misery that is the lot of the many, and because I want to change the world so that every human being can realize the beauty and happiness that life *can* offer. . . .

Poetry, while good for the soul, did not provide a satisfactory outlet for Angelica's energies. Poverty and alienation could be described in poems, but poems and songs would not ease the lot of the poor and the alienated.

232

The only way Angelica knew to achieve that unchanging goal was to work in the socialist movement. But what movement? Pride and a sense of honesty would not allow her to work with the Bolsheviks, even outside Russia. As a member of the Communist Party, she was unwelcome among the other labor movement parties. In fact, as she discovered soon after her arrival in Stockholm, the conservatives in Sweden felt that she ought to be unwelcome in Sweden no matter what her chosen politics. One stricture on her admission to the country was that she agree to refrain from any political activity. In Angelica's case, the constraint was tantamount to agreeing that she refrain from living. Since there was little possibility of any change in that provision, Angelica determined to leave Stockholm as soon as possible.

A visa to Italy was out of the question, and amid the turmoil and red scares of the early twenties, she could expect an equally cold reception in almost every European capital. She chose Vienna, because the social democrats in power there might grant her a visa, and because the low cost of living would enable her to get by without a regular job. Political friends used influence to obtain her a visa, a task which became much easier as the news of her break with the Comintern became public. After waging their own struggle against the communists at home, the Austrian social democrats were delighted to have a distinguished and disenchanted ex-communist as a guest.

In Vienna she took a room in a cheap boardinghouse, set up her little icons on the table, and took up the only work she knew—teaching foreign languages. She was still so weak and ill that at times, on the trams or even during lessons, she would collapse from exhaustion and pain.

The Russians, meanwhile, had not given up on Angelica. She retained her party membership, and as a "leader" she was frequently invited to functions at the Soviet embassy in Vienna. She went, and the receptions which were meant to lure her back to the fold only added to her disillusion. To attract commercial interest and to facilitate diplomatic relations, the Russians would lavish caviar and champagne on these receptions. ". . . Proof of the revolutionary decay of Russia itself, the revival of petit-bourgeois spirit," wrote Angelica. At a reception on the anniversary of the Bolshevik revolution that Angelica attended, unemployed Viennese workers who showed up to offer their greetings were turned away. She left the embassy immediately.

When she spurned offers of money and readmission to the Soviet Union (on the sole condition that she recant on the Italian question), she was expelled from the party for her "Menshevik" approach and her collaboration with "social fascist" newspapers. Her membership, the decree stated, had been an error from the beginning. She had, of course, never belonged to any Menshevik organization; the "social fascist" newspaper was *Avanti*.

Angelica began writing books in Vienna. Two she did for the Freethinking Press: a collection of Marx and Engels' writings and a pamphlet on Marx and Engels as Freethinkers. They were careful and competent, but little more than hack jobs. She also wrote a book on *Erziehung der Massen zum Marxismus* (*Education of the Masses to Marxism*), ostensibly a handbook for socialist agitators, but really a clear statement of Angelica's beliefs on socialism. Only through systematic agitation, she argues, can the masses be made into a class-conscious segment of society with a truly socialist goal. She continues with specific suggestions on how to address different audiences in different situations, spicing her discussions with historical examples—many at the expense of Mussolini or the Bolsheviks. What is interesting about her little book is its lack of faith in the "inexorable process of history." Agitation, organization, and didactic instruction are more important than any understanding of or reliance upon the workings of historical dialectic. As theory, the position owed more to her ideas of devoted sacrifice and charity than to any deep theoretical appreciation of Marx.

From Vienna Angelica watched closely as Mussolini rose to power in Italy. When the net of repression tightened under the fascist regime, especially after fascist thugs murdered Giacomo Matteoti in 1924, she initiated clandestine correspondence with the Italian socialists who were beginning to flee the country. Working in St. Tropez and later in Paris, Angelica became a one-woman reception and job placement committee for these émigrés. In Paris, she accepted the editorship of *Avanti,* now a newspaper in exile.

Because, as she put it, few outside Italy knew the truth about Mussolini, she wrote a book, *Wesen und Werdegang des Italienischen Faschismus* (*Reality and Development of Italian Fascism*). Its language is the language of her speeches, direct and simple; its documentation, considering the fact that she could not go to Italy and had little access to Italian sources, is impressive. Written in part to warn that Austria and Germany may be following in Italy's tracks, the book makes the point that the Italian workers were, in effect, duped into following Mussolini. Although overwhelmingly against fascism, they are so repressed that no visible rebellion is possible. Matteoti is her hero, and she tries to suggest that the flight of socialists from Italy is not a sign of weakness in the face of Mussolini but a precursor of the coalition that will be formed against him.

It was not her last book on Mussolini. During the second world war, in New York, Angelica wrote *Il Traditore,* an eight-part serial presenting the life of Mussolini and the history of the fascist movement in a series of playlets. Some of the scenes are from her own memory of Mussolini, and while time has sharpened her perceptions and the negative cast of her portrayal, they are on the whole accurate. The latter half of this pamphlet history—written in both English and Italian, for the benefit of the Italian-American community—is pure fiction, concocted solely to demonstrate that every move of the fascists (and especially of Mussolini) is cowardly, pusillanimous, and destined to failure. She published the pamphlets herself, and advertised that the whole set could be bought, autographed, for one dollar, by writing her.

From Vienna, then Paris, then New York, Angelica followed every cause of the turbulent twenties and thirties—the rise of the Nazis in Germany, the Italian invasion of Ethiopia, the war in Spain, the purges in the USSR—but always as an outsider, without the institutional support of an effective movement. For twenty-five years she wandered from cause to cause, from movement to movement. In Paris, she worked to reunite the fragments of various Internationals left in the wake of the Bolshevik split of the socialist movement. The efforts were short-lived and unsuccessful. In time, the Nazi takeover of Austria and the imminence of war caught up with her, and, like so many of Europe's socialists, she fled to the United States for the war years.

In New York she became interested in the Italian-Americans. To earn a living she wrote for any sympathetic publications that would take an article. Somehow she published a collection of her poetry, but she could not set roots in New York, and as soon as the war ended she headed for Italy.

Italy was home. Though well into her sixties, Angelica affiliated herself with the socialists and offered herself as a propagandist for the Socialist Party. As the various Italian parties vied to fill the vacuum left by the collapse of fascism, she journeyed from one end to the other of Italy, speaking to groups of every description.

In a way, it was a return to the days when Angelica first committed herself to socialism. But things had changed in what had been almost half a century. The single great movement was gone. It was not even international. In Italy the socialists were one of many parties, with no more than the most tenuous links to the other European socialist parties. And after the Mussolini years, it was difficult to call up the spirit and exuberance of the rallies and demonstrations of the turn of the century. Most Italians had seen too many demonstrations, heard too many speeches and too much cheering. Given the poverty and chaos that followed the war it was difficult to make promises that could distract the unemployed and homeless from the wretched reality around them.

Night after night Angelica would return to her little student's room, with its icons. Over the years the collection had diminished, as disillusionment had purged those who had once been heroes. August Bebel was still there, because he was of the working class and the leader of the largest mass party of workers. Rosa Luxemburg was there, because she had gone down fighting without compromising. Labriola was there, as a great teacher. And Jaurès, who had fought war with words.

There were times when even the old heroes could not sustain Angelica, as her faith in the workers waned to the level of her disenchantment with the socialist leaders. Postwar prosperity brought motor scooters, television sets, refrigerators, and cars to Italy. Workers became consumers, eager to acquire their own share of the increasing wealth. There were still strikes and demonstrations of unity, but the goal of those actions was no longer revolution or social change. Increased wages, increased consumption, and an improved standard of living had become all. Even the revolutionary rhetoric was dropped as the socialist party became a parliamentary labor party.

As the socialist party lost its revolutionary impetus, the Italian communists began their remarkable ascendancy in postwar Italy. In municipal elections they swept certain towns, then proceeded to demonstrate an efficiency of government that in turn earned them more strength at the polls and enough power to tread a delicate balance between their own policies and the line emanating from Moscow. They quickly became the largest communist party in Western Europe; at each election they seemed to be the great challenger to the ruling Christian Democrats.

No matter what changes might come over the Italian Communist Party, Angelica remained aloof, never forgiving it the sins of the fathers. Ironically, when she was taken to a rest home in 1964, after a nervous breakdown, the only available place was in a "red" village outside Rome. Her nurse was an ardent communist, and a photograph of Big Brother Togliatti, the communist leader, hung over Angelica's bed. She was too ill to notice. In the evenings visitors would gather to sing *Bandiera Rossa,* and Angelica could for a few moments forget the last fifty years and remember only the great days of the militant party. She experienced recurrent fears about "the Great Shadow and the Beyond," but with the camaraderie of a few friends from the Democratic Socialist Party she could sometimes sing and forget.

Everyone expected the nervous breakdown would be the end. But Angelica would not give up so easily. After a year she recovered sufficiently to get herself another little student's room in Rome. A merciful forgetfulness made the year of breakdown seem but a moment during which her "nervous system was a bit disobedient." She wrote an article on May Day in 1965, and at eighty-seven notified the party that she was ready for another lecture tour.

Later that year, she died in her little room, with the icons still on the table.

BIBLIOGRAPHICAL
N O T E S

Although my research occasionally took me into archives and other obscure materials, the notes which follow do not pretend to be a complete bibliography. Rather, they are a description of the sources I found most directly useful for this study, and which might be helpful to a reader interested in pursuing the subject further. First citations for works give complete bibliographical data; subsequent references are by author and short title. I have cited English editions where possible.

General

Despite the extraordinary recent production of studies of Marx and Marxism, there are still vast gaps. No major biography of Marx appeared between Franz Mehring, *Karl Marx* (London, 1936) and David McLellan, *Karl Marx: His Life and Thought* (New York, 1974). The researcher must still make constant reference to Karl Marx and Friedrich Engels, *Werke,* 41 vols (Berlin, 1956–68), a rather complete edition of the published works and correspondence to and from Marx and Engels, including many letters to and from family members; the notes and glossaries are excellent. Other important sources are the reminiscences in *Mohr und General* (Berlin, 1970), an edition which is much better than either *Reminiscences of Marx and Engels* (Moscow, n.d.) or *Erinnerungon an Karl Marx* (Berlin, 1953). Finally, there is some important material—in a few cases, material available nowhere else—in Werner Blumenberg, *Karl Marx in Selbstzeugnisson und Bilddokumenten* (Hamburg, 1966); the English edition, *Karl Marx: An Illustrated Biography* (London, 1972) has excellent notes.

The writings of Marx and Engels are, of course, available in many English editions, although there as yet exists no complete English edition. I have generally used the Moscow Foreign Languages Publishing House or International Publishers editions.

237

The history of Marxism, especially in the period of the Second International, also has some blank areas. Although Georges Haupt, *La deuxième internationale 1889–1914* (Paris, 1964) has catalogued the important documents and bibliography, there is still no adequate study of the International. James Joll, *The Second International 1889–1914* (New York, 1966) is brief and selective; Julius Braunthal, *History of the International,* 2 vols (New York, 1967) is more extensive, but increasingly partisan, especially in the period of the First World War and after. The closest to an adequate study of the theoretical and organizational disputes of the International is probably Peter Nettl, *Rosa Luxemburg,* 2 vols (London, 1966) which ranges far from its subject in clear and trenchant discussions of the tricky battles of the International.

The most useful published sources for the period are: Victor Adler, *Briefwechsel mit August Bebel und Karl Kautsky* (Vienna, 1954); Wilhelm Liebknecht, *Briefwechsel mit Karl Marx und Friedrich Engels* (The Hague, 1963); Friedrich Engels–Paul and Laura Lafargue, *Correspondence,* 3 vols (Moscow, 1959).

In a very different vein, Sheila Rowbotham, *Women, Resistance and Revolution* (New York, 1972) has produced an interesting survey of a number of figures and movements which are only touched upon in passing in these portraits.

Eleanor Marx

The Marx family papers were scattered after Tussy's death. Those she held went to Laura, then to the children of the Longuets, and are now under the control of Professor Émile Bottigelli in Paris. Other papers have found their way to the Institute of Marxism-Leninism in Moscow. Finally, those papers inherited by the SPD are now in the archives of the International Institute of Social History in Amsterdam.

Because of publishing arrangements between Professor Bottigelli and the Moscow Institute, I was unable to use the materials in Paris and Moscow. Fortunately, copies of many of the materials in those collections are also available in Amsterdam, where I found letters and other documents in the following archives: Marx-Engels, Marx Family, Kautsky, Lafargue, Guesde, Bruno Karpels, Liebknecht, Bebel, Bernstein, Schlüter, Van der Goes, Kleine Korrespondenz. I did most of my research among letters and memoirs in the archives, but many of these have now been published, as has some of the Bottigelli and Moscow material. Important sources for published documents include: Marx-Engels, *Werke;* Engels-Lafargue, *Correspondence;* Blumenberg, *Karl Marx;* and a number of articles: Bert Andréas, "Briefe und Dokumente der Familie Marx aus den Jahren

1862–1873," *Archiv fur Sozialgeschichte* II (Hanover, 1962); Émile Bottigelli, "Lettres et documents de Karl Marx, 1856–1883," *Annali dell'Istituto Giangiacomo Feltrinelli*, I (Milan, 1958); Bottigelli, "La rupture Marx-Hyndman," *Annali*, III (1960); Jean Longuet, "Lettres de Karl Marx à ses filles Jenny, Laura, Eléonore et à Ch. Longuet," *La nouvelle Revue Socialiste* 26 (November–December 1928); Longuet, "Lettres de Karl Marx à ses filles Jenny, Laura et Eléonore," *La nouvelle Revue Socialiste* 27 (December 1928–February 1929). Tussy's letters to Freddy were published in the *Labour Leader* (April 30, 1898 and July 30, 1898).

There has been much biographical attention paid to Tussy, though only some of it is serious. O. Worobjowa and I. Sinelnikova, *Die Töchter von Marx* (Berlin, 1963), includes some factual data published nowhere else, but it is generally shallow and hagiographic. Chushichi Tsuzuki, *The Life of Eleanor Marx 1855–1898* (Oxford, 1967) is based in part on the Bottigelli papers and other archives, but the volume is narrowly anglocentric. Yvonne Kapp, *Eleanor Marx* (London, 1972), of which only one of two projected volumes has appeared, is a model of thorough research and critical evaluation of evidence. The first volume, subtitled "Family Life," is a little obsessive in its attention to trivia, but it is unlikely that other researchers will add much to the materials Ms. Kapp has compiled. Pierre Durand, *La Vie amoureuse de Karl Marx* (Paris, 1970) and Luise Dornemann, *Jenny Marx* (Berlin, 1968), for example, offer little except "new" slants on old material. The novel by Michael Hastings, *Tussy is Me* (New York, 1970), while suggestive and sympathetic, takes such liberty with the historical record that it loses all credibility. Two shorter biographical studies are: Felix Barker, "Department of Amplification," *New Yorker* (November 27, 1954) and Lewis S. Feuer, "Marxist Tragedians," *Encounter* XIX (November 1962).

Some of those who knew Tussy have supplied memoirs: Havelock Ellis, "Eleanor Marx," *Modern Monthly* IX (September 1935); Eduard Bernstein, "Eleanor Marx" and "Was Eleanor Marx in den Tod trieb?" *Neue Zeit* XVI/2 (1898); Bernstein, *My Years in Exile* (London, 1921). I have also relied on many of the memoirs in *Mohr und General,* especially those of Wilhelm Liebknecht, Jenny Marx, Eleanor Marx, Franziska Kugelmann, Lafargue, Edgar Longuet, Engels, Aveling and Bernstein. Aveling wrote of his "experiences" with two of his "masters" in "Charles Darwin and Karl Marx: A Comparison," *New Century Review* (March–April, 1897).

Other memoirs and letters are: E. Belfort Bax, *Reminiscences and Reflections of a Mid- and Late Victorian* (London, 1918); H. M. Hyndman, *The Record of an Adventurous Life* (London, 1911) and *Further Reminiscences* (London, 1912); William Collison, *The Apostle of Free Labour* (London, 1913); Olive Schreiner, *Letters 1876–1920* (London, 1924); G. B. Shaw, *Collected Letters 1874–1897* (New York, 1965) and *Sixteen Self Sketches* (London, 1949).

The literature on the theater and labor movements of Victorian England is voluminous, but because Tussy and Edward Aveling were always on the periphery of both the theater and the socialist worlds, they are usually only touched upon in passing. I found the following books useful: Arthur H. Nethercot, *The First Five Lives of Annie Besant* (Chicago, 1960); James W. Hulse, *Revolutionists in London* (Oxford, 1970); Egon Erwin Kisch, *Karl Marx in Karlsbad* (Berlin-Weimar, 1968); Gertrude Marvin Williams, *The Passionate Pilgrim: A Life of Annie Besant* (London, 1931); Stanley Pierson, *Marxism and the Origins of British Socialism* (Ithaca, 1973); C. Tsuzuki, *H. M. Hyndman and British Socialism* (Oxford, 1961); Henry Pelling, *The Origins of the Labour Party, 1880–1900* (Oxford, 1965). The best book on the labor movement is E. P. Thompson, *William Morris: Romantic to Revolutionary* (London, 1955).

The writings of Tussy and Edward have never been published in a collected edition. A fairly complete bibliography is in Tsuzuki, *The Life of Eleanor Marx*.

Rosa Luxemburg

There are two important biographies of Rosa Luxemburg. Paul Frölich, *Rosa Luxemburg, Her Life and Work* (London, 1940) is a Marxist biography by a friend and sympathizer; although comprehensive in dealing with her German activities, Frölich downplays the disputes between Luxemburg and Lenin. Peter Nettl, *Rosa Luxemburg*, 2 vols, is a masterpiece of life-and-works biography. His researches in the most arcane languages and archives are a model of thoroughness, leaving few stones unturned. The result is a study so comprehensive and wide-ranging that the titular subject gets lost amid the complexities of politics and theoretical dispute. At the same time, Nettl gives perceptive analyses of some of the most important problems in the history of socialism, with matchless documentation of even the most obscure episodes. Much of the information he cites, especially the Polish materials, are available nowhere else, or are only slowly appearing in published editions. Many of the letters I have cited are quoted from Nettl, although in the case of letters and documents in the International Institute of Social History I have sometimes modified his translations.

Recently, Nettl's biography has been supplemented by further studies. Annelies Laschitza and Günter Radczun, *Rosa Luxemburg, Ihr Wirken in der deutschen Arbeiterbewegung* (Berlin, 1972) reemphasizes the central importance of the SPD and Germany in Luxemburg's thinking and activities—a fact sometimes lost sight of in Nettl's multifaceted biography. Lelio Basso, in his introduction to the Italian edition of her works and in *Rosa Luxemburg's Dialektik der Revolution* (Frankfurt, 1969) demonstrates rather persuasively that she had an intuitive understanding of Marxian dialectic.

Two other biographical studies which are insightful for Luxemburg's personal life are Luise Kautsky, *Rosa Luxemburg, Ein Gedenkbuch* (Berlin, 1929) and Henriette Roland-Holst, *Rosa Luxemburg: Ihr Leben und Wirken* (Zurich, 1937). As women, Luise Kautsky and Henriette Roland-Holst were often sensitive to problems that both Nettl and Frölich have treated lightly or not at all.

Rosa Luxemburg's writings are only recently becoming available in published editions. Only three volumes of the *Gesammelte Werke* edition were published: volume VI, *Die Akkumulation des Kapitals* (Berlin, 1923); volume III, *Gegen den Reformismus* (Berlin, 1925); volume IV, *Gewerkschaftskampf und Massenstreik* (Berlin, 1928). All were edited by Frölich, and his introduction is a useful guide. I have also used two East German editions: *Ausgewählte Reden und Schriften,* 2 vols (Berlin, 1951); *Rosa Luxemburg im Kampf gegen den deutschen Militarismus* (Berlin, 1960). The *Rote Fahne* articles are collected in Harry Wilde, *Rosa Luxemburg: Ich war—ich bin—ich werde sein* (Vienna, 1970). The Spartacus letters have also been published by the Institut für Marxismus-Leninismus in East Germany: *Spartakusbriefe* (Berlin, 1958). There are three important collections of letters: *Rosa Luxemburg Briefe an Leon Jogiches* (Frankfurt, 1971), *Briefe aus dem Gefängnis* (Berlin, 1920), and *Briefe an Karl und Luise Kautsky (1896–1918)* (Berlin, 1923). I used the latter in the English edition, *Letters to Karl and Luise Kautsky* (New York, 1923). Nettl offers an extensive bibliography of published and unpublished writings in Volume Two of his biography.

In English, there are the *Accumulation of Capital* in several editions and Bertram Wolfe, *The Russian Revolution and Leninism or Marxism?* (Ann Arbor, 1961); the latter essay is "Organizational Questions of the Russian Social Democracy." Also, two recent collections of writings: *Selected Political Writings of Rosa Luxemburg,* ed. Dick Howard (New York, 1971) and *Rosa Luxemburg. Selected Political Writings,* ed. Robert Looker (London, 1972). Of the two, the Howard edition is better, with particularly intelligent organization, substantial selections, and excellent translations; I have incorporated a number of the translations from this collection.

Rosa Luxemburg's life, ideas, and activities were so closely identified with the Second International that the secondary sources for her biography are really the literature for the International. I found most of the materials listed in the General section of these notes important. In addition, several standard works on the German left are illuminating: Carl E. Schorske, *German Social Democracy, 1905–1917* Cambridge, 1955); Peter Gay, *The Dilemma of Democratic Socialism* (New York, 1962); Werner T. Angress, *Stillborn Revolution: The Communist Bid for Power in Germany, 1921–1923* (Princeton, 1963). Some interesting new material has been added in the revised (German) edition of Angress's book, *Die Kampfzeit der KPD* (Dusseldorf, 1973). On the revolution, I relied on Arthur Rosenberg, *Imperial Germany: The Birth of the German Republic, 1871–1918* (Boston, 1964); Werner T. Angress, "Juden im Politischen Leben der Revolutionszeit," in *Deutsches Judentum in Krieg und Revolution 1916–1923* (Tübingen, 1971); Gerhard P. Bassler, "The Communist Movement in the German Revolution," *Central European History* VI/3 (September 1973) as well as many of the sources listed in the notes of both Angress and Bassler. On Polish matters, I depended on Nettl.

Finally, a number of memoirs illuminate both the private and public life of Rosa Luxemburg: Karl Kautsky, *Erinnerungen und Erörterungen* (s'Gravenhage, 1960); Émile Vandervelde, *Souvenirs d'un militant socialiste* (Paris, 1939); Paul Levi, *Karl Liebknecht und Rosa Luxemburg zum Gedächtnis* (1919) [the funeral oration]; Clara Zetkin, *Reminiscences of Lenin* (London, 1929).

The most complete bibliography is in Nettl, although it is quickly growing out of date.

Angelica Balabanoff

Although her "memory" is sometimes questionable, I have relied heavily on Angelica Balabanoff's memoirs for the story of her life. The English, German and Italian versions are not translations, but different versions, although many episodes are repeated: *My Life as a Rebel* (London, 1938); *Erinnerungen und Erlebnisse* (Berlin, 1927); *Ricordi di una socialista* (Rome, 1946). Her *Impressions of Lenin* (Ann Arbor, 1964) also covers much of the same ground. Events described in more than one memoir are usually essentially the same in each; for quotations I have used whichever version came closest to plausible speech. In any case, these recollections of ten or twenty years are scarcely exact quotes. Where her version of events differs sharply from the known facts, I have tended to discount her, or to explain her special perspective.

Her other writings are also useful as a form of autobiography, especially: *Il Traditore: Benito Mussolini and his "Conquest" of Power* (New York, 1942–43); *Sozialismus als Weltanschauung* (Jena, 1930); *Erziehung der Massen zum Marxismus; Psychologischpädagogische Betrachtungen* (Berlin, 1927); *Wesen und Werdegange des italienischen Faschismus* (Vienna, 1931); *Marx und Engels als Freidenker in ihren Schritten, ein Hand und Kampfesbuch* (Berlin, 1930); two volumes of her poetry: *Tears* (New York, 1943), from which I have taken the poems quoted in the text, and *To the Victims of Fascism* (New York, [193?]). I used none of her Russian writings in this study.

Although works on the Second International and the Russian revolution often mention her, the references are usually in passing. Because she eventually rebelled against both Mussolini and the Bolsheviks, and because her official party positions were generally token titles, the literature on both fascism and communism tends to underplay her role. She is never mentioned in Mussolini's autobiography. Works on the history of socialism frequently quote her observations, but even studies of Italian socialism rarely assign any significance to her activities. The closest to a biographical sketch is Bertram Wolfe, "Angelica Balabanoff," in *Strange Communists I have Known* (New York, 1965), a reprint of his introduction to the American edition of her *Impressions of Lenin.*

I have, however, found the following works useful, in addition to the material on the Second International cited earlier in these notes. On the war years, there is a collection of documents compiled by Angelica Balabanoff, "Die Zimmerwalder Bewegung 1914–1919," *Archiv für Geschichte des Sozialismus und der Arbeiterbewegung* XIII (1926), which should be supplemented with Olga Hess Gankin and H. H. Fisher, *The Bolsheviks and the World War* (Stanford, 1940). For the same period there is R. Grimm, *Zimmerwald und Kienthal* (Bern, 1917); *Die Zimmerwalder Bewegung,* ed. H. Lademacher (The Hague, 1967); Merle Fainsod, *International Socialism and the World War* (New York, 1969); Leon Trotsky, *My Life* (New York, 1960).

The Mussolini bibliography adds little to her own narrative of her relationship. On the Italian left: Maurice F. Neufeld, *Italy: School for Awakening Countries. The Italian Labor Movement in its Political, Social, and Economic Setting from 1800 to 1960* (New York, 1961); *Die Sozialistische Partei Italiens und die Kommunistische Internationale* (Materialsammlung) (Petrograd, 1921). The latter work, and C. Kabakchiev, *Die Gründung der Kommunistischen Partei Italiens* (Hamburg, 1921), give the other side of the story Balabanoff relates so thoroughly.

There is very little literature on the Third International, and what there is has generally been written without access to primary sources. Jane Debras, *The Communist International 1919–1943: Documents,* vol. I (London, 1971) collects the major documents for the first years, but documents do not tell the story of the machinations that Balabanoff and John Reed witnessed. Branko Lazitch and Milorad M. Drachkovitch, *Lenin and the Comintern,* vol. I (Stanford, 1972) and Franz Borkenau, *World Communism* (Ann Arbor, 1962) are the best histories, as Braunthal, *History of the International,* is very one-sided in his antagonism toward the Bolsheviks. Biographies of Lenin provide little confirmation or refutation of the anecdotes in *Impressions of Lenin.*

INDEX